Salt of tł

Rosaura Revueltas as Esperanza Quintero in *Salt of the Earth.*

"How shall I begin my story that has no beginning?...
Our roots go deep in this place... deeper than the mine
shafts...."

SALT OF THE EARTH

The Story of a Film

HERBERT BIBERMAN

Fiftieth Anniversary Edition

New York • Sag Harbor
Harbor Electronic Publishing
2003

www.HEPdigital.com

For Gale Sondergaard and our thirty-five years

*The author wishes to acknowledge his profound
indebtedness to Miss Alida Sherman for the
organization and editing of this book.*

© 1965 by Herbert Biberman © 2003 by Sonja Dahl Biberman
First published by Beacon Press, Boston, 1965
Library of Congress Control Number: 2002109150
ISBN 0-9707039-4-5 (eBook)
ISBN 0-9707039-3-7 (paper)

Printed in the United States of America
Amazon edition

This print version of the book does not include an index. Readers who need an index are directed to the eBook version, which is fully word-searchable.

The original edition of *Salt of the Earth: the Story of a Film* included the screenplay by Michael Wilson. A newly reconstructed edition of the screenplay is now available separately.

CREDITS
Editors: Anne Sanow, Charles Monaco
Cover design: Dimitri Drjuchin

A NOTE ON THE TYPE

This edition is set in Adobe's release of Meridien. Designed in 1957 by Swiss typographer Adrian Frutiger for the French foundry Deberny & Peignot, Meridien's large x-height enhances legibility, while its Latinesque serifs and flared stems give it a classical Roman elegance. One of the pioneers of "cold type" design, Frutiger is perhaps best-known for the influential Univers family. The display type is Bodoni. The type was set by UNET 2 Corporation.

CONTENTS

Publisher's Preface

You are about to read an extraordinary story. The film *Salt of the Earth* is a unique cinematic landmark, and grows in importance with each passing year, but the saga of the making of the film, and the lengthy tribulations of the filmmakers to get it distributed, is even more remarkable. *Salt of the Earth* is a classic of American movie-making— one of the first films to be added to the National Film Registry by the Library of Congress. *Salt of the Earth: The Story of a Film*, director Herbert Biberman's dramatic and wise saga of the film's notorious passage into history, is likely the most revealing and instructive narrative of the film business in the last fifty years. The story begins during the dark days of the blacklist and the Hollywood Ten, takes us through the adventurous production of an exciting and resonant film, continues with the valiant struggle to get the film seen, and concludes with the lengthy and persistent battle to achieve retribution in the courts.

Born in 1900, Biberman attended the University of Pennsylvania and Yale, worked for his father's textile business, then became involved in the Theatre Guild in New York. In the mid-thirties he set out to try his luck in Hollywood. He quickly found a niche as a director and screenwriter of B-movies (*One-Way Ticket*, 1935; *Meet Nero Wolfe*, 1936; *King of Chinatown*, 1939).

In the late summer of 1947 he was one of nineteen Hollywood filmmakers called to testify before the House Un-American Activities Committee in a show-trial meant to discredit leftist influence in American movies. Although nineteen were subpoenaed, only eleven testified. (Bertolt Brecht left the country after his testimony.) To a man they refused to discuss their previous political affiliations, or to "name names"—rat on friends and acquaintances who may have been members of the Communist party at one time or another.

In November of 1947 ten filmmakers (eight screenwriters, two directors)[*] were declared in contempt of Congress and sentenced to prison. They began serving their sentences in 1950. Eight were imprisoned for a year; Biberman and director Edward Dmytryk got off after six months. Dmytryk quickly turned, "named names," and regained his career. But it is still unclear why Biberman was offered a half-pass.

A few days after these citations for contempt of Congress were issued a meeting of studio executives in New York at the Waldorf-Astoria hotel issued a declaration supporting the aims of the House Un-American Activities Commitee and banning the Hollywood Ten. This "Waldorf Declaration" was the basis for the blacklist that followed. Hundreds of writers, directors, actors, and other filmmakers were prevented from working in the Hollywood studios from that time on. Some had been members of the Communist party in their youth, some had not: all were tarred with the same brush, and numerous careers were cut short. The paranoid terror of the blacklist lasted into the 1960s.

The House Un-American Activities Committee had been instituted in 1938 at the instigation of Congressman Martin Dies. Ostensibly, it was to investigate security threats from both the left and the right, but since Dies was an ardent supporter of the Ku Klux Klan, only the left was subject to the Committee's star-chamber scrutiny. By 1947 J. Parnell Thomas had assumed the chairmanship. He realized immediately that Hollywood was a great target of opportunity.

His moment in the sun was brief. He was soon convicted of taking kickbacks—this at a time when members of Congress were generally free of such scrutiny. He soon found himself serving time in Danbury prison along with Ring Lardner, Jr and Lester Cole—two of the Hollywood Ten. Only in America!

The House Un-American Activities Committee (known as "HUAC") returned to Hollywood in 1951 attempting to harvest another round of publicity, but by this time HUAC had been superseded by Wisconsin Senator Joe McCarthy. His Senate sub-committee

---

* The 10 were Alvah Bessie, Herbert Biberman, Lester Cole, Edward Dmytryk, Ring Lardner Jr., John Howard Lawson, Albert Maltz, Samuel Ornitz, Adrian Scott, and Dalton Trumbo. The group originally included the German writer Bertolt Brecht, but Brecht fled the country on the day following his inquest. The remaining 10 were voted in contempt of Congress on Nov. 24, 1947.

had unearthed "205 card-carrying Communists" in the State Department, he claimed. His list trumped HUAC.

This paranoid witch-hunt was to last another three years, despite the heroic actions of people like Senator Margaret Chase Smith of Maine, whose "Declaration of Conscience" on the Senate floor in 1950 strongly challenged McCarthy's sleazy tactics. HUAC had focused on Hollywood. McCarthy moved on to government. Eventually, McCarthy was brought down by the media—ironically HUAC's prime target. When he took on the Army in 1954 he had met his match. The televised hearings fascinated the country and displayed McCarthy's increasing megalomania. In one of the signal moments in television history the nation watched as the Army's counsel, Joseph Welch, confronted him: "Have you no sense of decency, sir?" After that moment the fever broke; "McCarthyism" entered into decline.

But that did not help Herbert Biberman—or any of the hundreds of other blacklisted filmmakers. The unofficial ban lasted well into the sixties. Scores of careers came to an abrupt halt; marriages broke up; the psychological distress that followed appearances before the committee was linked to numerous premature deaths, including those of actors John Garfield and Canada Lee.

Not everyone suffered, however. Numerous directors and actors found work—and sometimes greater success—in Europe: Joseph Losey, Jules Dassin, and Lionel Stander, for example.[*] Screenwriters, who accounted for well over half the blacklist, were sometimes able to find work using fronts. There was an embarrassing silence at the 1956 Oscar ceremony when Robert Rich won the Academy Award for Best Screenplay for *The Brave One.* No one stood up to claim the statuette: "Robert Rich" was Dalton Trumbo's pseudonym. Four years later Otto Preminger broke the ban by giving credit to Trumbo for the script of *Exodus.*

The Ten had relied on the First Amendment, protecting freedom of speech, rather than invoking the Fifth Amendment against self-

---

*The blacklist colony in Europe in the fifties and sixties is well described in Bernard Gordon's 1999 memoir *Hollywood Exile: or How I Learned to Love the Blacklist.*

incrimination. If they had "taken the Fifth" they might have avoided prison.

At least as important as the personal suffering created by the blacklist was the severe chilling effect the witch-hunt had on freedom of speech, most obviously in Hollywood but elsewhere as well. Just after World War II Hollywood enjoyed a brief flowering of socially conscious films (*The Best Years of Our Lives*, *Gentleman's Agreement*, *Lost Boundaries*). One of these—*Crossfire*, a tough indictment of anti-semitism—may have sparked HUAC's interest in a Hollywood show-trial: both its director, Dmytryk, and its producer, Scott, were among the first group called to testify. Was there an anti-semitic element to HUAC's hearings? Undoubtedly: at the time, men like J. Parnell Thomas would have been hard-pressed to differentiate between Jews and Commies, and a hard-hitting movie about anti-semitism would be just the thing you would expect from subversives intent on undermining American values.

Although they were landmarks, there were very few of these socially conscious films in the late forties. Conversely, the studios produced numerous HUAC-inspired red-scare tracts in the early fifties: *The Red Menace* (1949), *I Married a Communist* (1950), *I Was a Communist for the FBI* (1951), *Big Jim McClain* (1952). The political freeze had set in, and didn't lift until the late 1960s.

In this context, the production of *Salt of the Earth* is even more surprising. It is as if Herbert Biberman and his fellow blacklistees, producer Paul Jarrico and screenwriter Michael Wilson, were somehow insulated from the fifties freeze. Their film about a union's struggle for recognition continued the socially conscious trend of the immediate post-war years—and redoubled it. *They* were following a straight line; it was the rest of the country that went off on a tangent.

Since it attained general distribution in the late sixties *Salt of the Earth* has become a cult favorite for two main reasons: it is the only blacklisted film, and it is a precursor of modern feminism. Now, fifty years after it was made, the reputation of the film continues to grow as a new generation discovers its heroic qualities. But let's take it out of that context—imagine an alternate reality where HUAC and McCarthy did not have the profound effect on public consciousness that they did during the 1950s.

The film still stands as a landmark. It is the best—perhaps the only—example of American neorealism. There were lots of gritty, on-location, realistic movies in the late forties and early fifties. But *Salt of the Earth* is the only film that has the operatic emotions that made Italian neorealist movies so thrilling. Because it pays as much attention to what is happening at home as to what is happening on the job site, and because the women of the film turn out to be the ultimate heroes, it is rightly regarded as a feminist classic. But it needs to be noted that in this regard it is a logical extension of forties films. The women of *Salt of the Earth* just had the misfortune to be born into the frozen fifties, the aberrant era of Doris Day and Marilyn Monroe. If the film had been made five or ten years earlier they wouldn't have seemed so unique.

Finally, the film prefigures the genre of docudrama that was still twenty years in the future. In combining a real story, played mainly by non-actors, with a strong dose of Hollywood pizazz and classic scripting it stands as a model that has yet to be equaled. Again, we are reminded of Italian neorealism: think of *Salt of the Earth* as a bridge between *Shoeshine* and *La Strada*.

Herbert Biberman spent much of the 1950s struggling to complete *Salt of the Earth* and get it shown. His main enemies in this endeavor were the Hollywood unions—the ultimate irony for what is probably the most effective pro-union film ever made. From the late fifties through the mid-sixties he was involved in litigation to retrieve some of the revenue lost from the film's blacklisting. He earned his living during these years as a real estate developer in the Hollywood Hills. Before his death in 1971 he made one more film (*Slaves*, 1969), whose reception was luke-warm. In the end his great work remains *Salt of the Earth*—not just the film but also the eloquent narrative you hold in your hands. When I asked his sister-in-law Sonja if Herbert was depressed or disappointed by the long struggle to get the film seen, she quickly replied, "Herbert was never depressed. He was always active: he did what needed to be done."

Writer Michael Wilson eventually received credit for his anonymous work on such classics as *Friendly Persuasion* (1956), *Bridge on the River Kwai* (1957), and *Lawrence of Arabia* (1962). With public credits including *A Place in the Sun* (1951, Academy Award), *Five Fingers* (1952), and *Planet of the Apes* (1968), he is clearly one of the key screenwriters of the post-war period—certainly under-appreciated. He died in 1978.

Producer Paul Jarrico outlived his colleagues by a couple of decades. He spent much time during his later years working to restore credit to numerous blacklisted writers who had, like Michael Wilson, worked anonymously during the lengthy period of the blacklist. For this work he was honored at a luncheon outside of Los Angeles on October 28, 1997, marking the fiftieth anniversary of the debut of the HUAC hearings. He was killed in a car crash on his way home that day.

In 1982 Jarrico, having inherited the stash of left-over copies of *Salt of the Earth: The Story of a Film* from Herbert Biberman, approached us to put the book back in distribution, which we did. In 1989 Aleen Stein, co-founder of the Criterion Company, produced a CD-ROM essay on the film which is still in print. Later she issued a VHS edition of the film and finally a DVD-Video, both of which are available.

Now with this publication of the fiftieth anniversary edition of Herbert Biberman's book we have come full circle.

Special thanks to Sonja Dahl Biberman, Herbert's collaborator and sister-in-law, for allowing us to reprint this remarkable book. It is both a classic story of American filmmaking and an essential twentieth-century American political text.

James Monaco
Sag Harbor NY
February 2003

When the book *Salt of the Earth: The Story of a Film* first appeared in 1965 it was just a few years after Hollywood had first begun to confront the blacklist. The repressive winds of HUAC and McCarthy were still blowing. The publisher, Beacon Press, an independent Boston-based house known for courageous enterprises, still felt it necessary to try to explain why they were publishing Biberman's story. They prefaced the book with the following "Publisher's Note"—unusual at the time. The querulous, diffident tone of this unsigned note starkly indicates how powerful and long-lasting was the chilling effect of the red-baiting attacks of the late forties—more than fifteen years later. We reprint it here to complete the historical record.

PUBLISHER'S NOTE [TO THE FIRST EDITION]

There is and has been for a number of years disagreement over the right of a man to speak his mind. For instance, just how dangerous is it to allow a company of men and women to make a movie?

Salt of the Earth is a film about a strike. It takes sides. This book, *Salt of the Earth*, is the story of the difficulties resulting from a difference of opinion, a difference of belief. It is told by Herbert Biberman, who was a participant in the action. He directed the film and he has fought through all the ensuing battles. He was a Hollywood director, one of the "Hollywood Ten." He spent six months in jail for contempt of Congress because be refused to answer questions about his political beliefs and particularly about his membership in the Communist party.

Yet Mr. Biberman's willingness both to state and to act upon his beliefs is suggested by a clause in his 1957 contract with the Beacon Press which stipulates that this book shall not be published until after "the litigation with respect to *Salt of the Earth* now pending in the United States District Court, Southern District of New York... has been finally determined." Diligently, quietly, and vigorously, Mr. Biberman and the company which made the film have pursued the legal remedies available under our judicial system for eight years before the Federal courts. The verdict was returned by the jury in November, 1964, after a ten-week trial on which Mr. Biberman reports in the final section of this book, pointing out, "By all reasonable standards we had a fair trial. Our jury was conscientious, our judge scrupulously judicious."

Herbert Biberman would certainly agree that other men have suffered more for their beliefs, but it seems to the Beacon Press that his account of the past seventeen years of his life raises some important questions, some proper doubts, and even illuminates some of the dark places in our recent history.

Foreword
1964

FALSTAFF: What, upon compulsion? 'Zounds, an I were at the
            strappado, or all the racks in the world, I would not tell
            you on compulsion. Give you a reason on compulsion!
            If reasons were as plentiful as blackberries, I would give
            no man a reason upon compulsion, I.

                                                            I Henry IV

"They came here—the exile and the stranger, brave but frightened—to find a place where a man could be his own man."

                            President Lyndon Baines Johnson
                                      Inaugural Address, 1965

I

The door of the jury room in the federal courthouse, Foley Square, New York City, closed behind the twelve men and women of the jury. The judge had entered the robing room. The various counsel, four for the plaintiffs, sixteen for the defendants, toyed with papers, stuffed them into briefcases and sauntered into the corridor. There was nothing to do now but wait for the verdict in the case of Independent Productions Corporation and IPC Distributors, Inc., against Loew's, Incorporated, et al.

We, the plaintiffs, who had made the film, *Salt of the Earth,* had waited a long time for this verdict. Eight years before, we had brought suit, seeking an injunction and treble damages for the destruction of the film's value, charging violations of the anti-trust laws. Twelve years before (our complaint alleged) the motion picture industry had conspired to prevent us from making the film. Failing this, it had conspired to prevent us from showing it. But the case had its origins even before this, in the years 1947–1954, when some two hundred men and women of Hollywood were blacklisted, were denied the right to work in the motion picture industry.

We had been thought foolhardy, egotistical and capricious to undertake this litigation. We had only twenty thousand dollars to finance a lawsuit against sixty-eight defendants. Anti-trust suits rarely reached trial in less than three years. This one would probably take five. We were certain to be opposed by fifteen to twenty of the ablest law firms in the country with limitless funds behind them. Even those who were still owed the money they had lent us to make the film urged us to forego the suit.

It had not taken three to five years to reach trial. It had taken eight. The trial itself had been long and costly.

The verdict to be turned in by this jury was only one of the decisions being rendered at that time. Goldwaterism had just been rejected at the polls. A few years before McCarthyism had also been rejected, but the legitimacy of dissent had not been reestablished. Our legal action had been undertaken as a step in that direction; and, if damages were won, we would be able to repay the corporation's ten-year-old debts of a quarter of a million dollars, plus interest.

The courtroom was empty. Its hard, square contours transformed it into a kind of audio-visual memory chamber. Memory is a haunting, magnetized commitment to history, to the often unobserved dominance of morality in the lumbering life of man. The austerity of the courtroom, in that anxious moment, merged with the ancient passion for justice which is the root meaning of our land, however often its bedeviled moment-to-moment reality seems to betray it.

The barrenness of the large room dissolved for me into another barrenness, that of my small cell in the Federal Correctional Institution at Texarkana, Texas, the night before I was to be released. My fellow prisoners were scattered about the cell-block. Some, within their cells, were at work on wooden frames, knitting purses from skeins of silk thread. Others were in the corridor, sitting against the walls or standing in groups, talking. The showers were going full tilt. Here and there, checkers could be heard being slapped down on boards. I was nervous. I wished that night dissolved and gone. Around me were men with a year, two, three left to serve. How does one take leave of other men's prison-time?

I remained in my cell, pretending to be occupied, when two of my fellow prisoners entered.

"You know, Mr. Biberman, you been a mighty quiet fellow in here. Never did try to propaganda us at all. Now you leavin' t'morrow. How 'bout givin' us a little sample of the real stuff t'night. We a' askin' for it. How come y'all got kicked out a' Hollywood?"

There was laughter outside and another inmate popped his head into the cell.

"Don't let them git you in trouble yore las' night. They tryin' tuh mess you up, so you git shot and thow'ed in ter solitary. Anybody got on'y one night's time... go to sleep."

The corridor came alive with entreaty. And I went out into it. In the cell directly across from mine sat one of the wittiest and one of the sickest men in the institution. He was Mexican-American, native-born. A dope peddler, he sold junk to teenagers. He was personable until he fell into a depression when, on the least pretext, he would lash out brutally. Busily at work upon his frame making a purse of delicate and exquisite design, without even looking up, he said, *"Bee-bear-man*, go to sleep!"

But I began. I told of a young inmate with whom I had talked the first day in the institution. He was in for stealing a car—"just for a little ride." He asked me why I was there. When I said it was for contempt of Congress he jumped a foot. "Contempt of Congress! Kee-rist!"

I told of our subsequent walks together, and of how, one day, in the yard he had stopped suddenly. "I don't git it," he said. "Why, then you got more freedom o' speech in here 'n you hed out there."

The men didn't laugh. I continued.

"I had never thought of it that way," I said. "But, tonight, you kindly asked me to talk—about anything I wish. I'm not sure they will allow it outside. But I'm going to try. Not to get even. That place out there belongs to *me*, too. The best I've got is what it's going to get. In my own job. Making movies."

The attentiveness was almost intimidating. Even the checker players stopped. I went on to talk of crime and the complex origins of it. I stated my belief that any social order that caused, or even could not prevent, in so many young people, the feeling that they must engage in crime as a way of life, as a means of extracting fulfillment from it, was co-defendant. And because I believed that, I believed that revenge must be social or it wouldn't come off. Attempted personal revenge upon society was bound to end tragically both for the individual and for society. This was a little prison. The big prison was outside. One left here, as from the frying pan into the fire, unless one entered the big prison with social purpose.

And I was through. There was a pause and then, from the cell directly across, from the throat of the junk-peddler, came a husky call out of the silence.

"You'll be back, Bee-bear-mann! You'll *be back!"*

The inmates turned upon him with ferocity.

"You God-damned, lousy junkie..."

"You shet up or I'll ram your frame up your..."

Out of the tumult, his reply came, husky, loud and firm:

"He peddles worse than I do! *He'll be back!*"

The plane took off into the big prison. It suddenly seemed more difficult outside than inside. What was life going to be like —what had happened to the U.S.A. in these months?

Before me the land I had longed for was rolling out. The land beyond the fences. Night came on. I fell asleep. When I awoke, the amazing expanse of neon signs which is Los Angeles was a carpet under us. I was almost *home* again.

As the plane descended for its landing, I scrutinized the buildings below, searching for landmarks. In turning we seemed to be swooping down upon a very familiar mass of structures—*Metro-Goldwyn-Mayer* Studios!

The studios! Would I ever enter one again? Would I ever sit before a camera, directing a…. Depended on what kind of country was below me! Didn't I know? No! You can't find out about a country in its jails, any more than you can in its Congresses. You don't find out about a country in its extremities but in its center, in the ratio between its people's discovery of themselves and their acceptance of those who stifle their self-knowledge. All the jail-dreaming carried no answer. It was too special. This was the place, below me. But I had been there. Perhaps *all* this questioning was stupid. Inside and out! I was fifty years old. If I hadn't found out what kind of country I lived in up to this point…?

The plane's wheels hit the runway—and I was in it.

II

In and across my bed, that first night at home, the winds blew the tangy aroma of desert air. The slight, oppressive heaviness in the chest, which had begun when the handcuffs were locked upon my hands after sentencing in the court house in Washington and which never left me throughout my imprisonment, was still there. I was not yet home. I felt more a guest in my house than an inhabitant of it. Feeling that, and out of a consequent sudden, deeply drawn breath, my nervous system contracted and exploded as I remembered that as I lay there eight of the Hollywood Ten were still held in five prisons from Connecticut to Texas. Were they also awake thinking of Eddie Dmytryk and me—out? The story of our sentences—eight sentenced to a year and Eddie and I only to six months—remained a mystery.

As a "free" man, of some twelve hours standing, I felt shame that such men were incarcerated in the United States of America. *Alvah Bessie,* novelist, screenwriter, Guggenheim fellow, veteran of the International Brigade in Spain. *Lester Cole,* screenwriter, officer of the Screen Writers Guild. *Ring Lardner, Jr.,* screenwriter, Motion Picture Academy Award for Best Original Screenplay of the Year, 1942, executive board member of the Screen Writers Guild. *John Howard Lawson,* dramatist, screenwriter, essayist and critic. First president of the Screen Writers Guild. *Albert Maltz,* dramatist, novelist, screenwriter. O. Henry Award for the best American short story, 1938. *Samuel Ornitz,* novelist, screenwriter, historian. *Adrian Scott,* screenwriter, motion picture producer. *Dalton Trumbo,* novelist, screenwriter, poet, essayist, member of the executive board of the Screen Writers Guild, United States accredited war correspondent in the South Pacific.

I remembered Alvah Bessie, that Sunday afternoon in the fall of 1947, at a reception given in Hollywood for a lady member of the British House of Parliament. He came toward me waving a pink slip of paper.

"Did you receive one?"

"No."

"What's wrong with you? Didn't you rate?"

The next day, I discovered that I also rated. A pink slip. A sub-poena to appear before the Un-American Activities Committee of the House of Representatives of the Congress of the United States. One of nineteen issued. A barrage of propaganda accompanying them, issuing from the committee's representatives. This was to be a "big show." We understood that. We also understood many things that were not being ballyhooed.

Blithely, following the war's end, many of Hollywood's film makers, of assorted political points of view, had begun to walk the road toward the fruits of victory with the American audience. It was a widening avenue of increasingly realistic, more mature and complex subject matter; the emotional reaches of America's postwar yearnings, democratic yearnings.

Out of the blood bath the world would emerge not merely rescued, but reborn. If its birth had been violent and punishing, it was decency that had triumphed. The new world, reasonably, had to be more than secure. The motion picture was the universal medium to expose this new world of victory to the peoples of the world. Making films was creating life.

We felt genuine pride in the industry when such films as *The Best Years of our Lives* and *Crossfire* appeared. They were important steps toward making the newly won peace popularly secure. They gave us a sense of national and even global identity. That they were both enormously successful at the box office made the executives optimistic that pictures that held audiences in high esteem seemed to be held in high esteem by the audiences.

The sudden announcement in the late summer of 1947 that the House Committee on Un-American Activities was undertaking an investigation into the alleged "infiltration of subversive propaganda into motion pictures" was a shocking, bald notice of a fierce battle ahead for control of the medium. Films were apparently too influential to be permitted to remain an oasis of popular expression.

The larger part of Hollywood understood the threat and was alarmed. It began slowly to gird its loins. So, also, did a miniscule part of it—the committee's agents within it.

We nineteen recipients of subpoenas knew that, without our having been consulted, a sizable decision had been lowered upon us. We also knew that it was not uncomplicated.

It was palpably clear that we were not going to a hearing but to a judging—upon us—and through us upon the industry and perhaps even its vast audiences. We were then being set up, only to be knocked down, with the reasonable possibility that if we fell, a great deal more might fall with us.

Seven thousand persons gathered at the Shrine Auditorium in Los Angeles to wish us well on our journey and success in our undertakings, which were as yet by no means clear to us.

In the developing atmosphere we knew that to challenge the committee in any fundamental way was to risk some personal danger. If we refused to permit the committee to violate the First Amendment through interrogating us in the privileged areas of thought and association, we would risk a contempt citation. But such a citation would permit us to take the committee to court and seek a constitutional judgment upon it for its contempt for the First Amendment. Without a viable First Amendment, freedom of communication loses its meaning. If a committee of Congress can label certain thinking "un-American" and can forcibly pry one's mind open to discover and punish the thinking, then it can also outlaw ideas it dislikes, through intimidation. Not one's conscience but one's fears then became the determinant of attitudes and associations.

The Supreme Court had not yet ruled on the subject and there was some hope of success. We were not tilting at windmills.

In Washington, one of our attorneys, genuinely concerned for us in the first days of the hearings, earnestly suggested that we invoke the Fifth Amendment—refuse to testify against ourselves and thus avoid the risk of jail. The nineteen men addressed demurred without exception. If we invoked the Fifth there would be nothing in contention. We would not be challenging the committee and could not take it to court. We made it clear to our many attorneys that we had not come to Washington to defend ourselves. We had come there to defend the First Amendment—and to challenge its enemy, the House

Committee on Un-American Activities. That was the job we wanted to get on with, side by side with everyone else in the industry.

At that very moment we learned something that rather deepened our insights. It came from Mr. David Niles, a man knowledgeable in the Washington scene, through a screen writer who was a mutual friend.

"David wants you to know," he said, "that Eric Johnston was made president of the Motion Picture Producers Association by major financial interests to turn Hollywood into a blurb factory for the political era based on the bomb." Even before the war had ended, the message continued, big business had begun preparations to create an American world. High upon the list of instrumentalities for deployment to this end was Hollywood. But whereas other media had begun to convert to new political commands, Hollywood had not. This was held to be due to the presence in Hollywood of so many Jews—Jews and those other "artistic elements." These two groupings had emerged from the war with some kind of soul-scars, due no doubt to the wanton slaughter of so many millions of Jews by the Nazi nationalists. And, it was believed that within them existed a psychological incapacity to face and carry out the kind of film-making required in our own postwar period. And, by now, it was further believed that even if these elements protested that they were not psychologically incapacitated, they required total supervision and rather rigorous direction.

Eric Johnston was to bring about the swiftest possible erasure of the infantile, postwar sentimentality that was running wild in Hollywood, and to substitute for it a tough-minded Americanism and to watch out for the Jews. We were advised to watch out for Eric Johnston.

The night before the hearings began, our attorneys called upon Eric Johnston. They inquired about the rumors the committee had fed to the press that an industry-wide blacklist was imminent. Johnston called the rumor nonsense, a libel upon him as a good American. "I will never be party to anything as un-American as a blacklist."

But the following morning the committee made a bewildering revelation. The previous spring the committee had met secretly with the producers. Eric Johnston had proposed the immediate institution of a blacklist, which the producers adamantly rejected. Then, said the committee, the producers had sought to bribe it into abandoning the investigation of Hollywood. The producers arose in high dudgeon, declaring that the accusation was a lie. They had rejected a blacklist because the allegation of alien ideology in films was false. They had been steadfast to their obligation to their audiences: to hire the best creative talent they could find, without regard to the private views and political opinions of that talent.

For the duration of the hearings, Mr. Johnston seemed to go along with the members of his Producers Association. But we watched him.

Twenty or more witnesses appeared to give evidence regarding the infiltration of subversive elements into the motion picture industry. One who "testified" to the evident delight of the committee was a White Russian emigre, Miss Ayn Rand. Louis B. Mayer, head of Metro-Goldwyn-Mayer Studios, was, she implied, a near traitor because during the war, when the Soviet people were miring the Wehrmacht in their own bodies when they had nothing else to throw into its path, Mr. Mayer had made a film called *Song of Russia*. And in it, Miss Rand said, he had dared to show Russian people smiling. "It is one of the stock propaganda tricks of the Communists to show these people smiling," she said.

Only two years after the monumental victory over fascism, we listened to these witnesses decrying the rewards of victory, turning America's face away from the "bad thoughts," the "infiltration" of anti-fascism. How did the country suddenly pass into the hands of intellectual gnomes matching men to labels? Labels expose nothing. They obfuscate. For days, we heard talk of Communist devils. Communists are devils. Then would come the question, "Are you now or have you ever been a devil?" In what fashion was this different from "Jews are enemies of the Reich. Are you now or have you ever been a Jew?" Or, "Niggers are inferiors. Are you now or have you ever been a nigger?"

Constant vilification unnerves one. Yet, somehow, all of us who were examined stood against the committee and refused to answer questions concerning our personal beliefs and associations. We were cited for contempt of Congress. Press opposition to the blatantly staged hearings was growing apace, and suddenly, without warning, the hearings were called off at the end of the second week. Only ten of the nineteen had been called when the committee adjourned *sine die* but showing signs of real defeat. We returned to Hollywood, and those of us who had been employed went back to work, some under new contracts and at increased salaries. But we continued to watch Eric Johnston. We did not have to wait long.

Within a few weeks an announcement sent a paroxysm through the community. Eric Johnston had ordered the producers to a special meeting at the Waldorf–Astoria Hotel in New York. Protests from the producers were unrestrained. They knew they were being assembled to preside at the dissolution of Hollywood's authority over its own product. More than one producer declared that if he were the only one to refuse to capitulate to Johnston's Munich, he would do so. Hollywood's anger flew with Hollywood's honor to the Waldorf.

Some fifty assorted producers, executives and lawyers met in battle for several days. When they asked Johnston to square his pressure upon them to capitulate to the defeated committee with his previous public bravado before the committee itself, he replied with uncharacteristic modesty that he was "only a messenger." He came from their boards of directors and financial institutions with a request. The producers had only to "fish or cut bait." Any who wished to be known as soft on Communism in the motion picture industry could vote against his proposals.

By the second day all present understood that their individual jobs and access to money were directly at stake. The open rebellion subsided. But that was not enough for Eric Johnston. He demanded a more visible jettisoning of anger and manhood. He demanded that they all stand—so they could witness each other's total capitulation. And then he lectured them. A vote was nothing. He wanted implementation, committees out of their number to carry out decisions. Thus it was that the document that was known variously as the

Johnston Policy and the Waldorf Declaration came into existence, a
policy which committed an entire industry to an illegal conspiracy to
bar men and their work from the American marketplace forever:

> Members of the Association of Motion Picture Producers deplore
> the action of the 10 Hollywood men who have been cited for con-
> tempt by the House of Representatives. We do not desire to pre-
> judge their legal rights, but their actions have been a disservice to
> their employers and have impaired their usefulness to the industry.
>
> We will forthwith discharge and suspend without compensation
> those in our employ, and we will not reemploy any of the 10 until
> such time as he is acquitted or has purged himself of contempt and
> declares under oath that he is not a Communist.
>
> On the broader issue of alleged subversive and disloyal elements
> in Hollywood, our members are likewise prepared to take positive
> action.
>
> We will not knowingly employ a Communist or a member of any
> party or group which advocates the overthrow of the government of
> the United States by force or by any illegal or unconstitutional
> methods.
>
> In pursuing this policy, we are not going to be swayed by intimi-
> dation or hysteria from any source. We are frank to recognize that
> such a policy involves dangers and risks. There is the danger of hurt-
> ing innocent people. There is the risk of creating an atmosphere of
> fear. Creative work at its best cannot be carried on in an atmosphere
> of fear. We will guard against this danger, this risk, this fear.
>
> To this end we will invite the Hollywood talent guilds to work
> with us to eliminate any subversives; to protect the innocent; and to
> safeguard free speech and a free screen wherever threatened.
>
> The absence of a national policy, established by Congress, with
> respect to the employment of Communists in private industry makes
> our task difficult. Ours is a nation of laws. We request Congress to
> enact legislation to assist American industry to rid itself of subver-
> sive, disloyal elements.
>
> Nothing subversive or un-American has appeared on the screen,
> nor can any number of Hollywood investigations obscure the patri-

otic services of the 30,000 loyal Americans employed in Hollywood
who have given our government invaluable aid in war and peace.

The ten men of Hollywood who had been cited by the committee
were promptly fired and declared unemployable in perpetuity
unless…. The producers returned to Hollywood. But the gates of Hollywood were not opened to the committee for almost three years.
They had to await the outcome of the legal battle of the Hollywood
Ten against their congressional citations.

The black market in their services began ten minutes after the
Waldorf declaration received the unanimous agreement of the members of the Producers Associations. Not every producer engaged in
black market dealings with members of the fired Hollywood Ten.
Some were afraid of the wrath of the committee if they were discovered. But others took advantage of the excellent business opportunity
offered to obtain scripts at one-twentieth to one-tenth of their value.
Why forego the benefits of the old adage, "It's an ill wind that
blows…"? Besides, if caught, it could always be protested that it was
an act of pure charity. Those poor fellows.

The Hollywood Ten litigated through the courts, wrote pam-
phlets, toured the country, appealed for resistance to the committee's
attempt to cancel out the individual liberties enumerated in the First
Amendment.

The lower court found against us. The court of appeals upheld the
lower court. We were not distressed. This was a constitutional matter
for the Supreme Court to rule upon. Our petition for *certiorari* was
accompanied, we were told by more valid briefs, *amicus curiae* than
had ever accompanied a plea for a hearing. Then, quite suddenly, two
liberal Supreme Court justices, Rutledge and Murphy, died. We knew
that we had spent three years in vain so far as *certiorari* was concerned.
Certiorari requires four votes. With justices Rutledge and Murphy gone
we received only two. We prepared to go to jail. The night we entered
prison, the Korean war broke out, with McCarthyism swift upon its
heels. What followed illustrated another adage, "Beware the cure that
is worse than…" But, there are so many adages.

And then six months later Eddie Dmytryk and I were out. And
eight of the ten were still in. What adage covered that?

III

Eddie Dmytryk had directed over twenty movies, among them *Golden Gloves, Confessions of Boston Blackie, Hitler's Children, Till the End of Time* and *Crossfire*. When we had returned from Washington, he and I attended the annual meeting of the Screen Directors' Guild, of which we had been board members, Five of the nineteen who had gone to Washington were directors and were present at the meeting during which partisans of the committee attempted to wrest control of the Guild. Two of the five were then members of the Board of Directors of the Guild and it was demanded of them by shouts from the floor that they answer the questions we had refused to answer or be expelled from the Board. The meeting grew noisy, ugly.

That night a new board member was elected, Cecil B. DeMille, who had come to early organizing meetings of the Guild and pleaded with those present not to organize. Organization was for laborers, not for gentlemen and artists. The producers were our friends and one did not organize against friends. On the skirts of the Un-American Activities Committee hearings, DeMille became a leader of a Guild that was transformed into a court of inquisition.

As Eddie and I walked out of the hotel, one of the most rabid of the directors present approached us, not at all embarrassed. "Don't worry kids. This'll all blow over. Between you and me they treated you boys like a bunch of niggers tonight. Wild men. But you know— get out of line and you get your ass in a sling with the producers." Walking around the parking lot across from the hotel until three in the morning, Eddie was raw, almost to the point of nausea. Not even words would come for a long time. When words came, they were like explosions of anathema. Each attempt to temper his bitterness was brushed aside like the mouthings of an innocent. That men with whom one had worked so long, tasting the dignity of building a Directors' Guild could....

"I'll never trust a human being as long as I live!"

"You can't say that, Eddie. That includes you."

I thought of Eddie the last time I had seen him in the West Street jail in Washington. The third day we were there. The first time we had been given yard privileges. Not yet having made canteen, unshaven, we looked like the stereotypes of inmates. Eddie... so enthusiastic. Jail was an extraordinary experience. Every writer and director ought to manage it somehow. So cocksure and exuberant that day. Most of the others, very sober.

Then, about a month before he was released from jail, Eddie issued a curious statement, very different in tone, a sort of half apology in deference to the war in Korea. Puzzling.

Eddie, his wife, Jeanie, Gale and I met. Just ordinary talk at first, jailbird talk of our institutions. Then of his trip across country, of his baby, of our children and finally of the matter of a letter to the parole board on behalf of the eight still in jail. His flat opinion was that it wouldn't do a particle of good, but, if I wished to write it, he'd sign it. And my question about his puzzling statement from jail, and his reply. He was going to work! He was broke and he was going to do the one thing he knew how to do!

"Herbert, I'm the same guy I always was. *But I'm going to work.*"

"Good," I said, and began talking of plans I had developed for independent production.

"I mean work for the studios."

"The studios? You think you can?"

"I hope so."

We had planned to spend a few days in the mountains, in the snow, where we could be with our families for twenty-four hours a day. The Dmytryks were going to come with us, but late that afternoon jean called to say the baby had a cold. They couldn't join us. We'd see each other when we returned.

As I composed a letter to the parole board, I tried to fathom Eddie's thinking. Work in the studios? Did he know something I did not? I remembered the statement from jail. I fended off a doubt which came to me about it. Eddie had always been passionate, voluble, yet curiously withdrawn in the midst of assertiveness. Now, however, I sensed a very intense, brooding quiet.

The day we returned from the country I was called by a woman who worked in the studios. I knew her slightly, a rather conservative lady whose passion for flowers ruled her life. She seemed in a state of considerable disturbance. Could she see me at once?

That evening at my home she stammered out that that afternoon upon her employer's desk she had seen a statement made by Dmytryk—he was an informer.

Curious how words we think we know escape us in any exactness of meaning in crisis. The word whirled about in my head. Informer! But the lady helped. In short gasps she blurted out, "He says that he was a communist but left the party. He names six others. You are one. He says you weren't villains but fools. That way he doesn't brand your hide deeply—just enough to save his own!"

Her voice quavered. A hallucination seized me. I stood before a great dam and saw a crack open in its broad face. It moved, slanting, down across the whole structure. I felt total immobility as I foresaw the immense waters which would sweep down and from which there was no escape. And suddenly I knew that the dam was me and the rent in its face was a rent in my stomach. Now, the committee had won. Not jail, not blacklist, not isolation, not poverty was their victory. This....

The lady had waited for some explosion from me. None came.

"Why don't you say something?" she asked. "How can you be so indifferent?"

I tried to gesticulate emotionally. But it was lacking in adequate drama for the lady.

"Is there any more ugly betrayal than of one's closest associates? of four years of common struggle—for decency? How can you just sit there?"

I wasn't just sitting. I was immobilized by a presentiment of a very great change in the structure of our lives ahead. How invaluable Eddie had become for them, the key with which to open the flood gates. Now the committee could call hundreds in the expectation of scores of informers. What a Walpurgisnacht! Lying to themselves in private about their previous political concerns, the informers would then be able to recant them and their friends in public. Men like

Eddie would not only review their own past from the point of view of the committee but would take it on themselves to condemn the lives of others, to open veins other than their own on order, an act which Shakespeare would not permit his blowhard clown Falstaff, even at the command of his beloved prince.

What was the axe that had split Eddie?

"I am going to work," he had said. "In the studios."

Work. Man's clue to himself. God-damn it, Eddie wanted to work, to use his talents. That was the axe. The deepest promptings can become our most heinous betrayers when the axe-man comes, his hands extended, ex-communication from work in one and capitulation in the other. What was Eddie to do? Retreat to a flower garden? Sell television sets? Become a bartender, a barber, as others would do? The need to work can penetrate beyond the needs of physical hunger from which, at most, one can only die. Creative hunger will not kill: it malingers and forces one to live in perpetual, self-lacerating non-life. And for what? To what palpable end? Who really gives a damn? A man can get tired dissenting. He wants to say yes too. Even to…?

Had Eddie become tired of fighting for people, of even believing that people were worth fighting for? Had he become sickened to discover how short-lived was applause, how lonely was reliance upon self, and with what scurryings people, capable of building an unqualifiedly noble life, ran for cover where they could defile themselves for such a little safety and for some money? Had these observations, these conclusions gathered into a near loathing of his species? Did he wish not only to separate himself from it, but, somehow, to wreak vengeance upon it for having betrayed it and himself?

Perhaps not.

But, at any rate, Eddie sent word out that he wanted to meet with "the toughest anti-communist in town." The man of the many anti-communist hats, Mr. Roy M. Brewer, International Representative of the International Alliance of Theatrical and Stage Employees Union (IATSE), and a few of his associates answered the call. The terms for Eddie's return to the studios were worked out. In the tradition of Hollywood movies the conditions for return to the "outfit" were tough. Associating himself with Brewer and other members of the Motion Picture Alliance for the Preservation of American Ideals, an organization which, in 1944, he, together with representatives of some twenty thousand workers in the industry, had described as "anti-labor and neo-fascist," Eddie undertook to expose his past friends, his past and himself.

Eddie went to work in the studios.

"I am the same man, but..."

"It is the same country, but...."

IV

Four months later, the petition campaign for the release of the eight men still in jail having failed—with only weeks remaining until the jail gates would open of themselves for the last of the Hollywood Ten—I again began to think about making a film.

Only a week later—after a hiatus of three and a half years the Un-American Activities Committee announced a second "investigation" of Hollywood and the issuance of some seventy subpoenas. The studios *welcomed* the investigation and officially promised full cooperation. The investigation was to become a national institution, like drag-racing.

Hundreds of questions were debated by thousands of persons in the "film capital of the world." How many victims were they seeking this time? How many informers did they have? Which was which? Where would this all end? But the most serious questions concerned motivation. Why—having announced "discovery" almost four years ago of a virulent, subversive fungus feasting upon that tender plant the "movies"—why had the committee not moved in to exterminate it, cell and spore, immediately after the first ten "spores" had been jailed? Why—the producers having capitulated to the committee and subjected every story and idea to microscopic scrutiny for three years, having cut every stem, leaf and tendril which reflected the reality of life—why were they still investigating "the infiltration of communist propaganda into motion pictures?" Or, was the industry, thoroughly coordinated, now to be used as a night-stick upon the rest of the country?

Answers came from individuals prepared to resist re-invasion by the committee. They also came from those prepared to enter what promised to become the biggest new business opportunity in Ameica.

The new "opportunity" was offered by the committee and industry on a silver platter. All one needed was a loose muscle in the oral cavity. One had only to pierce the reputations of intellectuals already long exposed for their indiscriminate softness toward their fellow human beings. In the incredibly infantile and fantastic belief that the era of Roosevelt was adult, defensible and American, they had not

only supported a war which the United States had had to fight in tan-
dem with a communist nation, but had committed the cardinal sin of
waxing enthusiastic about it. Utterly careless, they intoned in public,
published in the public press, even publicly organized for it. The pure
gold nuggets of proof of their anti-fascism lay about in such quantity
as to make exposure of them little more than a grunion hunt. It was
not even necessary to dig. One scooped as fast as one's energy permitted and the accompanying handfuls of sand also passed for the real
gold.

A new atmosphere was lowering upon this southern California
community and the phenomenon was observable on two levels.
There was the physical smog that dulled the five senses and the anti-
intellectual smog that dulled the desire to expose life. These accidentally simultaneous phenomena had contiguous origins in two indus-
tries: the refining of oil, and the distilling of entertainment. The oil
industry, although unwilling to spend the sums necessary for the
eradication of its acid, odoriferous outpouring upon the community,
had no desire, artificially, to worsen it. It did not actively enjoy
befouling its own nest. But to the accomplishment of that specific
end, the movie industry put its "best" brains to work. Intellectuals
became the trumpet soloists in the anti-intellectual jam-session for
which Hollywood was becoming synonym. The artists' job was to
wham the drum, not reason why. If conscience problems arose in
respect to total jettisoning of past reason, the industry came to one's
aid. It provided a lawyer who charted a path to legal absolution from
the committee. The fee was moderate. One had only to denounce
earlier "subversive" humanity as an adolescent foible and one's companions of that period as infantile. Any who persisted in defending
their former infantilism were an impediment to the nation's progress
or had become agents of Moscow, and the blood, in that case, was
upon their formerly ("when I used to know them") quite innocent
heads.

If the lawyer encountered psychological blocks in an individual
and required the assistance of a psychotherapist, one was made available. The therapist who undertook this task would minister to spiri-
tual needs by couching you, or with you, depending upon your sex.

The new atmosphere bred a new cult: Four letter words became standard in polite society.

From one director, who joined the jam session with only the ministrations of the lawyer, and who had been a very close personal friend, I received a letter which was almost unbearably self-punitive:

> I have come to recognize that I was not formed in the heroic mold. Unfortunately, my father and mother bred a moral weakling. I'm truly sorry, but because I am what I am, I'm going to work and get paid for my cowardice.

One unfortunate writer, who had somewhat earlier sought the solo tutoring of the therapist, took off across the Pacific Ocean in a single-motor plane with a quarter tank of gas. That was too brutally quick. Others malingered.

During the few remaining days before the last of the jailed men would be released into the midst of round two, I had the dubious pleasure of acting out the role of elder statesman. Among the first to receive a subpoena for the second round was my wife, Gale Sondergaard.

What would Gale do? Insist upon her rights under the "clouded" First Amendment—and go to jail? Was this resistance? Some counseled so. Fill the jails to bursting! Others questioned whether this would not help condition our fellow countrymen and women to mass jailings as well as mass blacklisting—until almost nothing done to anyone would any longer offend a people successfully "adjusted" to every sort of intellectual and physical barbarity.

And to these larger questions, smaller ones. The father had gone to jail. Now, the mother? And then the father again? Did we not have to prevent jailings so that the mothers and fathers of families might remain in the homes of their still young children? Did we not know by now that no debate was to be permitted, that our words would count for little *against* the committee, or *for* the country in this atmosphere? Was not resistance a matter of being around, to devise other means of fighting back?

"But what will people say if I invoke the Fifth Amendment and protect myself?" Gale asked. "Will they say that your imprisonment made me afraid? I'd rather stand on the First and..."

I watched Gale across twenty-one years of married life. When the competitive spirit had been parceled out among humans she had been off on a holiday. She wished to "best" no one. She had so often refused to participate in a game when skills passed beyond the border of enjoyment, and became combative. Making a speech, participating in argument, were anathema to her. She was happy when, as an artist, behind the veil of character, she could search for expression of human emotion and the juices of life could flow freely through her.

Subversive propaganda in motion pictures? Gale had won an Academy Award for *Anthony Adverse.* Followed by twenty-seven other films. Madame Dreyfus in *The Life of Emile Zola,* the Cat in *The Bluebird,* Empress Eugenie in *Juarez.* The first wife in *Anna and The King of Siam* had won her another nomination for an award and the respect, the affection, of the industry.

The cry of the dope peddler in the cell-block corridor at Texarkana, Texas, rang in my ears: "You'll be back, Bee-bear-mann!" Only Bee-bear-mann would be coming back as Mrs. Bee-bear-mann. "What are you in for?" "Contempt of Congress!" "Contempt of Congress? Kee-rist!"

I didn't wish to contemplate it. And for a most subjective reason. It was high time to get on with making a film. How long would we wait? We had to move forward. To take *one* positive, offensive step forward! First parole prevented it—now more investigations—and what next? We had to get on with something! But the argumentation was to no avail. This wasn't film time either.

I had to relive jail, because Gale *faced* it. I had to relive—its indignities....

The day Gale came to visit me in the jail in Texarkana I had finished my morning's work—unloading a truck load of hundred-pound sacks of potatoes, beans and flour. I was walking rapidly up the hall of the main building on my way to my cell-block. An officer, standing by the control room, called after me. "Biberman, get up to your cell! Put some *clean* clothes on! Your wife's comin' to visit."

I halted in my tracks for an instant. Under the exterior calm my insides were shrieking back at him, "Don't you tell me what to do when my wife comes! Keep your..."

I was in the control room, in the *clean* clothes I had kept guard-edly aside for this purpose for a week. Two officers came up and frisked me. My gorge rose. Why did my wife have to come to this…?

And then we were together. We were told we could kiss once and then there could be no further *fondling.* Her purse had to be on the table in full view of the officer. The officer sat close by to listen in. But Gale was there. It was all right. We were to have two hours together. After we had been together for an hour and a half, I had a need to urinate that reached insufferable intensity. I walked to the officer and told him so. He said if I left I couldn't come back. I told him that was insane. They could frisk me again. No! I demanded that he call the control room. I had to go—and I had to come back! The control room sent back word that if I left, *I couldn't* come back. And I had to tell my Gale that the *indignities* of the morning and the *indignities* attendant upon meeting her… And I left.

I was peering out of the washroom window in my cell-block, as I saw her walk to the taxi-cab and pull away. An inmate was standing near me, and he heard me burst into sobs.

"Perty rough sayin' goodbye, huh? Or ain't that it?"

"Not exactly. It's—little things, sometimes…"

"Naah, it ain't little things. It's the one big thing. You know why you're here and it burns you up. Me? I don't know why I'm here. And that burns me up. But we're both here. And what the hell does it prove?"

"That we've got a job to do."

"Not me. I wanna see 'em boil in oil. They take every god-damned beautiful thing in the world and turn it into shit and make us walk in it. I jus' wanna live long enough to watch 'em eat it!"

His eyes filled and he swallowed hard. Then he turned to look, out of the window, his hand fishing into his back trouser pocket at the same instant. He drew an envelope from it and handed it to me. I looked at the pictures of his wife and a stepladder of three of the handsomest blond boys it seemed to me I had ever seen; twelve, four-teen and sixteen. When I looked back at him, tears were falling down his cheeks. Then he ran to the bowl and was sick to his stomach.

In that slow, calm, shy, yet resolute fashion which was hers, Gale came to her own decision. "I'm going to take the Fifth. That's what it's there for. You know, darling..." There was an instant's hesitation. She searched for a phrase with which to begin. As she did, I was enraptured, as if for the first time, by the active poise, the inner and outer dignity of her. I marvelled that, in all the decades of our life together I had never seen her slouched, crumpled, either physically, emotionally or intellectually. I felt a newer, fuller love for her, an embattled, shared, fighting love. I wished only to walk with her into a more meaningful... and then Gale found the phrase and the thought.

"I've been lying here, thinking of the bond tours I made for our government during the war. And I know that when there was a speech wanted, with insides, they would ask me. And I remember one I made. It started like this: 'I learned from my mother's lips—lips that spoke with a Danish accent—that the earliest Americans thought that rape of the mind was as ugly as rape of the body. That they needed freedom of the spirit and the whole being—as they needed life itself. They needed it so much, that they even had a flag made, and to be absolutely certain that everybody knew what the image on the flag meant, they wrote words on it too. It said, *"Don't tread on me!"'"*

She reflected, and then repeated, *"Don't tread on me!"*

"You know, since I made that speech for the government, I think I am also going to say it to the government. And just in case they won't like it now, I am going to protect myself from being tread on by using the Fifth Amendment. Do you know, I'm beginning to like it."

Preliminaries were at an end.

Resistance was about to begin again.

Now, was film-making time.

Part One

AMERICA 1951

I

Among those declared creative outlaws under the industry's Waldorf declaration, following the 1951 Un-American Committee's renewed Hollywood melee, was Paul Jarrico. A screenwriter, author of *Tom, Dick and Harry, Thousands Cheer, Song of Russia* and *Las Vegas Story*—a record of startling Hollywood catholicity, he is the son of a lawyer, and love of justice rated high among his passions. No one languished in his presence, neither friend nor foe. Something recompensatory was being fashioned of whatever was going on. He nurtured his faiths into a posture of constant, positive expectancy. He would undertake tasks with the air of having accomplished them by the assumption of them. In the many years of our association I do not recall Paul having said anything was difficult. It had to be done? "See you later." He was on his way alerted to all the possibilities: of laughter, of illegal actions against us, and of people through whom our undertakings could be guaranteed.

Ten minutes after he was fired by RKO for refusal to answer those stock committee questions, questions which the committee swore could be answered with a yes or a no—emasculation guaranteed with either answer—he and Adrian Scott had begun to develop several stories for independent production. When we discovered that we were each of us proceeding toward identical goals, we determined to join forces. I called upon my attorney, Ben Margolis, to discuss setting up a company.

"Simon Lazarus has been talking to me about just this sort of thing."

That led us to Simon Lazarus. Simon had been a motion Picture theatre operator almost his entire adult life. In 1942 he had proposed the organization of an independent film production company to me, which he wished to set up and finance. But that was a time of war, a time in which we wished to be closer to the industry, its people and its war efforts. I rejected his invitation, perhaps not only somewhat abruptly, but also without recognition of the creative impulse that motivated him. Now, eight years later, I was talking with him again. I knew he was no longer the man of means he had been. I knew he could not finance the undertakings I would describe for him. But he could vouchsafe us something we needed as much as money. To discover that we were not creatively dead —in the appraisal of others than ourselves.

"The blacklisted! They're like gold laying in the streets. We'll make good pictures and we'll make money. Who is in the company?"

With that encouragement I outlined our thinking, enumerated the distinguished writers whom we could enlist. We would prepare screen plays, produce, direct, organize a company and staff it. Obviously we would have to borrow money for the production. But we would repay every borrowed dollar plus interest before we received any returns, support ourselves until we had completed the making of the film. Would he accept the presidency of the company?

"You have to ask?" he replied. "I've been waiting a long time to do something worthwhile. Yes, I'll be your president. And I'll sell a piece of property and give you ten thousand dollars to begin to operate."

He leaned back, shaking his head slowly in reflection. "What a mistake that we didn't start this eight years ago. You must never be afraid of independence. But I guess there's no danger for you any more. You got independence the hard way. But you got it. O.K. Let's go. And don't wait too long. Bring the boys here tomorrow."

Simon's eagerness to associate himself with our company settled the matter of production. It gave us confidence that the country in which we had grown up would permit us to use the skills we had developed over the years without using an axe upon ourselves or burrowing into the anonymous black market. There were alternatives to self-erasure. We were about to take an appeal to the people of the country, in films.

The first of these "people" was coming through the door of the Hollywood restaurant where I waited at the bar. He was a man with whom I had made a luncheon appointment, hoping he would help us finance a picture company of our own. But there was a stranger with him and my heart fell. I feared to impart what I had to say in the presence of a stranger, who might well warn my friend against being "caught dead" with so incredible a plan. The pleasantries over, the inevitable, "What's on your mind?" followed.

I talked of people first—blacklisted and severed from their life's work. I spoke of their talent. Then of the money a few of us had saved, available to the last penny to help build this undertaking.

The man I did not know took over. Light blue eyes peered from a ruddy, firm face. His questions came thick and fast. They were well conceived. For many of them I had no answers and said so. His questions continued. I knew I was dealing with a man whose mind was trained to search out flaws. He found many of them. I asked that he stop searching for others. I was not prepared to defend the plan as a normal business undertaking. It was a plan "in extremis" and had to be seen in that light.

"Do you mean to tell me that you're going into something without knowing that it can work out?"

"If we don't we'll never begin."

"Do you expect me to put money into this moving picture venture without its making any practical sense whatsoever? You want to make a product—which you don't even know you'll be permitted to make—and the sale of which seems even more dubious. What's the point of all this?"

"I don't think the people of the country go along...."

"People of the country! They'll never even know you failed. These stories you're talking about. They sound pretty radical to me. Why don't you make a nice mystery story?"

"The country has a surfeit of them now. The only thing radical about our stories is that they're about real people."

"What's that got to do with anything? Movies are for entertainment."

"I agree. But I think you're as entertaining as any businessman I could make up."

"What's entertaining about me?"

"You've been good for me. You've played the role of businessman excellently. You've pointed out a number of flaws. Having them pointed out will be very helpful. I thank you."

"You mean you're going ahead with this?"

"We have to! A few men have declared us creatively dead. We have permission to walk around and talk to you and breathe and eat and sleep. But we are not allowed to communicate—not as long as we live. We are going to try. We have that much faith in the people of this country—faith that they will make it possible. I want to thank you both for listening to me and I don't hold it against you that you don't find our plan prepossessing."

"I'll give you five thousand dollars," he said, "to begin with."

Before I could look at him to check on what I thought my ears heard, the man I had made the date with said, "I'll give you twenty-five hundred."

"What?" said the ruddy-faced man. "I said I'd give five thousand. What do you mean you'll give twenty-five hundred? You invited me here. If I give five thousand, you'll give five thousand, too."

"Okay. I'll give five thousand."

"To begin with!"

"To begin with."

The stranger looked back at me.

"Do you know why I've given you this money? You're a fighter. Maybe you're a radical. Maybe very radical. And I don't go for that. You might even be a purple Communist. But I think you think what you're doing is right. Then go ahead and do it. But make it a little funny, huh?"

"It will be entertainment."

"That's a promise."

"Yes. It's a promise. Naturally, I don't want your money now. Our company is not yet organized. But there is a matter we must discuss. When I accept your money, we'll have to give you a note. If you would rather not be on record in the company's books, I can have the note made out to me and then endorse it over to you."

"Why should I not be on record?"

"I have to be very frank about this. The Un-American Activities Committee might....

"... ask me how I see fit to invest my money? I'd like to see them try! I'd like to meet the man in this country who will tell me where to earn a dividend! I'm getting interested in this now. *I want to be on your books."*

My friend said, "I don't."

"Okay. Give me your money. I'll be on the books for ten thousand—for the time being. "

Then he thought quietly for a moment.

"Do you mean to tell me that somebody might actually come to me and ask me if I dared put my money in what my judgment dictated to me was a fine business proposition?"

"They might—because of us."

"Do you mean to tell me that somebody might come to me and tell me I can't make any money through you?"

"It's possible. My advice is that you not be on the books. I don't see what benefit you can derive from it."

"That's *your* advice?"

"It is."

"I don't accept it. I started to say I'd raise my loan to seventy-five hundred. But let's not do it that way. I'm going to get a group of businessmen together and raise quite a little money for you. I'm beginning to enjoy this. I may not have as much money as some of the businessmen in this country who oppose you, but I've earned it with just as much sweat and with just as much relish. I'm glad I bumped into you here. Give 'em hell. Who do they think they are anyway? Telling you whether you can work or not! Telling me where to invest my money! Waiter! The check!"

The following day I received a call from him. I was to meet him that evening at his house. He would have a group of friends there.

Within a few weeks we had thirty-five thousand dollars pledged. One-third of the budget of our picture. All from businessmen. It wasn't easy to get. But in most instances, when the chips were down, the men would not refuse to gamble on a democratic America.

Paul Jarrico, Simon Lazarus and I met with our attorneys, Ben Margolis and Charles Katz. We opened a bank account. We deposited thirty-five thousand dollars. Independent Productions Corporation now had capital. Only sixty-five thousand more to raise and we could make a film—if we had a script, a crew, equipment, and a cast.

II

Four months later we had several stories in work. They were going badly. We were worried. We had spent fifteen years in Hollywood. We knew stories written for effect. Did we measure up to the requirements of stories about real people and real situations? In one instance the story chosen simply would not illustrate the people in it. It was the wrong structure and background for what we hoped to express. In another the idea in the story came out as an idea—in discussion—and would not dramatize itself. We had fifty thousand dollars in the bank by now. Money, it turned out, was not our problem—not at that juncture. We were the problem. We were discovering the vast distance between intention and skill. We were meeting daily and all day and all night and making very little progress.

Toward the end Paul Jarrico had gone away on a few weeks vacation with his family. He had heard of an extraordinary strike in progress in New Mexico. The strike had been called against New Jersey Zinc in Bayard, New Mexico, by Local 890 of the Mine, Mill and Smelter Workers Union. This old and militant union had been expelled from the C.I.O. for alleged Communist influence. The local union membership was largely Mexican-American. Several months before, when the strikers were faced with a Taft-Hartley injunction prohibiting the miners from picketing, the women of the local union's Ladies Auxiliary had taken over the picket line from their miner–husbands and were holding it with dramatic bravery and resourcefulness. The Jarricos drove there.

Ten days later Paul came back to Hollywood, filled with the sights and sounds of that little town in New Mexico. His eyes glowed as he regaled us with descriptions of the women, the men, the community; a feast of incidents, told with the creative enthusiasm of a writing man who had seen a "story."

"This is it," said Paul. "All there, ready to study, live. If we could only get Mike to write it!"

Mike was Michael Wilson, screenwriter, freshly blacklisted, and brother-in-law to Paul. Winner of an Academy Award for the screenplay A *Place in the Sun*, he had also been nominated for an award for his screenplay *Five Fingers*. Quiet, intense, soft-spoken, precise, he was forever curling a lock of his prematurely iron-gray hair with his forefinger. When he was spoken to, his steel-blue eyes lifted, shot a hard glance at whoever addressed him, and then he replied tersely. When the intensity of look and speech subsided, a wry gaiety appeared. He was never off alert. Observation at three hundred sixty degrees was a compulsion in him.

If there was a profoundly funny way to put something Paul Jarrico was attempting it. If there was a profoundly incisive way of putting something Mike Wilson was at it. Paul never saw anything but potentialities. Mike saw difficulties standing squarely upon the Adam's apple of all possibilities, and would proceed, soberly, to the rescue, because he hated to let a good possibility down. Mike and Paul were fast friends. When the three of us were together there wasn't enough fear around to put on the point of a needle. How good it would be to have him.

But Mike was, at last, deep into work on a novel. It meant a great deal to him. Would he give it up, and go to Silver City, and take on a screen play without any assurance that six months of punishing work would ever be realized in a film?

He took on the assignment, but with one proviso. "Fellows, we've got to give up trying to write stories about real people from our point of view. I think that's why the stories you have been doing are not coming off. If I do this story, I want to do a story from the point of view of the people of Local 890. And if I do this story, they are going to be the censors of it and the real producers of it... in point of view of its content. If you think something's great and they think it's lousy, they're going to win. And vice versa. I may have to spend a lot of time there. And I can't make any promises about how soon this script will be done. I've got a lot of reorientation to do. Terms satisfactory?"

The terms were satisfactory. And Mike left for Local 890. He was there for a number of weeks. When he returned he said, "It's all there and nothing's there. It's not a matter of situation. It's people. It's a story of people and the conflict is very complex. There are battles for equality taking place there on so many levels I can hardly unskein them yet myself."

He shifted in his chair. He didn't really want to capsulize his concept yet. But he was going to—a complex, many-peopled screen play—in a paragraph.

"Well, the core—it's something—something like this: A love story. A Mexican-American miner and his wife. In love. And divided—by everything outside themselves. He, consumed by hatred of the discrimination that surrounds his people and his family, Can't think of anything else. She, feeling ignored—overburdened—despairs of life itself. Their situation becomes intolerable. The men strike. And they hold fast. The company—finds a legal maneuver, and prepares to break the strike. The men are lost. Desperate women, suddenly appear out of nowhere—so far as their husbands are concerned—and offer to take over the battle. And do. And overnight—they become important. The struggle for equality moves to a new level, which includes the old. Because the men can't overcome company discrimination against them unless they overcome their own against their women. A people will either unify itself for the real struggle—or fail in it. That's it! The theme: The indivisibility of equality. The story: A husband's struggle to accept as his equal the wife he loves. A wife's insistence that love include respect. The resolution: The women lead the men to victory on all fronts because in social struggle *they* call on and embrace every living soul in their community—the men included."

Mike clenched his teeth and said, "Now—go away and leave me be."

Two months, three months went by. Mike was dour, silent and curling his forelock furiously. But there was nothing for us to read. And then one day there came a treatment. We hung on with our figurative fingernails as we read. And afterwards, when we had completed it, we knew, the way you know that you're breathing, that it breathed. And we said, "Yes, Mike...." But he paid scant attention to us, although he listened. He took off for Silver City.

When he returned, several weeks later, we knew by his eyes, by his face, and by the reduced speed with which he twirled his forelock, that he had passed his own first test. "There have got to be some changes." Then came the stories of his conferences with the people in Silver City.

In the treatment, when the women take over the picket line and the men are left to handle domestic chores, Ramón, the strike captain, a male supremacist, starts having an affair with a young widow. This, Mike informed us, had to be changed. The men objected to the sequence. What about the women, we asked. The women had insisted it stay in.

"Oh, you're all so pure!" they said. "You don't do things like that?"

The objecting, adamant men said, "Maybe a few have. But that doesn't make it true. It shows the men up in a bad light."

"It stays in," said the women. "Let it be a warning."

"Is this story to insult us?" asked the men.

Mike said, "It's going out because of another reason. It isn't typical. But beyond that, it raises the old stereotype of the sensual, promiscuous, Latin male. It's a phoney."

Then he discussed another scene in the treatment. Just before the strike began, Ramón, with part of his last pay check, knowing it was to be the last in quite a while, bought a bottle of whiskey. The men hadn't time to comment on this scene before the women objected, "Our husbands are not drunkards," they said.

"That goes out too," said Mike.

"You see," he said to us, "these are perfectly legitimate dramatic scenes and illustrations. In a script in which you're after drama for its own sake, they'd be perfectly acceptable. But we're dealing with something else. Not just people. _A_ people. And you don't necessarily express them through naturalistic detail. You have to really synthesize them, all of them; the weaknesses and the virtues, until the individual expresses a real element of the whole and something not atypical of the whole, even though a variant part of it. The point is this: discrimination has forced these people into a conscious as well as unconscious unity. They have respect for themselves as a whole, because they've learned that the individual doesn't get anywhere by himself. The fact is they're a people. It's a beautiful thing to see and to reflect. I'm a little in awe of the job. I've got a lot of work to do."

Six months later there was a second draft of a screen play. And we believed in it. Not without reservations, but with absolute faith in its final form. And the miners and their wives believed in it. We took it to the International Union in Denver, and they believed in it. After a year, and two previous failures, we had the basis for a motion picture. Now we could move the script into final shooting form—and organize the production.

Simon Lazarus, as president of our company, Independent Productions Corporation, called upon Mr. Roy M. Brewer, the international representative of the International Alliance of Theatrical and Stage Employees union in Hollywood. It represented almost all the back-lot workers in the industry. Simon Lazarus, who had been a theater exhibitor in Los Angeles for thirty years, was one of the first to recognize this union, and he had supported its efforts to organize the theater projectionists. He had asked for the assignment of meeting with Mr. Brewer. An official of a local of the union accompanied Mr. Lazarus, proud to vouch for his pro-union history. Simon Lazarus asked Mr. Brewer for a crew for our picture. Brewer, Simon reported to us, told him that the Hollywood Ten had been run out of the industry for good. He also told Simon that no one who refused to cooperate with the Un-American Activities Committee would get a crew or make a picture and that if Simon proceeded with such people Simon would be destroyed.

Roy M. Brewer, rehabilitator of Eddie Dmytryk, "toughest anticommunist in town," was above all a man of many bats: International Representative of the I.A.T.S.E. in Hollywood; Chairman of the Hollywood AF of L film council; Chairman of the Motion Picture Industry Council; Champion of the "rehabilitation" (blacklisting) system for the motion picture industry; the industry's volunteer liaison man with the American Legion; leading light of the Motion Picture Alliance for the Preservation of American Ideals. Mr. Brewer was the man of destiny in this time of expiation for past over-zealousness by present, conducted, gut-spilling. Many of the producers had allergies to blood. But they didn't have to look far for someone with stomach for it. Their boy was waiting in the wings, wings which he had had some part in setting into position. The producers gave him all the titles, all the chairs, all the pleasure of power. Hence, despite the fact that he was only a lowly international labor representative in a community which worshiped status, he was able to say to Simon Lazarus, with all the authority of a monarch, that if he proceeded with such persons, he would be destroyed.

To Lazarus's reply that the right to engage in business, to employ and associate himself with others, was his, that the union could not deprive him of that right, that he wished a contract and a list of available men, Mr. Brewer retorted that if Lazarus knew what was good for him, he would get out of this thing before it was too late.

How were we to obtain a crew? We were not going to make any pictures, so the labor "leader" of Hollywood had decreed! What were we to do? Sue the union, since their refusal to provide us with craftsmen was illegal under the Taft-Hartley law? But we attacked Taft-Hartley in our script. Shoot with a non-union crew? We had a moral right, since a union crew was denied us. But it was wormwood in our mouths. We must look for a cameraman first.

Paul searched. Many liked the script. The idea of the film was challenging to them. But it was clearly dangerous. They feared they might lose their union cards if they worked with us. It was tough, but they couldn't voluntarily end their careers, could they?

The summer was passing. The good weather was rolling by. Go to Mexico? Make the picture there? No! This picture was going to be made in the United States of America. Attempt to obtain a Mexican cameraman? A Mexican crew? Would they be permitted into the country? Wait a minute! There was a *documentary* union in New York, Paul suggested. It was affiliated with the CIO. Get them.

I was off to New York. This had to be done quickly. There was casting to do, and much work with Mike on the script from my own, the director's, point of view. I wasn't altogether pleased with the character of Ramón. In elevating women to their proper rank as equal individuals we had denigrated Ramón excessively. It was almost as if we couldn't raise women without trampling on the men. The men had lessons to learn. But they were brave and determined working men. Ramón, thematically, carried the line of ancient struggle of his people. He had to retain the full measure of his valor as well as carry the full weight of his weakness. It was not there—yet!

In New York the documentary union people were most interested. But terribly afraid. What would happen to them if they worked with us? We were—well—*hot!* And they were just then in negotiation for merger with the I.A.T.S.E.—the very union which had just refused us a crew. They talked and talked and finally agreed. The following day they called for more discussion.

I understood their dilemma. And they understood it. It was a crippling business for them: to wish to make this film. To have respect for the thing wished for. Not to know whether or not to fear their fears. And to be afraid to find out! Could I give them ten days? By then they'd know. I couldn't wait that long in New York. Well then, yes—they would come. The details would be ironed out. I returned home to casting.

From the very beginning, the role of Esperanza, the leading woman's role, had been designed by Mike for Gale Sondergaard, my wife. For Ramón we had decided to use a well-known Hollywood actor who also was blacklisted. One of the purposes of this company was to engage the blacklisted in their professions again. And now, before we had even really begun, we were jolted by recognition of a primary obligation. We had thought of ourselves as "the blacklisted." And we were the veriest newcomers. Culturally and socially, as well as politically and economically, vast numbers of our American people had been blacklisted for centuries. Had they not been, we might never have been. Were we, the new blacklisted, to blacklist the older ones? Keep them unexpressed and unfulfilled? We were preparing a film of the Mexican-American people. But we had selected two "Anglos" to play the leads! Oh, we had planned to use Mexican-Americans in all the small parts. But we couldn't entrust Mexican-Americans with the *important* Mexican-American roles. The Hollywood tradition! And we were carriers.

The first humiliating recognition of our discriminatory inheritance was sufficient. We knew what we had to do. Perhaps the hardest task for me was breaking it to Gale. For months she had been growing, slowly, happily, into this role. Her immediate reply was, "Of course. How unfeeling we have all been!"

On the heels of that realization the documentary crew in New York notified us that they required a twelve-week shooting schedule. We had planned on six. To me their demand was a refusal wrapped in the bows and ribbons of polite escape. My colleagues disagreed. They believed I was unsympathetic to the new problems we posed to film people who knew only about documentaries. They were unfamiliar with the technique of a story-film. Our kind of shooting was more organized, swifter. I was to return to New York, and explain all of this. However, whatever the compromise, our film must be made with a union crew. Summer was rolling by with terrifying speed. What came first, a crew or a cast?

I flew to New Mexico for two days, made some tests of various miners and their wives and daughters, and flew back with the film. Most of our company opposed the use of non-professionals in the leading roles. The roles were too complex, too delicate in nuance. I did not agree. I remembered unforgettable performances of equally non-professional Chinese in the play *Roar China* that I had directed for the Theatre Guild in New York.

But, as a necessary precaution, we telephoned friends in Mexico and asked them to search for two leading actors and supplied details concerning the roles. Then we returned to the question of non-professionals enacting them. It seemed to me that my colleagues were confusing two distinct categories—the actor who plays a character foreign to him and a people who enact themselves.

To back up my opinion, I related an incident of the final dress rehearsal of *Roar China*. The Chinese in the cast had been recruited from the restaurants, laundries, gift shops in New York's Chinatown. It had been a long and arduous day. On the stage was a battleship with rising guns, around which sampans moved, in eleven inches of water in which men drowned.

The technical problems were so many that we rehearsed scenes in the order in which the technicians could solve them, rather than as the action demanded. A young Chinese student played "Number One Boy" on the British battleship. Early in the play he was to be shoved off the gangplank into the water and be saved by a sampan. Later in the play, in deep, personal depression, he was to hang himself before the cabin door of the captain of the ship. We had rehearsed the hanging scene first and, because of faulty rigging, he had come within an inch of losing his life. He was, for some time, in a state of traumatic shock. But we had only one day in which to complete the full rehearsal. This was the inescapable commercial pressure upon us. When we proceeded to the scene in which he was to fall into the water, breaking the impact without any hurt to himself, he was incapable of doing it.

He extended his hand to break his fall, revealing the depth of the water to be what it was—eleven inches! In the next attempt he landed on his feet, then on one foot, then on the other hand. An hour had gone by. I was at my wit's end. I tried a hundred suggestions. They failed. I sought to cajole him into recovery, argue him into it, upbraid him into it. And finally, in a state of utter compulsion myself, I asked him whether he wished me to pull off my clothes and show him how to do it. I weighed twice as much as he! If I did not fear to do this "simple" fall, why should he? As I spoke I pulled off one article of clothing after another. Finally I stood upon the gangplank in my shorts and, declaiming loudly upon the simplicity of the action and forgetting where I was and what I was doing, I *dove* into the eleven inches of water and landed on my nose!

I arose with blood streaming down my face and onto my body, all the while proclaiming the "simplicity" of the fall, and offering to do it again. The Anglo actors on the stage were convulsed with laughter at my athletic dive, the flowing blood and my utterly ridiculous assurances of the success of my demonstration. Not a single Chinese on the stage, and there were more than seventy, so much as smiled. Then without any perceptible sign of his intention, a very old Chinese with purest white, silky hair and soft, flowing beard took one step toward the young man and barely touched the side of the youth's arm. The young man walked to the platform, closed his eyes, and fell flat upon the water. The Caucasian professionals ceased laughing.

The relevant point in this story for us was that for the Chinese playing in it, *Roar China* was an act of love and pride, not of commerce. They weren't making careers for themselves. They were seeking to build affection in the heart of Americans for their country of cultural origin and its people. This was their dramatic stature. As they achieved it they not only "outplayed" the Caucasian professionals, but in scenes which included both groups it was only barely possible to see the professionals on the stage. The Chinese developed a homogeneity, a group presence, that endowed each individual with stature that was a gift from the whole. It brought a power in relaxation to them that few *actors* achieve. If they brought less skill, they brought the authority and dedication of their own persons and that incomparable thing—the reality of a people.

As I finished telling this story, our friends in Mexico telephoned. They had the perfect actress for us: Rosaura Revueltas. In addition they spoke of a Mexican actor who had left Mexico City only a few days before and must now be in Hollywood. If we could get him for the role—there was no one more suited to enact it as actor, person, and physical type. We expressed our interest in Miss Revueltas whom I had once met. We would communicate with her soon.

That evening I met with the actor. The following morning he had read the script. He proclaimed it the role he had been waiting all his life to play. We warned him that playing this role might permanently close Hollywood's doors to him. He dismissed the warning without concern. Did we realize what it meant to him to be able to express his national pride, his love of a character such as Ramón, the heroic struggles of his own people? He'd rather play this role than ten of the fattest Hollywood could trot out! At two days' notice he'd be ready to leave for Silver City.

Some time later, when I was ready to leave for Silver City, I called him. He asked to see me at breakfast the following morning. What a different fellow than the one I had first met. Apologetic, morose, he told me his problem. His agent had warned him against any association with us. It would sound the death-knell of his Hollywood career, which, miraculously, was just about to begin for fair. His agent had told him he had two parts for him in two studios, one part to follow the other. I must not misunderstand—he wanted terribly to play Ramón—he was born to play it —but! Renounce Hollywood?

And two roles? Even if they were just the same old Hollywood Mexicans! They were—it was—he meant—didn't I? I assured him that I
did. I asked him to forget Ramón. Forgetfulness was the price everyone paid for remaining in the good graces of Hollywood that year,
even to play a Hollywood Mexican. "Someday!" he said. "Yes," I
replied, "Someday, someday!"

Mexican-American actors in Hollywood! The few with standing
had either feared to talk with us, or, if they did, protested that their
standards of living imprisoned them in the need to "keep in good
with Hollywood."

I had read with a number of the bit players of Mexican origin.
They were eager to join us, but because of the size of the role, not
because of its meaning. They had little to lose or to offer. Pride in
their cultural background was forgotten or had been abandoned. The
men read "refinement" into the indomitable cultural militance of
Ramón. The women brought Hollywood smiles and middle-class
intercession to the unerupted volcano of Esperanza. They had lost the
art of touching a neighbor's arm as the old Chinese had done in *Roar
China.*

As I entered Paul's home to report on the loss of our Ramón,
there was a telephone call for me from New York. It was a spokesman
of the documentary crew to say that it was not joining us to make the
film. After a full round of peripheral niceties I asked the spokesman
for the true reason. In the ensuing silence I volunteered a question.
"Is it the same old fright? The I.A.T.S.E.? I have to know!" A tension-
filled pause. Then... "Yes."

I hung up the phone and sat shaking my head.

"I knew it when I left. It's hopeless. They're immobilized."

Paul and Mike spoke very quietly. We had to have a union crew.
The documentary crew was the only one we had a chance of getting.
I must return to New York. I must convince them.

"But..."

"We have to have them! We simply have to have them. You
ought to go back right away. Crew comes before cast. How soon can
you leave?"

III

En route to New York for another go at the documentary crew, I stopped at Silver City to scout locations. Those in which the "live" events had taken place were photographically magnificent and every one *boldly on public property!* Where would we go if the mine superintendents persuaded the local authorities to eject us?

I returned to the union hall and laid my concern before the local's officers. We must find a privately owned five-hundred-acre ranch to which we could escape in case of difficulties. Large doubts were written upon their brows. Who among them knew anyone with a five-hundred-acre ranch? And especially anyone who would be willing to turn it over to a union project? Sitting in on the discussion was an Anglo miner, sixty or thereabouts, a man who had done almost everything a man could do in one lifetime. He told us he knew of a man, Alford Roos, rather elderly, who lived quite alone on a very large ranch, "a thousand acres or more, over in Vanadium." Roos was an independent mine owner, had a lot of land under lease to some of the big mines. He was a brilliant man in many ways. Could read Arabic. Said he had been converted to Mohammedanism. He had been an explorer, archaeologist, inventor, writer—and was a very independent person. Couldn't tell what he might do. Might throw you out, even shoot at you. But if I were willing to take the chance....

Did he know this gentleman? Yes, he had done some surveying on his property a few years back. Would he feel free to call him on the telephone and ask for an appointment for us? "Do it right now," the miner said. He called and made an appointment immediately.

From the main road to the ranch house it was a mile drive down the bumpiest little dirt road an automobile had ever traveled. The house had to be approached by way of the kitchen door. On the ground immediately surrounding it was a mass of steel rails, old ore cars, barrels, pumps, drills, iron pipes and other invaluably authentic "props" for such a film as ours. The ranch house was located in a valley with gentle sloping hills rising at every angle away from its center. A half-mile down the deep, rocky arroyo that was the bed of the valley, the shaft of a mine was visible.

We knocked on the back door of the house and it was flung open immediately. There stood a very short and very thin man of seventy or more. He was dressed in an old T-shirt, trousers and a pair of sneakers. He looked at us for a long second, his small black eyes no less set than his hard, unshaven chin.

"Come in! Whisky or beer?"

He turned and led us through his kitchen into his living room. We told him beer as we walked in and he disappeared for refreshments. The room was more a museum than the living room of a dwelling. In one corner stood an assortment of some fifty rifles of various vintages. In another corner about the same number of spears. The walls were a mass of pictures from all parts of the world and heads of various animals. A solid gold Inca shrine gleamed with the reflected light of the late afternoon sun. Rough uncut stones were scattered on the tables, some having the outward aspect of precious varieties. Every chair in the room was covered with a rather old and, in some cases, very far gone animal skin. And over the whole of this room and its contents was spread a layer of cigarette ash an eighth to a quarter of an inch thick. We sat down on the edge of chairs.

The gentleman returned with the beer and began to talk as if we were honored guests who, having heard of him and his collections, had come to visit both as interesting landmarks of the area. His speech was New England, incisive, well enunciated and fashioned out of a large vocabulary. His black eyes darted as he spoke and his jaws clamped together frequently. He gave every indication of having a trigger-mind. When he paused in his description of his possessions, I spoke. I said that we had called on him to ask something of him and that I wished first to inform him about myself. I believed a man ought to know with whom he was talking.

"Who are you?" he asked. His eyes set and his jaws set and his small springy frame set and he was as quiet and attentive as he had been garrulous a moment earlier.

I told him our Hollywood history, the nature of our film, and finally placed before him our desire to use his ranch as an escape to private property if we encountered difficulty on public property. I was then, and am now, no poker player. But as I spoke I made a mental note never to be drawn into playing the game against him. His face and every muscle were rigidly sealed against expression. Involuntarily my eyes sought the exits as I developed my story. I finished by adding that if our visit disturbed or embarrassed him we would leave.

He held his silence for a long moment, his unmoving eyes on me. Finally, he spoke.

"You're one of that Hollywood gang?"

"I am," I said, and was tempted to repeat my earlier promise of readiness to leave at once, when his second question came.

"You've been in jail?"

"Yes, sir. I have been."

"WELL! PUT IT THERE, OLD BOY, OLD BOY!" And with this he leaped up from his chair and shook my arm almost out of its socket! His seventy-year-old grip made me cringe. And his enthusiasm was no less fierce. His face was now aglow with dancing fires. Then he invited me to sit down again. He told me his views, past and present. He was a militant, arrogant, unregenerated Jeffersonian living presently with anger and shame. Then he stopped, held his peace for a moment and abruptly addressed me in a most businesslike tone.

"What do you want?"

"I want your ranch to escape to if we have to. We'll pay for the use of it."

"Escape, hell! You come here and shoot the whole damn thing here. I'll stand at the top of the hill with a gun in my hands and say, 'Yes, I've got the whole gang here. What're you going to do about it? This is a thousand acres of Jeffersonian America and don't any reactionary, un-American hoodlum put his foot on it!'"

A half-hour later I had left the ranch with a contract in my pocket and a thousand acres of the state of New Mexico enrolled against the censors and silencers. All that for one dollar down!

As I flew from New Mexico to New York over this great blossoming land, I found myself singing, and smiling as I sang. We had a script, fifty thousand dollars, a location site, a union of miners. And I began to outsoar the plane. This flight was one of the happiest times in some years. I felt more than the joy of battling for the country below me. I enjoyed again a feeling of residence in it. And I owed it to

Alford Roos, independent mine-owning "Mohammedan," Scandina-vian-American, American. Perhaps what made me happiest of all was the deep-seated knowledge that at that moment Alford Roos was just as happy as I. I had found a man willing to be engaged against the benighted. *He* had been "found out," though buried in the confines of a museum-ranch house, a mile off the main road of a town of a thou-sand inhabitants, way off in the copper-laden hills of New Mexico. And he was happy to have been discovered. How many like him were stashed away in the America below me, in those endless prairies and villages and cities; individuals whose outraged national pride stuck in their gullets, but who did not know what to rally around?

IV

The New York documentary film workers now suggested postponement of the shooting until the following spring. Negotiations with the I.A.T.S.E. had slowed down. They could talk again. They offered as argument that we were already into the fall of the year and weather would be bad. I submitted weather reports that indicated the month of December in New Mexico to be without major precipitation, and January usually beautiful. I had a hunch they were talking political, not physical, climate. I insisted upon December. But a few days later I left New York with their agreement based on a compromise schedule of eight weeks and production to begin in January.

My colleagues received the news with gratitude. I had succeeded in spite of my previous doubts. When I said that my doubts still held, they smiled with pardonable reservations concerning my sportmanship.

And then, as on so many occasions—fireworks! Our collaboration was no bed of roses! No passive agreement directed at a boss to keep a job, and no fierce contest for personal advantage. Battles raged for the points at issue—but for them, not for us.

There was one thing we never argued about—what we were undertaking. It was one thing and we were one in seeking it. But as to a quality in the script, the achievement or failure of mood, or point in the direction of a scene, the battles were long, fierce and always resolved. Not on the ground that one or the other was the supreme authority, even in his particular field. But, if discussion did not bring agreement, then on the basis of a majority vote. It was difficult to take, at the beginning and, for that matter, also at the end. But we came to rely upon it, increasingly, as security for the end object, against our own individual weaknesses, even in the areas of our greatest individual strength. If we couldn't find one supporter, we swallowed our conviction and lived with and worked toward that of the majority.

And so it was in the matter of casting. I was outvoted. The company's decision was to use professional actors in the leading roles. It was necessary to go immediately to Mexico. We hoped that Rosaura

Revueltas would prove a proper choice. She was Mexican. She was a professional. I was also to find an actor to play Ramón, and then go directly to Silver City to cast the smaller roles and, finally, begin rehearsals.

After two days of work with Rosaura I signed her to a contract. I gave her a letter for presentation to the American Embassy in applying for a visa, stating that we had employed her. The visa was granted. Rosaura was Esperanza.

Rosaura Revueltas de Bodenstedt: A remarkable woman in an extraordinary household. She had had few years of schooling, having been born into the family of an impoverished small shopkeeper. Her mother, the daughter of a miner in northern Mexico, had borne many children. Of them, five had survived into adulthood. Rosaura's oldest brother had become Mexico's greatest composer, but had died at an early age. Her second brother had become one of the most gifted of the newer Mexican painters. He also died at an early age. Her only living brother was a leading novelist and screenwriter. Rosaura had played but three roles in the Mexican film industry but had won national awards for two of them. She spoke English, French, German and Italian, as well as her native Spanish—all self-taught. She was an accomplished dancer.

Her husband was German by birth. He had been a flyer in World War I. At its end, surfeited with German militarism and Emperor-worship, he left Germany. Speaking of his native land, his features firmed. "In Germany, everyone spoke of military courage. The German soldier was the most courageous in the world. But there was one thing that was lacking in Germany, always lacking—*civic* courage. Nobody spoke out. Not really. And without civic courage, what does a country have? Parades? Brass bands?"

He met Rosaura in Mexico when she was sixteen. They were married almost immediately. Now at thirty-five she had an eighteen year old son, six feet two, as lean as a birch and preparing to enter medical school. He and his father spoke all the languages Rosaura had taught herself and at table their conversation was, paragraph to paragraph, in one of five alternating tongues. Each chosen, one gathered, only to suit the precise mood to follow.

With Rosaura's help, an intensive search was initiated for an actor to play the leading role. The United States of America is large and powerful and Mexico is small and weak, and their borders meet. Our script honored people of Mexican cultural background; was an expression of their racial vigor, the Mexicans understood. But it was an insufficient solvent for their fear of the censorial attitude in the United States.

As I read with the few Mexican actors available to us, I came to appreciate that the Mexican-Americans of New Mexico were not Mexicans. They were a product of the struggle of their root culture and the struggle of their United States living. Dual struggle brought them dual strength and they needed it. They lived with their opponents—all the variegated partisans of inequality—face to face and day and night! Not one instant's surcease. The Mexicans, on the other hand, were a nation. They had sovereignty. No! Ramón, Mexican-American, was going to have to be found in the United States. Then, together with a Mexican actress, New Mexican miners' families, and blacklisted Hollywood film makers, we would begin a motion picture depicting the struggle for equality of a minority people in the United States—a struggle that succeeded.

Heading for Silver City, the road had begun to descend. The snow was changing into fog through which one could begin to see. I increased the car's speed. The houses on the outskirts of Silver City came into view.

It was now two years since prison—in a car driving toward Silver City. The long last night in jail indeed had ended. My liberty continued. And we were on our way to begin shooting a movie. No one had asked us to undertake this. It was our own idea. At least in part. Perhaps the largest part of every striving for liberty comes from outside oneself. From some indestructible popular intelligence or faith in it. It had nourished us for a year and a half. And in spite of the "times" behind us and around us, a final shooting script of "Salt of the Earth" was in our brief cases.

We dropped our bags at the lodge in Silver City and we drove another ten miles to Bayard. It was eight-thirty. The little town was dark and almost invisible in the unrelenting storm. The small unpainted wooden building which was the union hall showed little light. I opened the door. We entered. A miner in his work clothes, the sergeant-at-arms, barred the way. His speech was pure Oklahoma. "This here's a union meetin'," he said. Before we could reply, one of the officers at the other end of the small room nodded to him. We were permitted to pass through and took seats. The miner who had stopped us came to my side. "Excuse me fer stoppin' you. But I got t'know who's comin' in'y here." I nodded. "They wuz expectin' you, huh? You must be them movie people? That's O.K. I didn't know, and that's my job: t'know. Yer mighty welcome." Many of the persons present turned and nodded or lifted a hand a little. We knew most of them. The ladies smiled, shyly.

The president of the union was speaking in Spanish—Ernest Velasquez, a man of thirty-five, with glasses, shirt open at the neck and wearing a leather jacket. His voice quiet, firm. His tone though casual was clearly studied in its intention to communicate.

Almost all of the eighty or ninety men and women present were Mexican-American. There were ashtrays on the benches. No one crushed his cigarette out on the floor. One would guess they had built the hall themselves. Rugged, calm, gentle faces. On previous visits we had studied them for hours, as if they were paintings in a gallery. They weren't. As militant trade unionists as this country had bred. A Catholic people. Every house with its shrine and holy pictures. An intelligent people. No soft soap went far with them.

And that was the trail over which we had walked, flown and skidded until, finally, Paul and I sat in this union hall of Local 890 in Bayard, New Mexico, in Grant County, waiting to address the members and announce that we had arrived to begin filming their lives, albeit without a leading actor.

That night the documentary union people in New York telephoned that they were not coming to New Mexico. I was not surprised. Brewer and the I.A.T.S.E. had delivered a knock-out blow through decent, frightened people.

Paul told us not to worry, we would have a crew—on time. Knowing Paul, I knew with what persuasive and infectious confidence in people he would proceed. He left for Los Angeles at once.

In one sense, this picture was more Paul's than anyone's. Not alone that he had found this reality and suggested it as a picture, but that in every moment of everyone else's despair his stubborn optimism, humor and scorn for difficulties became a parachute that went up instead of down. Often his seeming obliviousness of catastrophe would become infuriating. He would smile blandly and say, "We've got it made." And then turn up with the most unexpected people, products of his faith in them, who would also turn up with the most unexpected people out of their faith—and we were off again. There was no job too ungrateful for him, and even if he were covered up to his neck with muck, yanking a half-ton drilling rig through it by a string, he would be every inch a producer and bring dignity to the craft. Many of his cracks are unforgettable: when a reporter asked him one day if our film were in 3D (three dimensions), Paul blithely replied that ours was in 4D. The reporter, somewhat flabbergasted, asked, "What the hell does that have?" Paul replied, "Content."

If Paul said we'd have a crew, and on time, we'd have one. It would necessarily be tatterdemalion, but so was the army of the American revolution, and *it* won. I wired Rosaura that there might be a short delay, but asked that she sit tight. As Paul would have put it, "We had it made." All we needed was a crew, a leading male actor and Rosaura, our leading woman, safely across the United States border.

V

Of our crew, recruited by Paul, some came from New York, some from Chicago, some from Denver, some from Los Angeles. Some were past members of the studio unions who had been expelled for opposing Brewer. Some were present members of his union who would not be dictated to. Insisting that he had no right to deprive them of work, they joined us, even at the risk of their union cards. Some had never worked in motion pictures before, but came from the field of television. Some had never worked on a story film before. Two were members of the documentary union. They wished to work with us and came. Three were Negroes. Although the Hollywood unions were 100 per cent Jim Crow, we were free to choose our crew out of representative parts of the population.

Some came for two weeks, some for a month, some for the duration. Some came anonymously, some timorously, some under their own full names. Some came because they would have died to make this film, some because they could learn from a new experience, some for the job, some strictly for the money, some because—in spite of all our explanations—they didn't know what they were getting into.

Where were we to house thirty people of mixed composition in Silver City? My brother, Edward, and my sister-in-law, Sonja Dahl Biberman, who was also the secretary of our company, had been scouring the area in vain for days. There were no accommodations, anywhere, for a mixed company. The lodge in which we were staying was everything we could have wished for. It would accommodate thirty. This was off season and the lodge was unused except by us. Because it was the best lodging in the area and the scene of local dinner-parties, we doubted its availability and had not broached the matter. But it had become a last resort.

After dinner Sonja and I chatted at length with the proprietor. He was a handsome, quiet, out-of-doors Easterner who had retired to Silver City with his devoted wife and charming daughters after many years of employment in Ohio as an automotive engineer. We had enjoyed each other's company from the outset. My family had arrived to spend part of the Christmas holiday season with me and, having the lodge to ourselves, we had moved somewhat beyond the relationship of host and guests. Now we were forced to essay a crucial foray—to win this castle as a home for our entire company. Our host was a man of erudition and of easily discernible conservative bent. We talked at length, seeking the most favorable entrance for our inquiry.

We drifted into discussing movies. He enjoyed them. I suggested that he would be interested in watching us make one. We were there for that purpose. We would have a company of about thirty men and women in Silver City for about two months. It had occurred to me that this might be a quite pleasant place for all of us to put up. We would take two meals a day in the lodge, breakfast and dinner. He gave me his rates. I computed the cost for thirty people for two months and the total sum was sizable. It was obviously a windfall for him at this time of year. He expressed his belief that they could make us very comfortable. We were welcome to use the large living room for our conferences and, in effect, take over the entire physical premises.

I casually disclosed that the members of our company would be Negro, Mexican-American and Caucasian. He replied without any pause, but rather carefully, that he was opposed to discrimination. He knew it was practiced fiercely in these parts, and there might be some repercussions, but he did not think, since we would be taking over the entire lodge, that it was his business to inquire into the race or color of our crew.

I felt we had it "made." And I was all the more shocked when, in describing that we were shooting the film in association with the Mine, Mill union, his face showed sudden apprehension. He supposed I knew how people in the area regarded the union? He was not anti-union. He had belonged to a CIO union some years ago. And he was not even against this union. But he was aware of public sentiment, at least among his clientele. He didn't wish to ruin his reputation in the area. Were we going to have people who refused to cooperate with Congressional committees too? And would we also invite leaders of the union to dinner occasionally? Would we have "meetings" there? He would have to think about this. It presented some very serious problems. Everything he had in the world was invested in this lodge. It was a lifetime nest egg. He would have to discuss such a step with his wife. In these times the smallest rumor, utterly without substance, was enough to put a man beyond the pale. He would really have to dig into this question. I agreed that he must because if we came to terms I would have to have assurances that he would not change his mind in the midst of production.

Sonja and I wandered out into the fine night air and discussed our chances, and what, in heaven's name, we would do if he said no. We were not going to separate our crew and house those of color apart. Parceling thirty people out among the families of the miners was utterly impractical from many points of view, including such simple ones as transportation and efficiency. As we talked, the substance of a proper presentation occurred to me. We returned to the lodge and sought out the proprietor.

I expressed my sympathy for the difficulty of his choice. And yet, was it actually such a difficult one? It had occurred to me that he might like to know that a week ago Paul Jarrico had gone to the largest bank in Silver City and deposited fifty thousand dollars. It was banked by our company to the credit of an account to be known as the Mine, Mill and Smelter Union Special Motion Picture Account. Paul had informed the officer of the bank of the nature of the company and the purposes for which its money was to be used. The officer was cordial and solicitous. He requested that Paul inform him of any way in which he could be of any help. That same afternoon, I had made tentative purchases of thousands of dollars' worth of corrugated iron sheeting, lumber and assorted supplies. The businessmen had expressed interest, even fascination, and shown honest desire to serve us. Why should only big business have the unqualified right to make money? Why not he equally?

If he housed us, and anyone questioned his purpose, it seemed to, me he had only to say that when the bank refused to take our money, and Kennecott refused to give Mine, Mill members employment, and the lumber companies withheld their lumber, he would join them by refusing us the use of his hostelry. And he might add, perhaps, that if he did refuse us prematurely, and we had no place to stay, we might withdraw our money from the bank and cancel our order for the lumber and deprive the community of an opportunity of dividing fifty thousand dollars. As to whether we were socially suitable, did he propose to demand of everyone who entered, suitcase in hand, if he had ever incurred the displeasure of a Congressional committee? He was not required to do so. I suspected he would dislike it. And I doubted that any of his guests would appreciate it as a gratuitously imposed ritual. As to our guests and meetings in his living room, the lodge remained his property and if our conversation at any time offended his sense of propriety, he had only to tell us so. Actually, since the meetings would be discussions of shooting of the picture, he might be very interested in them and I cordially invited him to join us whenever they took place.

He promised to let me know his decision the next day. The following morning he apologized for his previous hesitation. The lodge was ours, come what may. I knew I did not have to write it into a contract. He was a conservative, independent American—when he thought about it.

Casting began now in earnest, and was divided into three main parts: securing a Ramón, casting the large number of Mexican-American parts, and finding Anglos for sheriff's deputies. The roles of the sheriff, the superintendent, the mine's eastern representative and the foreman were to be filled by blacklisted actors from Hollywood.

In the script Esperanza says that finding scabs in Zinc Town was like looking for a rich man in heaven. Finding Anglos in Silver City to play deputies in our Mine, Mill union film was almost impossible. The few Anglos who belonged to the union were desperately needed to play themselves. And they were older men. The deputies in Mike's script were a very special article. They were patterned on the real thing, and the real thing was a lanky, thin-nosed, young Anglo-Saxon with a drawl and no hips.

But our problem was not confined to Anglo actors. Now that it seemed we were beginning, stage fright seized many of the Mexican-American union members and their wives. Some approached me confidentially and asked if I truly knew what I was doing. They were not actors. They were not Hollywood people. How could they make a film that other people would enjoy? What did they have to offer?

Perhaps I was endowing them with qualities they did not have. I must not romanticize them. They were only working people. And burdened ones. Good people, yes, but very simple people. They liked us, and that was why they didn't wish us to make mistakes.

A minority was most enthusiastic and persuasive with others. This was going to be an adventure for the union and the union's friends from Hollywood. Together we would find a way. Clint Jencks and his wife, Virginia, were unqualified enthusiasts. And this meant a great deal among the union members, for their love for Clint was almost equally unqualified. He was one Anglo who had never let them down. More than that they knew that he respected them, loved them, believed in them. If he said they could do it, well!

There were problems of another kind. Husbands, they discovered, were going to have other men's wives as their wives in the film, and vice versa. That was a little awkward. They wished to know why they could not have their own wives as wives in the film. It was explained that each individual had characteristics and was cast for them and that casting was a very creative element in a film.

Whatever theoretical agreement we may have won was dissipated when we announced our final selection of the film's husbands and wives. We had coupled one man and one woman between whose real families there existed antipathies as deep and ancient as had separated the Montagues and Capulets of Verona. The man protested that his real wife would not tolerate this union. Even for the film it was unacceptable, intolerable, against nature. But his wife startled her husband by swiftly agreeing to our casting of him. No reason was offered nor asked for. It was all too evident that the wife believed that the family feud would act as a safeguard for her husband. The entire company would watch his scenes with infinitely more than customary interest, and thus effect a kind of chaperonage. Following this, the families changed mates without any further embarrassment. And as for the family feud, making a film dissolved it more swiftly than had all the bloodletting of Romeo and Juliet.

In the little town of Fierro, two miles from the Roos ranch, there was a dance hall. It was one of the two where Mexican-Americans could dance. And it was patronized exclusively by them. On Saturday

night every able-bodied man and woman, young and old, who could
afford it, came to Fierro. I went to observe, as an aid in my casting.
Three hundred couples danced, and the band played loudly, yet one
could hold a conversation with one's neighbor without yelling. In all
the time I was there, there was not ever a drunk in that hall. If a man
came with his wife, he danced mostly with her. If a man came with a
young lady friend, he danced mostly with her. Tables surrounded the
dance area and between dances they were filled with the dancers,
who ordered drinks and talked.

Everyone dressed up for the evening. The women wore lovely
frocks, some of them homemade. Men and women alike were grace-
ful. Many of the women were ravishingly beautiful.

Mrs. Molano came, whom Mike transposed bodily into the character of Mrs. Salazar in the film. She was fifty-five, had iron-gray hair
and was married to a miner who was ill with silicosis, of which her first
husband had died. She was hearty, proud of her people, a sinew of the
union. During the women's tenure on the picket line, she rose every
morning at four. Finishing her household chores by five, she would
begin knocking on the doors of the other houses, rousing the women
within for picket duty. And when they would cry out to her, "Mrs.
Molano, why are you up so early? You will get sick!" she would reply
that she was up and moving at five to prove to them they could be on
the picket line at six.

There was nothing we needed that Mrs. Molano was not certain
we could get, because she meant to see to it herself. She was pleased
that the film was going to be made. She thought these were fine working men and women and that one could profit from coming to know
them. And one day, when I was rather beaten with problems, she came
to me and said, "When you feel discouraged in your life afterwards,
you come to us. We will always give you courage. Because we always
have our backs against the walls, we have never a way to go but forward. We cannot afford to be downhearted. You will see. We will finish
the picture."

And there was Mrs. Ramirez, who had been the picket captain of
the women's line. The union and the auxiliary had planned a dinner in
honor of the women on the first anniversary of that momentous event.

At a meeting to organize the dinner the president of the union had said they would require many committees and first of all a food committee—and what lady would volunteer to head that committee? Mrs. Ramirez rose and, addressing the chair, asked if the celebration were to honor the women? Of course! Then she believed the chair should ask what *brother* would volunteer to head the food committee because, personally, she expected to *sit* all through the celebration and be honored! And she was. The evening of the dinner the men were at the tables serving the food and cutting the hams and sweeping the floors. And they did so because they wished to. They were honoring their women because when the chips were down these women had been saviors of the union and of its gains for their families.

And Floyd Bostick, southern Anglo, looked at them with wet eyes and said, "By God, I'd die fer those women, 'n'd think nothin' of it."

And Adolfo Barela, tall, massive, young, handsome, well-spoken, college-bred, said, "I tried leaving here and going out into the country when I came out of the army. But I'm Mexican-American and I didn't get far—and I missed my people. My father was dying of silicosis and I knew that if I came back I'd probably end as he was ending. But then it occurred to me that maybe we could see to it than no one died of silicosis. They were my people and if I could do anything for them, I wanted to. So I went back into the mines. It gave me such a boot during the strike to throw the Anglos' stereotype of us right back into their teeth. Sometimes we can use it to our own advantage. I was out trying to build support for the strike among the Anglo workers. And whenever any of the deputies would catch me where they didn't want me to be, they'd shove me up against a wall and ask who I was and what I was doing. And I'd shrug my shoulders the way those Hollywood directors make Mexicans shrug their shoulders and say *'No sabe, nada.'* And they'd let me pass. And then I'd get a little sick to my stomach thinking what power ignorance has when it can wear two pistols over its thin hips. And later, when I saw what these women were doing, these women of ours, I was glad I was here, glad I'd come back. They made a man proud of what he came from."

Their sturdy pride showed in Joe T. Morales, giant, Indian, father of six great sturdy sons, who came to me and said, "If you don't

mind—in that scene where the foreman calls Ramón a 'dirty greaser'—
I'd take that word out. Because somewhere, if somebody saw the film,
they might get the idea that people could come here and call us names
like that. And that would be too bad because somebody might get
killed. We have no ill-will for anyone but we've passed the point where
we stand still for insult. Why don't you show the foreman about to say
it—and stopped before the word is out! Then people will understand."
We did just that.

Sometimes a casting problem was solved by pure luck. One day in
the union hall an Anglo walked in to talk to Clint Jencks. When I saw
him, my hope became almost physical. There was the deputy Vance, in
the flesh! Tall, angular, blond, the twang, the narrow hips, everything.
While he was talking to Clint I made signals with my hand indicating
that I had to meet him. I discovered that his name was Rockwell and
he was no deputy. He too was a miner. And a union man, although,
because of the nature of his work, he was not a member of this union.
When I had told him of our need of him in the film, he said quietly,
"I'd shore like to do it and git my licks into them mine owners for what
they done to these people. I'd shore like to pay my respect to those
womenfolk of these people here. They deserve anything a man could
offer. These are shore great people."

He took the script, came back next day and said he shore would
like to do it but it called for him to beat up one of the union men. He
couldn't beat up a union man the way the script called for because he—
well, he just couldn't do it, that's all. But it had to be done by someone,
I explained, or there wouldn't be a picture, and wasn't it better to have
it done by a friend? He said that shore sounded reasonable and he'd
think it over. The next day he came back and asked did I know that he
just wouldn't be able to live in this town if he played a mean Anglo—
those mean Anglos would lay for him until they got him—they were so
mean. But even so he'd do it—but in the script he had to haul off and
hit Ramón. And he didn't want to do that because he'd not like to have
it on his conscience if he really hit him the way the script described it.
He shore wouldn't like to have that on his conscience.

I assured him there were techniques for delivering blows. He
would only barely touch Ramón yet the effect of it would be there. He

said he'd have to be awful sure it was foolproof. I asked him to come back the following evening. We would be holding a group rehearsal and I would give him the proof. I went back to the lodge and practised, because in all my years in films I had never directed such a scene. In Hollywood such scenes were turned over to trained stunt-men. I knew I had to have a theory so I invented one which seemed plausible. After study I concluded that in the delivery of the blow one went from relaxation through energy to relaxation so that at the moment of striking, one's arm, hand and fist, were again completely relaxed. Lining up pillows, suitcases and chairs, I practised and practised until, whether the theory was any good or not, the practical application worked perfectly.

Then I found a brother in the union to whom I showed the technique of reacting—the turns of the head, the slump of the body and the grunts—still all theory. That evening the Anglo miner arrived, but not alone. He brought his brother. A replica of himself. He brought his brother along, he said, because he just wanted him to see this thing. There were now two Anglos available to us, if our performance earned them. And we performed. It worked like a charm. Everyone applauded wildly. Then I revealed the secret and asked the Anglo skeptic to try it, and not to fear to give it all he had. He did and he was magnificent! The tiny ball rang with cheers, while both he and his brother signed for the film. Naturally they brought their wives and children too. Great day! Our Anglo problem was solved. Because these were the important roles and with the Rockwell brothers with us we found the few other Anglos we needed. The brothers and sisters of the local said, "The movie brings us friends."

When the picture was over the Rockwell brothers did leave the Silver City area. Rocky had been right. It had become too hot for them. They piled their families into their truck and took off for parts north. But they had paid their tribute to a people they respected, and had left, on film, two performances which professionals may study with profit. And they did so not for any reckonable profit, but for love of a fighting people.

VI

Early in January Rosaura crossed the border of the United States at Juarez-El Paso and flew into Silver City. She was met at the airport by a delegation from the union auxiliary. Mrs. Molano presented Rosaura with a bouquet of flowers, welcomed her, and expressed the union's pleasure in having a distinguished Mexican artist join them. Suddenly we were almost a going operation. All that remained was to find a Ramón.

Paul had returned from Los Angeles. The crew was scheduled for intermittent arrival according to the need for various of the technical departments. The negative film had arrived. Arrangements had been made for processing our film at the Pathé Laboratories in Hollywood. Paul arranged for a theatre in Bayard to run our rushes each day.

With Sonja's assistance the organization of the union, by the production committee, began. Eight members of the union and auxiliary and seven members of our company and staff. The committee was so organized that in the event of any dispute it was guaranteed that the union could outvote the company. The production committee, by mutual consent, was assigned absolute authority over all aspects of the filming including the content of each scene. This was not a union demand. It was our company's demand. Its purpose was to insure that the finished film, to the limit of our ability to achieve it, would represent their point of view—truth as they understood it—a picture of life as it looked from where they stood. Because every precaution was taken to ensure this result, obviously no such division—vote was ever necessary.

Paul, Sonja, Ernie and Braulia Velasquez, Eva and Cente Becerra, Adolfo Barela and Virginia Jencks, union men and women, organized committees in every small surrounding community, to gather the people necessary for the day's shooting, baby-sitters to care for the children of those women on the set, miners to alert those working in the various mine properties, crews for construction.

After eight hours in the mines, whether on the day, night or graveyard shift, the men required came to the Roos ranch to erect the mineshaft and adjacent buildings, or to the Fierro dance hall, where the interiors were being built under the supervision of technicians from the Hollywood studios. And everything they did was done with never-ending quiet, never-varying modesty.

One evening, at the construction site on the Roos ranch, some twenty miners were piecing together the skeleton of the mine shaft by moonlight. Since it was necessary for me as their director to understand these stalwart people I questioned one of them about their unfailing humility. Was it only the customary modesty of working people? Yes. With a little something added. This was a people living surrounded by "superiors," he explained. A loud laugh, a gusty conversation, an exuberant party, brought the Anglos down upon them for disturbing the peace. Through insults, beatings and jailings, they had learned long ago that their enjoyment of each other had many limits, included among which was a limitation on volume. But the quieter the tone of voice, he added, the more you put into it.

Then I understood better something that had happened the last evening Gale had been in Bayard. We had read the screenplay to the members of the union and their families. At its conclusion we received modest applause, which to our ears spelled flop. Beads of perspiration gathered on our foreheads as we sauntered down from the platform. Turning to the first group we passed I asked for an expression of opinion. "It was—*perty* good," came the reply. The beads grew larger and more numerous. To a second and third group the same question and from each the same answer. "It was —perty good."

Across the room I saw Vincente Becerra. He was an outspoken, frank soul; a young man with real enthusiasm. From him we would receive the low-down. We strode across the hall, I seized him by the shoulders and demanded, "Cente, for God's sake, tell me!" His head nodded slowly, keeping time with his calculated speech. "Well, Herbert, it was *perty* good." My lower lip fell against my chin. But he had not finished. His head continued to nod slowly and then he added reflectively, "You know, I think that was about the best thing I ever heard in my life."

The following day, at the formal union meeting which was to discuss the reading and pass on the script for production, I made a new kind of speech. And I received a new kind of response.

"Brothers, we have come to know each other, *a little*. I know *some* of the things in your lives that you would like to have many people know.

And we Hollywood people have some things we would like known. We are not so far apart as some people would like to keep us. If you'd like what you heard last night told to the people of the country who don't know you—so they can know you are their friends—I think they and you and we will all profit. That's all culture is—people talking to each other— finding out about each other. It may not seem like much, but it's a lot. And you're part of it, if you wish to be. The decision is up to you."

A miner rose and called out vigorously, "Brother Chairman, I move we make the movie." A stirring round of applause almost drowned out the seconding. The reading of the script *had* been a flop from which we learned a great deal. Our job was not to bring courage to them, but to photograph theirs.

There remained only Ramón. I had scuttled from one end of Grant County to another. I had read with dozens of members. I had followed the hunch of anyone who had one. "There's a brother who lives in a canyon north of Santa Rita." "What about so and so, he's a good union brother." I explained that it took more than a good union man, although that too was necessary. It required more than a good speaker, although that might help. The part needed a man with control, yet a deep feeling and a desire to have that feeling represent—out of himself—all of them. They knew what I meant, but they didn't know just the man. They were not actors; they had warned me.

I knew that I was growing panicky. Ramón was not all there in the script. The necessaries were there, but characterization would come only if the script was largely filled out in performance—in damned good per- formance. Ramón was not the hero in the ascendant, structural sense that Esperanza was the heroine. But the whole inside of the story swung around him. Played literally, the role would lose the powerful dissatisfac- tions which drove him, his deeply hidden adoration of his family, his knowledgeable, demoniacal defense of the union and his great concomi- tant capacity for gaiety. He was complex in mood and motivation. He was long history. His growth was the theme vindicated. Had I come a cropper this time? Had I taken on a too impossible creative task in relation to a non-professional?

Rosaura and Sonja had asked me several times to read with Juan Chacon, the newly elected president of the local. I had shaken my head vigorously. Johnny was much too shy, too small in stature, too sweet and retiring for Ramón. Ramón was—and I was off again. I had found one man in the Miembras area who was far and away the most promising physically. But he had too small a voice for Ramón. But…

I pointed him out to Rosaura and Sonja and their only reply was to ask why I did not read with Johnny. I was beginning to become annoyed. I had been casting all my adult life. There were certain attributes for a role! I asked them to come to the hall the following day and I would read with the Miembras brother. I wished very much to have them hear him. They asked if I would not, please, give a script to Johnny and have him read after the brother from the Miembras. Somewhat sullenly and protesting that this was not the time to burden me, I agreed.

The next afternoon before the reading, I asked Rosaura and Sonja—if they liked the Miembras man and saw possibilities in him, as I was certain they would—to clear their throats gently when he had finished. That would be a signal to me and I would make appointments with him for rehearsals because we simply had to begin work on the Esperanza–Ramón scenes.

The reading over, I waited for the throat clearing. It didn't come. I was annoyed but I was also relieved. He was not Ramón—no one knew that better than I. I thanked him and we waited for Johnny. Not a word was said between us. They felt my gloom and did not add to it. Johnny came. He read. His reading was utterly pedestrian. He was ill-at-ease, as well he might have been. But the clearing of throats which followed resembled an orchestra tuning up. I told Johnny that he had been selected by the ladies for the role. Johnny fell two steps backward and said, very honestly, "Oh, my God!" My own feeling exactly.

And that was how we cast Ramón.

The following day Johnny came to the lodge and he and Rosaura and I began to read together, to discuss the character in the context of actual scenes. One had to be careful not to urge too many concepts at one time. I had three weeks in which to help him turn himself inside out. Every atom of the buried experience and feeling of himself as an individual and as a part of his people had to be realized. We had to find the general in the specific, rather than the specific in the general. Technique, interpretation and transformation had to be discovered as interrelated aspects of a single development. But there were other hurdles; perhaps insoluble ones.

After three hours of intensive study of him, I was frightened out of my wits. Johnny had two ingrained mannerisms which were impossible to cope with. At the end of each sentence, and sometimes at the end of each phrase, he licked his lips. He obviously did not know it. Also, when he listened to someone speaking, he repeated the speaker's words with him, his lips moving silently, his head bobbing slightly. He was obviously not aware of this either. Reference to these habits accomplished nothing.

When lunch was over, I asked Johnny to walk out to the veranda of the lodge with me, alone. I undertook a drastic solution of the problem. The cure couldn't wait. It had to come quickly or fail. I told him that he had two very serious shortcomings. I described them. They had to be eliminated swiftly or it would be impossible for him to play this role. I asked him if there would be any point in my telling him so if I did not believe they could be eliminated. Obviously not! I had had other similar experiences. I knew how to help him. Because of that I could be blunt and direct in describing the problem.

"Johnny, in the movies we don't need your mouth or your lips." Later on this afternoon I would like you to throw them away, but completely. The only things we need in you are your eyes. Every last bit of your whole being's concentration is in your eyes. You remember with them, think with them, love with them, fight with them. And in order that there be no possibility of doing anything with anything but your eyes I want you to throw away your mouth and your lips, and your ears too.

"Now, one other thing. When you leave me in a little while, I would like you to go to the top of that mountain behind us. I want you to stay there for several hours. I'd like you to spread your legs, get a good, comfortable stance, and remember everything that has taken place in the valleys below you for three hundred years. And everything you remember I want you to see. Is that clear, Johnny? Not just remember it in your brain, but see it in your eyes. And everything you see I'd like you to feel yourself in the middle of. See yourself right square in the middle of it, with your eyes! And as you stand there, seeing yourself, seeing this country, seeing its history, seeing its struggles, seeing its strength and promise, I want you to talk back at it, and with *words*, spoken by your eyes. Not looks, remember, but words and sentences and deep feelings, pledges, *spoken with your eyes.* If you do this you'll come back tomorrow no longer John Chacon. Not even Ramón. But the vital spark of the people of this valley out of which we will make Ramón. And also it will be raw material that has been cameraized; that thinks and feels and lives and talks in such a way that the people who look at you can think and feel and live and talk with you—in your eyes. Okay, Johnny?"

He nodded his head and left, without words. A very important beginning! I watched him cut around the lodge and make for the foothills to the mountain behind. I went up to see Rosaura. I was somewhat self-conscious before her. After all she was a professional, and I was concerned lest the morning's work had been very discouraging to her. What I had forgotten was that she was an Indian, and Johnny was an Indian, and this was not an "engagement" for them. They had not taken on this task provisionally. They were confident of making it. I was not nearly so certain. I couldn't eat and I couldn't sleep. All I could feel was Johnny on that mountain top, and the necessarily brusque way I had sent him there and the loneliness of it for him and the terrible burden he had had thrown upon him.

At nine-thirty the next morning we began to read—that is, Rosaura began to read. Johnny's eyes fastened upon her as if she were the whole, vast terrain of Grant County—and his lips were gone. They no longer moved as she spoke. When his responses came his eyes were fastened upon her and the words were secondary, his tongue did not once lick his lips—and never did again in all the time we rehearsed or shot film.

Each day the chunks we digested became larger, until we rose from our chairs and began to read while moving through the roles. And then it was all gone again—all of it! It was like starting all over. But this time it was not frightening. Before Johnny was only another step of growth. And he went up to the mountain, this time script in hand, with instructions to play his role walking. And he walked it and walked it until his feet also belonged to his eyes and moved with and toward what he saw—and then progress became fantastic. The chunks were now the size of boulders.

The script never left his hands. He studied when he got up and when he sat down and when he ate and when he slept. He studied for all the people of his culture and of his social order to whom expression had been denied. This was not playing himself only; this was art, creation; the representation of a culture in an individual. A torrent of impulses, some conscious, some instinctive, emerged from him as emotion, as expression, as truth, as art. He developed a pedagogical approach to his artistry which I had never observed in an actor before. When a scene was finished in its shooting, he would go off alone and work. But not upon the next scene. Upon the one finished. As if now chewing it to shreds, to drain the last bit of masticatable marrow from its bones, tasting the accomplishment as foundation for the next. And scene after scene drew rounds of applause from crew and the Hollywood members of the cast. The union men and women came to me and asked, "Johnny is perty good, eh?" They did not know jealousy. They believed more in themselves because of him.

In the intense cold of the last days of filming indoors, the cameras froze and for days we lost time. When we began again, in order to make up this valuable, costly time, I undertook to shoot the long climax scene between Rosaura and Johnny quickly. I rehearsed it throughout. For Johnny it was a most complex scene, filled with the minutiae of business which had to be timed with absolute exactness so that it would match the subsequent closer shots. I had determined to shoot the entire scene at middle distance. And did. Then I realized what I had done.

No actor could remember all that business for later shots. I recalled one piece of it in which Ramón inserted a bullet into the chamber of his rifle. The actual sound punctuated the scene magnificently and I knew it might take twenty tries to get that again. But, gambling, I decided to take the new angle and later shoot many cut-away scenes so that in assembling the film I could cover up the inevitable mismatches. We began. Every tiny thing he had done before, even the beautiful timing of the cartridge into the chamber, was there again. And later, in the long months of cutting the film, mismatches were a problem, but not with Johnny. Never once did we have to cut away from him. And the likelihood is that he may never make another film, artist that he is, because he is Mexican-American, because he belongs to a militant union with a record of battling too hard, too long, and because he made the mistake of discovering his great talent with us—dangerous people with whom to associate.

After months of cutting and attempting to exhibit the film, after having seen it perhaps five hundred times, I never ceased to stand in awe of the technical, human and artistic magnificence of so many of these "non-professionals": Henrietta Williams, in so many scenes; arising to ask that the women be permitted to take over the picket lines; her reading of the line, "These changes come with pain"; the frosty morning when the women's picket line had dwindled to a mere thimbleful. I will remember their unsuspected artistry for its proof of the unimaginable sum of untapped human beauty which exists in people.

Nor did we have to wait so long for the rewards of their capacities. The filming presented a surfeit of problems, but they were all possible of creative solution. We lacked many elements of Hollywood production and we missed them. Our equipment was second rate; it was all we could obtain in Hollywood. Our crew was inexperienced in many departments—and there were many departments missing altogether. We had no script clerk. Without a skilled one, a production is lost. In the trained memory and notebook of this individual is every atom of information concerning what has been shot—what is missing—and of the relationship of people, things, angles, lenses, locations, etc. We trained the wife of one of the members of the crew and she worked eight hours and studied eight hours of each day.

We had no assistant director. For weeks I had to function in this capacity as well. Finally, one of the actors doubled in brass. We had no full-time wardrobe department. We had no full-time wardrobe man. Our transportation department was inadequate and many days we did not begin shooting until almost noon because somehow the actors had not been gathered and the cars and trucks had to begin their tortuous rounds at ten o'clock to fetch those we discovered to be still missing. These were some of the things we did not have.

But what did we have? We had a people before the camera, and men and women who loved them behind it. We had three Negro crew members who were at long last fulfilling a dream—they were engaged in making a motion picture, and fighting to learn how against a more equitable future for Negroes. One of the Negroes, the assistant cameraman, was also the still photographer and the visiting trumpet player in the orchestra at the Fierro Dance Hall on Saturday night. We had a blacklisted head-grip formerly at Paramount Studios for fifteen years, who was a splendid teacher of his craft. Carpenters were graduating on all sides of him after an intensive four-hour course under his tutelage.

At the end of the day shift, lines of miners climbed onto unfinished sets, stole a few moments for rehearsal between chores, or watched the designer—a painter from Hollywood, blacklisted—pull a puppet from his box and give an interlude performance of which they never tired: a senator inveighing against the *out-ra-geous* people making that *out-ra-geous* film, *Salt of the Earth*.

And all day, every day—the women! They saw to it that we were never without a dozen of their number, just in case. To act as technical advisers, to leap into any scene that required background people, to provide audience and encouragement, to mother and wive the production, to hold our hands in their hands and our eyes with theirs and keep our courage high when our thin, middle-class patience showed holes. Mrs. Chavez, Mrs. Flores, Mrs. Espinosa, Mrs. Iguado. And interlaced among them, our women-actresses: the serious, gay, true and beautiful artists: Angy, Clorinda, Henrietta and Virginia.

Generous, patient, but fiercely proud. Prudent, jealous of what was theirs and scrupulously tidy. I never felt any need to limit an artistic goal for them, men, women or children. They understood because their culture was a rising curve. And they were no pushovers in the matter of aesthetic judgment.

One such problem momentarily assumed sizable proportions. The sheriff and his assistants, in the real struggle, were ignorant, vicious toadies, and, realistically portrayed, would have demanded a stretching of the imagination of the most willing to believe in human animality. It was our desire to generalize these minions of the law in isolated mining communities. The men and women who had known the real article in life and bore mementos of them in vivid scars feared that we were too greatly minimizing reality. They feared the miners and their wives would appear aggressive against little provocation. We explained that our purpose in this story was not to expose villains but to dramatize protagonists. Enough that the villains were representatives of distant operators, doing a job, sometimes without relish. And, in the persons of the most backward, with a kind of sporting pleasure which was more believable, and in a sense more fiendish, than blatant brutality. We found agreement and approach.

In shooting the scene at the mine head, in which the foreman and Ramón tangle and the strike is declared, the compromise proved to be a realistic synthesis of all the factors involved. Both the miners and the Anglo actors from Hollywood who played the company representatives were so carried away with the verisimilitude they created for each other, that I allowed the scene to play on for some six hundred feet. It grew and mounted in dramatic tension with that exciting extra quality a scene takes on when the actors have forgotten who and where they are. I was directing the scene from the roof of a low building and, in my own excitement, almost fell off it. When the scene was concluded I leaped down and physically hugged all the participants, only to discover that the cameraman, unprepared for a scene of such duration, had run out of film after three hundred feet. But that three hundred feet was enough. For as many takes thereafter as I wished they recaptured the realities previously so deeply felt and transmitted. The miners congratulated the actors on having "made them so mad!" And the actors thanked the miners for having been, as one of the actors put it, "like a magnificent drummer in a jazz band, beating the trumpet up and up until..."

But that evening at the union hall, Paul Jarrico and Sylvia, his wife, who was visiting us for a few days, were present during a discussion among the miners. Several officers of the union were critical of the treatment by the Mexican-American union members of the Anglo actors who played the anti-union roles in the film. The realism of the scenes, they explained, had made some of the miners who had participated in the real scenes hark back to them and carry their emotions into the periods between filming. That was disrespectful. The members must understand that this was a film, a work of art. They must respect it, and all who participated in it. That especially included Anglos, whether from Hollywood or Silver City, who were playing the roles of opponents of the union. To them no remarks must be addressed, such as had been made to their counterparts in real life. Not even as a joke!

After the meeting Cente Becerra asked Sylvia why she could not stay on for the entire production. They were always pleased to make new Anglo friends and believed her prolonged stay would profit her and them.

The men gathered to talk about the crew that had come from Hollywood. The Negro and the Anglo people of the crew worked so well together that the miners had thought they had been working side by side for many years.

The spirit of the set penetrated swiftly into the community. The lingo of motion picture making even established itself in Mary Lou Castillo, aged five, who played Estella, Esperanza's daughter, and who had christened me "El Biberman." On the Roos ranch one morning, when the wind was blowing six-inch rocks up hill and everything on the set was battened down to prevent its being swept away, Mary Lou had asked Sylvia Jarrico to accompany her to the privy which had been erected on the location. Once she was inside, her panties lowered and seated upon the wooden board, she turned her head toward the violent whistlings of the rampant wind outside and shouted at it, "Quiet, for a take!"

The most persistent problem was the most simple. The miners, even those who spoke English better than Spanish, retained a rhythm of accenting words which was of the Spanish rather than English. Many colloquial Americanisms lost their flavor because the accent was on the verb instead of the noun or adverb. Johnny could not protest: "Work *alone*," so that its meaning came through. He would accent "work" rather than "alone" and often an hour would be spent helping him get it. And the set would ring with dozens of people saying it for him until the simple two-word phrase intoned around the location was like a mystic chorus. But once he got it, like everything Johnny "got," it was there for keeps.

But the most pressing decision upon me had been the style of shooting. It was obvious that the use of dollies and intricate moving camera shots was precluded. We did not have the manpower or a wide enough skill in the use of the equipment we had. But one could not shoot negatively. One had to feel creative possibilities within the areas of technical approach determined upon. If one did not use a fluid camera, the stationary camera had to have an orientation.

I began to look at the work of Mexican painters and engravers for clues of composition which might stimulate ardor for an arrested camera. One evening, before the beginning of shooting, I was examining a folio of Rivera's murals, when I recalled an evening spent with him twenty years before in New York. A group of theater people had gathered to meet him and someone had asked him how he could paint for multi-millionaires; did not the limitations they imposed cripple him? He reacted to this question with a kind of shock as if the questioner were artistically illiterate. He replied that all artists work under limitations, of many kinds. The very concept of unlimited freedom was non-existent, absurd. Limitations were the first command upon artists. Only when the artist knew what were his limitations was he free to work. I had been as cynical of his reply as others that evening. But as I remembered it, I began to discover its extraordinary application to our problems. We were making a film of a gentle people. Their rhythms had to be preserved. If I pushed them too hard for speed of delivery, their actual quality would be falsified. And yet their own normal speed of delivery and reaction was too slow for the screen. The screen, a magnifying instrument, demanded a greater-than-life pace to keep it from lagging behind the speed at which an audience could assimilate. Then it occurred to me that if I were to shoot many distances of the various scenes and pretty much from the same angle we could cut straight in upon scenes and straight out of them. By rapid cutting I would be able to eliminate interstices of pause and thus speed the pace of the film with pieces which yet retained the normal speed of the real people. Because there were no changed angles, the audience would not have a sensation of abruptness and of being yanked about. It would permit, in this direct approach to scenes, the use of jumps from very close to very full shots, for emphasis. And I could vary my approaches in terms of low and high shots rather than changed angle, remaining within this very simple set of limitations. As I began to enjoy the prospect of such use of the camera I ended by thanking my stars for my limitations. Had I used a mobile camera, I would have had infinitely less potential for frequent cutting. Because of the camera movement, the cinematographic speed I could now obtain would have been impossible. I would have had to choose between artificial and damaging acceleration of the actors or surrender of the pace itself.

The overall advantage of my accepted limitations would be a film in which the camera work was unobtrusive and the scenes were more in the visual tonality of the realistic story we were photographing. Limitations, properly understood, were indeed a first creative step. In this instance they evolved a style which, as I reviewed it later, was most singularly fortunate for this particular subject.

VII

The film's production became a leaven in the countryside. Within a few weeks a change began to creep over the entire community. The proprietor of the lodge had indeed received a few weak challenges. But they dwindled off and were not renewed. The body of men and women in the crew and staff, and the miners and their families, began to win new respect in the community. And not for themselves alone. Also for their union and for us, their friends, who were now widely known as Hollywood expatriates, unfriendly to the Un-American Activities Committee and, in my case, a jailbird. All shared the spreading warmth. Little by little we began to be accepted for ourselves. The local newspaper's unconcealed barbs fell on barren ground. Perhaps the greatest compliment to the entire community, Mexican-American and Anglo, came when Will Geer, who played the role of the sheriff, was invited to address the Horticultural Club of Silver City. The star of many Broadway shows, a featured and highly respected character actor in innumerable Hollywood films, he had, after being blacklisted, opened a nursery in Topanga Canyon.

He was something of a scholar on the subject and the invitation to him was an acknowledgement of that fact, as it was an acknowledgement of our acceptance by the Anglo ladies of Silver City. After his speech, the president of the club, a leading socialite of the community, suggested to Will that she would be pleased to invite some of the ladies of the union auxiliary to luncheon to discuss their cooperation in beautifying the area. Perhaps a program of gardens could be developed. She thought it high time all the ladies of the community came to know each other.

One Sunday, when we required a large picket line of men, I was startled and delighted to see in the camera finder as I checked the scene the figure of our lodge's proprietor moving in the line along with the miners. Several other Anglo-Americans from the community were there to observe and participate in this increasingly popular project.

When we required a church for exterior and interior shooting, we visited the priest of the Catholic Church in Hanover. He was cordial, interested and in every way helpful. "The church doors are never locked. Enter whenever you wish and be at home." He instructed the actor who played the priest in the christening scene, gave him the necessary robes and acted as technical advisor in the shooting. The Dean of the cathedral in Silver City made the parochial school playground available to us for another scene. And he, a militant Irishman, became a frequent visitor to our locations and between us a friendship developed. He was a well-read man, and since I had long possessed a deep affinity for Irish literature and speech and history, we found wide grounds upon which to range in our talks. A saloon keeper of Central, the chief politician there, and the ranking Mexican-American politician of Silver City became acquaintances upon whom we called for assistance and from whom we received it in full measure.

For three weeks we tasted America: A land of people making up their own minds, finding much to admire in each other without fearing their own judgments and confidences. It was a promising country. It contained all the necessary elements to make it again the light of the world. It was capable of healing old wounds, of discovering the external bias which had inflicted them, and of laying foundations of understanding to prevent their recurrence. Life in that America was increasingly pleasurable, rewarding and profitable. For three full weeks a neighborly, democratic way of life began to shine through a community of many cultures, races, classes and conditions of living. The community was moving toward peace and security. It was actually on the verge of becoming a community.

And for that sin it was punished!

The denouement came slowly, and somewhat absurdly. One day we read that Walter Pidgeon, president of the Screen Actors Guild in Hollywood, had received a letter from an Anglo lady, resident in Silver City, "revealing" the presence in Silver City of a "Red" motion picture company. She asked Mr. Pidgeon how the unsuspecting Mexican-Americans could be rescued from seduction into the Communists' filmic toils. The modernistic superiority of this good lady was not wasted upon the miners and their families. Nor was Mr. Pidgeon's immediate "revelation," in return, that we had nothing to do with the motion picture industry and that he was referring the matter to higher authorities. So far it was amusing and routine.

But on its heels came a column of Victor Riesel. This lifted the Pidgeon item into the journalistic stratosphere. He nominated Mr. Pidgeon for an Oscar for "discovering how Red is a valley not too far from the Los Alamos atomic proving grounds." "When you try to hide secret weapons," said Mr. Riesel, "you find concentrations of Communists." Paul Jarrico, he reported, had imported two carloads of Negroes [we had three Negro crew-members, breaking the Hollywood lily-white crew pattern] and deployed them for their first shooting, a sequence which starts with mob violence against them. And, soon, he continued, some four hundred Americans of Mexican descent were being skillfully handled by Herbert Biberman and Gale Sondergaard [who, with our children, had actually been in Los Angeles since leaving Silver City seven weeks before after a brief visit with me at Christmas time].

The following day two singular statements were made in Hollywood. In an interview in the Hollywood Reporter I.A.T.S.E. president Roy M. Brewer, chairman of the Hollywood AF of L Film Council, said, *"Hollywood has gotten rid of these people and we want the government agencies to investigate carefully."*

The second statement was made by the Motion Picture Industry Council, to which belonged the producers, the talent guilds and the unions—organized for the purpose of coordinating industry-wide blacklisting efforts—euphemistically known as the "clearance" program. This statement was signed by Steve Broidy, president of the council and of Monogram Pictures:

> "None of the motion picture companies represented in the MPIC has any connection, whatsoever, with this picture or the organization of individuals making it. The studios and groups composing the MPIC membership do not recognize this operation or its product as reflecting their own views, interests, or policies."

Never, in its entire history had such a declaration of outlawry been issued against any film by the motion picture industry.

The following day the *Silver City Press* stated that a member of MPIC was in Silver City to "investigate" the film. Then came a two-column, page one editorial carrying the title, "It's Time to Choose Sides." Despite this invitation to "action," the communities of Bayard, Hanover, Central and Silver City remained unprovoked. But the unruffled sensibilities of the people of these communities were to be subjected to more rigorous experiences.

After the day's shooting, on February 23rd, I arrived at the lodge one evening to find two immigration men waiting. They asked to see Rosaura. I asked the reason and was told that it was a routine check on her papers. Rosaura had not yet returned from the set. I asked them to wait. Having driven from El Paso in a fairly high, snowy wind, they were chilled. I asked if they would accept some whisky. After the second drink Rosaura arrived. We adjourned to her room and the gentlemen questioned her about her crossing of the border. Everything seemed in order. They asked for her papers. She gave them. They scrutinized them meticulously and asked why the passport did not bear a stamp. Rosaura said she could not answer that question.

She described the scene of crossing the border. She had flown to Juarez in a Lamsa plane. There she and a large group of young girls bound for a Catholic school in the United States—her only co-passengers in the plane—had been escorted to a Lamsa limousine. They had driven to the United States border, where the limousine stopped. An immigration officer approached the car. He asked them to take out their papers and extend them through the window of the car. He passed by, examined each one cursorily and waved them across the border.

The immigration men asked her to describe the man. She did. She also described the driver and even the porter who had taken their bags from the plane to the car. The inspectors recognized them. They had another drink and asked if they could have her papers. She turned to me for advice. I suggested that the officers had a right to them and that she surrender them. As the men left one of them stopped in the hall and repeated his previous statement, that this was only a routine matter, not to worry about it, nobody wished to hurt anyone. The papers would be returned after they had been seen by the chief.

They left.

The following day word came to the set that Congressman Donald L. Jackson of California was speaking on the floor of the Congress, attacking *Salt of the Earth* as a "new weapon for Russia... deliberately designed to inflame racial hatreds and to depict the United States as the enemy of all colored peoples."

That evening we listened to the twenty-minute speech of Congress-man Jackson, broadcast by the local radio station. He described our film as an arm of Moscow's foreign policy. "If this picture is shown in Latin-America, Asia, and India, it will do incalculable harm, not only to the United States but to the cause of free people everywhere.... For instance, in one sequence, two deputy sheriffs arrest a meek American miner of Mexican descent and proceed to pistol-whip the miner's very young son." (That no such scene ever existed in script or imagination was no defense. There it was, stated as fact, over the airwaves of the entire United States. What defense is there to such a statement by one who ought to know—a member of Congress?) I will do everything in my power to prevent the showing of this Communist-made film in the the-atres of America," Jackson concluded.

The speech was displayed on page one of the *El Paso Herald-Post* and other papers throughout the southwest. Adding up the long sequence of events which had been building so neatly to this speech, we knew we were in for a bad time. The question was, what could we do about it?

There were many things we had to do immediately. Among them was to rearrange our shooting schedule to give Rosaura's remaining scenes first consideration. We also had to face certain problems within our own ranks. One of the members of the crew became jittery and wished to leave. It took all our powers to persuade him to stay. He remained—like the proverbial spoiled apple in the basket. In an effort to counter the effect of Congressman Jackson's speech we sought to buy time on the air. The radio station refused to sell us any. Now we began to notice a drop in attendance of the families of the miners on the set. This required immediate attention as well. People were logically afraid. We had both to win back those we had lost and to keep those who remained.

But we were faced with other, even more serious, matters. Pathé Laboratories in Hollywood notified us that they would no longer process our film and were returning our cash balance. Every effort by Adrian Scott to find another laboratory in Hollywood failed. To make a motion picture without being able to review each day's shooting, through view-ing "the rushes"—the prints of all the previous day's work—is to shoot as if blind. One may not take for granted even that the film was properly exposed, that the scene is in focus, that the microphone does not show in a corner of the scene, that the sound is audible, that the clothes match, that the props are there, that the actors have performed well, even if they seemed to have been brilliant to the eye. Seeing rushes makes it possible to correct error through retakes. Without viewing rushes, making a film is like playing Russian roulette. With an inexperienced crew and cast it is to court disaster.

Months later, when we finally saw our developed and printed film, we discarded two whole scenes because of gross inadequacy. We discovered that the single most effective shot in the film was a double exposure. We lost both scenes because I had taken only one shot of each. We spent a week in the cutting-room trying to edit around some mismatching of clothes. The finished film still contains evidence of our failure to see rushes for half the film shot. In one scene, still in the film, a tall, thick iron pipe, on a stand, is badly visible. It is a light standard. It shows because whoever was operating the camera panned too far over and caught it. We were not able to cut the scene out because it was necessary for transition, but we wince whenever we view it.

There are passages of sound at which we also wince. For, following Pathé's example, the head of the company from which we rented our sound equipment notified us that he would not transfer our sound tape to film. We were *persona non grata* with the industry, we were informed by him, and it would jeopardize his good relations with the motion picture companies if he continued to service us.

Newspapermen began to descend upon us in numbers. We had to make firm policy concerning when and where we would see them, to prevent the shooting day from being lost, and the set turned into a newspaperman's quarry.

Congressman Jackson's speech was rebroadcast by the radio station many times each day and the newspaper itself became a horror sheet of incitement to vigilante action. All this took very little time to develop.

Within twenty-four hours a number of us received anonymous telephone calls telling us to get out of town or we would be sent out in black boxes. Similar calls, we discovered the following day, had been made to union officers and to Clint Jencks. The following night while his family slept, a number of shots were fired into his car, parked outside his

house. We called on the sheriff of the county. He was newly elected and
had been supported by the Union. He had served as sheriff several terms
ago and had been re-elected by a community ready for a change from
the sheriff who had led battle against the union during the strike.

We found him as disturbed as we. He pointed out that he had only
seven men to cover the entire county and that there was little of a positive nature he could do. The most important thing, he volunteered, was
to do nothing to inflame feelings, even against himself. Seven men, in
that huge county, were nothing to put any hopes in "if the skin of all this
tension ever breaks."

In the midst of these murmurings—not yet crystallized into vigilante actions—the immigration men returned. One would not have recognized them, they were that "serious." They refused whisky, although
the night was equally cold. They were accompanied by a lady. Rosaura
was not yet at the lodge, having remained behind on the set to gather
her wardrobe. I asked whether they had come to return her papers.
They had not. They had come to arrest Rosaura and to take her to El
Paso. There she would be offered voluntary deportation to Mexico. If
she refused she would be indicted for illegal presence in the country. I
told them that we would do nothing until we had obtained advice from
our attorneys in Los Angeles. They suggested that I get it quickly because
in one hour they were leaving with Rosaura, one way or another.

When Rosaura arrived we went to her room and I asked the officers
to tell us the reason for arrest. They said that her passport had not been
stamped. I asked what they thought she should have done when the
border official waved her by, as was common practice there. Should she
have *forced* the officer at the border to stamp her passport? Knocked him
down, taken the stamp away from him, and applied it herself? I asked if
all the girls now in the Catholic school were also being faced with the
alternatives they offered Rosaura? They replied to all of this with "serious" calm by saying that they just worked for a living and if they didn't
do what was required of them someone else would.

Paul Jarrico joined us. He asked what would happen if she refused
voluntary deportation. He was told that in the morning Rosaura would
be obliged to put up five hundred dollars bail against her appearance at a
hearing to be set. The bail deposited, she would be free to return to us,

under bail, until the day of the hearing. Paul asked what guarantees existed for this promise. One of the men read the paragraphs on the warrant for arrest. They did indeed stipulate what he had stated.

We reached Ben Margolis in Los Angeles and he advised that Rosaura had no legal right to refuse arrest even if there was no basis for it. We were to post bail and keep him advised. Paul arranged to follow Rosaura in his own car, his request that he be permitted to accompany her in the immigration car having been denied. The matron was to be Rosaura's escort on the ride. We asked for thirty minutes so that Rosaura might have a bite of dinner. She had been working in the cold since the noon meal, some seven hours before. The request was refused. They would provide dinner for her in Silver City, which they did. Following this they drove to El Paso and subjected her to a relentless grilling during the several uninterrupted hours' drive. They demanded "information" concerning everyone in the company as well as herself.

In El Paso, they proposed to jail her. Paul's remonstrance, as sturdy in this instance as his optimism in others, caused them finally to agree to lodge her in a hotel with a guard in front of her door twenty-four hours a day.

In Silver City I stood outside in the cold long after the two cars had pulled away from the Lodge. I tried to find some rationale for this shoddy melodrama. Was all that surrounded us from Washington through Hollywood to El Paso and Silver City the result of a single shrewd conference of minds? If it was, everything had worked to perfection. They had thought they knew the length of our schedule. At the end of five weeks they would catch us with most of our money gone and the film incomplete. Much deadlier to intervene then than earlier when our money was unspent.

They reasoned that two-sevenths of Rosaura incomplete would leave a hole unpatchable. But they had miscalculated by a week. We had not only enjoyed our five weeks in Silver City; we had made the most of them. The problem facing us was not what had already been stolen from us, but whether the next ten days would be. If they were, then we were lost, truly.

What were their further plans? Were we dealing with shrewd, or powerful but intrinsically stupid men? Did they lay their plans forever without taking other equally real, living Americans into consideration?

The *Silver City Press* began to whip up a demand for popular action against the film. Simultaneously, among letters to the editor, most of them unsigned, one called upon *him* to do more than use words. The editor replied to this letter, stating that the writer had been guilty of "asking George to do it."

The following days were tense. The wire services hounded us for stories and sent reporters to visit us. We determined to limit our replies to simple releases: we were shooting a film of the lives of the miners in the area with their cooperation.

Several small establishing scenes were necessary for the film; simple shots of a car driving through a town. We had selected the small community of Central for them. With the atmosphere growing difficult, we decided to photograph these scenes at once. Our production manager called upon the mayor of Central and asked for permission to make the shot. The mayor, a Mexican-American, agreed instantly. Our production manager then asked for the permission in writing. The mayor protested that this was not necessary. But our representative, under instructions to insist upon it, got it.

In the morning, early, with a small crew, I drove into the Central area and set up our camera in the street. A body of some eight men, several of them armed, strode toward us, ordering us to "get going." I told them that we had permission to take the picture and was about to offer them the mayor's letter when the spokesman of the group, a brother of the district attorney of the area, told me the mayor did not run the town; they did. They were a Citizens' Committee and they were not going to allow a bunch of Communists to photograph their community. I asked them to wait until I could find the mayor, and sent the production man to find him. His office was only a few feet away, but he was not there. By this time the men were becoming unruly. If we didn't move right away, they'd throw us out. I asked our crew to pack up. We left.

On our way to the Roos ranch, the mayor overtook us. He apologized. But he also complimented us for having avoided difficulty by leaving. He regretted that there was such a pitch of feeling among this group of hot-headed individuals. But he couldn't placate them at the moment. In a day or two he would have things in hand again and we would be able to proceed.

As we slept that night, seventy-five vigilante—patriots were meeting secretly in the little village of Central, plotting to burn us out of this community.

The following day Mike Wilson remained at the lodge. He kept in touch with El Paso and the Roos ranch. Bail was offered in El Paso. But the immigration authorities refused to accept it. They didn't have to live up to the law, their promises, or the small print on the reverse side of the warrant. Paul telephoned Ben Margolis who flew into El Paso some hours later. But it was to no avail. The immigration men would not release Rosaura. Ben Margolis and Paul Jarrico engaged a local lawyer and together banged away at the law, still in vain. Mike joined them.

The union decided to send Joe T. Morales, one of the union actors, to Washington to seek the intervention of the New Mexican congressmen and senators. At a press conference in El Paso, Ben and Paul were attempting to unfold the story. They described the exemplary character of the people of the union and suddenly, the door to the hotel room opened and Alford Roos and an Indian, six-feet four, slim, stoic, with the bearing of a king, entered the room. Joe T. Morales had looked in on the conference en route to Washington. Joe talked, quietly, majestically. Alford Roos talked, volubly and passionately. And the papers, almost without exception, carried stories condemning the arrest and the promises and the new charge. But it was not possible to rescue Rosaura by debate.

Reporters were legion that day at the location on the Roos ranch. They demanded entrance to the set. It was refused. They hired a single motor plane and buzzed the location all day. I rearranged much of the sound shooting so that it might make sense silently if the buzz of the plane was so deeply imbedded in the sound track as to make it unusable. Messages came to me all day. Albuquerque, New Mexico, was on the phone—a strange group of people was skirting the crest of the hill above us—there was a vigilante parade of autos moving from Bayard to Silver City—El Paso was on the phone. I disregarded all of this. To each message I would turn my back and indicate to the cameraman, "The next shot is here—three-shot-favoring Ramón." "The next shot is here—very close."

And finally I asked that no further messages be given me. I had to make time—time—time! With Joe T. Morales gone I had to give certain of his lines to other people—and Mike was not available. Mike was so adept at this kind of translation. But this was no longer a question of technical excellence. It was a matter of getting images on film. Even as I tore from one set-up to another I knew that one day, months off, when the film was exhibited, there would be those who would say, "... in spots the sound track was not quite professional." I burst into a short hysterical laugh. They would be right. It would not be "quite" professional. And they would be right to say so. And I would not try to explain. There is no explaining technical inadequacy in a Hollywood world. But I would not be embarrassed by the criticisms. All I wished now was to get thirty-five scenes shot today, despite the plane and the reporters and the messages, despite everything. I found a young woman who resembled Rosaura from the back and I literally dragged her from one spot to another to get missing pieces of shots of scenes of Esperanza and Ramón over her shoulder and across her half profile. Her skin was very light and it bore no earthly resemblance to the color of Rosaura's. I called for make-up and applied it to her face and neck and ears. And thus it happened that the only player who used make-up in the entire production was the double for Rosaura's ear.

The following day again the same tensions. That evening we received reports that following the parade of thirty-five vigilante cars with signs calling upon the community to rid itself of Communist conspirators, spies and saboteurs, the vigilantes had called upon the Silver City Chamber of Commerce and the local post of the American Legion and asked for support. Both organizations refused it, categorically. Seventy-five vigilantes had met the night before and twenty-four hours later they had not won a single new recruit.

Who were these people? The handful of little shopkeepers; the sour, self-appointed representatives of the great mining companies, to whom the word union was synonymous with subversion. To them anyone of dark skin who wished to lift himself above the level of slavery was a dog worthy only of the rope and faggot. Behind them were the local mine superintendents who looked upon any activity which cemented the relations between the miners and other elements of the community as "the revolutionary rising of those people." There were the politicians defeated in the last election, a handful again. And then that stalwart group of permanent scabs imported for pay whenever the mine superintendents required them. And some backward sheepherders from the hills. To this conglomerate body was added the salt and pepper of the drunks and dipsomaniacs of every hamlet in the area. Vigorous imbibing of fiery fluids spurred them on to more heroic deeds.

On the third day the rumor came to us that, believing the film to be stored there, the vigilantes planned to burn the Roos ranch to the ground that night. This brought the union into immediate action. Eighteen men were assigned to guard the ranch with rifles. Twelve of the men were ex-G.I.'s and six were older union men, actors in the film, who insisted upon being part of the guard. The union asked the sheriff to deputize these men. He refused, believing that if he did so the vigilantes would also demand deputization and the situation might inflate to disastrous proportions if he refused them.

Because we had to, we tried again to photograph a car passing through a town, the shot which had been prevented in Central. We chose a spot directly in front of the union hall. We planned it carefully so that it might be filmed with a minimum of public attention and within a matter of minutes. When all the instructions had been given, the camera was hastily unloaded from a truck and set up. Just as the signal was given for the camera to turn and the car to start forward, we saw two carloads of men driving hard upon us. As we finished making the shot the cars were brought to a swift, screeching halt in front of us and some dozen men leaped out. They made for the camera, knocked it over, and then began slugging their way through our ranks.

Sonja Dahl Biberman, her English accent under the most rigorous control, was moving about among the largely youthful contingent of attacking vigilantes, saying, "Now if you don't stop this, I will take down all your license numbers." Nothing could have been more effective. She was attractive, ladylike in voice, and she succeeded in breaking up the mass character of the attack. Two men singled out Floyd Bostick and were punching him over the heart. She rushed there and Bostick was able to wring himself loose. I was busy with several of the crew righting the camera and lifting it into the truck, safe from more serious damage. The finder was broken and we were obliged to finish subsequent shooting without one. The camera stowed, I came back to the embattled group and shouted that we would leave immediately. One of the older vigilantes said, "You had yore camera pointed right at our ballpark. We spent f' thousand dollahs buildin' that park and we don't wan' no Roosian commonists takin' pitchers o' our ball park." I nodded my understanding and we started for the union hall. But the bully boys had not had their fill. They followed us. At the entrance to the union hall they were joined by another contingent headed by the president of a bank. We had foolishly neglected to make any deposits there and perhaps he was properly indignant, although he stubbornly denied it. He was a patriot, he had told others in the community, not a subversive like the bank in Silver City. He wouldn't have taken any of our Russian money.

As the two groups met, the big-bellied man who had defended the pristine honor of the ball park saw Clint Jencks walking toward the union hall. Holding his belly with one hand, he ran after Clint, grabbed him by the shoulder from behind, whipped him around, and hit him savagely in the eye; a large ring upon his middle finger struck squarely in the center of the eye. Johnny swung back at him. Several of the attacking group drew pistols, but somehow we completed our withdrawal into the union hall.

As soon as possible we left for the Roos ranch. We had gotten our shot and had paid for it with a broken finder and some ugly bruises. In the few minutes inside the union hall we had come to the conclusion that even if the rumor concerning the burning of the ranch had been false, it was by now probably true.

After dinner at the lodge, the crew talked our situation over and decided to share guard duty with the miners. Volunteers were called for by the crew's shop steward. I had formidable quantities of work ahead in preparation for the next day's shooting. I felt, frankly, that guard duty was not the best use of my time, and I wished heartily that my raised hand would not be accepted. But it was. I asked to be on the first watch so that I might be back in time to do my necessary homework. This was agreed to.

With a young member of the crew I took off at about seven-thirty in a convertible for the Roos ranch some fourteen miles away. I had never developed a decent respect for the reality of violence, or for its logically concomitant emotion, fear. It never occurred to me that riding to the ranch in a convertible was stupid. I had no realization that from behind any bush in the fourteen miles of utter darkness a rifle bullet might sing out at us. My companion had been through four years of battle in the Pacific and had equally little respect for the lurking dangers. We had been given light signals to be flashed by our headlights so that we might gain easy access to the ranch. We stopped at a liquor store to pick up some candy and a bottle of whisky for the guards, and rode through the cold, bleak darkness at sixty miles an hour; another stupidity. Our fortune was better than we deserved—we arrived at the ranch.

A small central building which we used as a kitchen for our noon meal had been turned into the guard house. We opened the door and walked in. What I saw made me wish to laugh out loud. The interior of the little adobe building reminded me of nothing so much as a movie set in which a third-rate western was being shot. There were no lights. Six men were standing, each with his back to a wall, beside a window. They leaned on rifles or shot-guns and their eyes peered into the darkness outside. But any inclination to laugh was wiped out in short order by the soberness of the actors. There were no words of greeting. We came in, unloaded the candy and poured drinks in paper cups for all of us. Then we sat down. I asked where the other guards were. The younger men were deployed around the hills doing extended formations to flush out any vigilantes in the neighborhood.

Silence again. I saw Floyd Bostick rubbing his chest lightly. Recalling how he had been pummeled that afternoon, I asked if he were in much pain. The ribs were a little swollen, that was all; made it a little hard to breathe. I noticed two guns by him and commented upon them. Oh, he said, he had a rifle for distance, a shotgun for closer range, and he pulled a hammer out of his hip pocket and raised it for me to see—"this" for real close quarters. There was a moment's pause and then Floyd spoke again. His voice was normally quiet and soft with the accents of the South, in which he had lived his entire life. Now it was even quieter and softer because of the pain when he breathed and spoke. "They can beat me up, mebbe," he said, "and mebbe they kin kill me. But they cain't make me take a step ba'k'ards in this town. Ef I'm still here, I'm goin' to the post office fer my mail in the mornin' with my gun in my hand. An' they better give me the street."

There was a pause again. A little behind me was Iguado, a Mexican-American miner of over seventy. He had a most majestic head; dark skin, firm, noble features crowned with white hair. In his own kind of soft, quiet, accented speech: "Dey get me may-be, but I get t'ree first." Again quiet. In that quiet I found physical fear. I found it in the grim, sober reality of men with families who without fuss were prepared to lay down their lives that night to keep the sets up for shooting the next day.

But as I looked more closely into the aged, bronzed face of Iguado, I saw profound fatigue of more ancient vintage than just this night. The shameful necessity confronting him showed in his eyes. I swallowed back my romanticizing of these men, ambushed in the darkness of their own country. What was glamorous in decent, hard-working Americans, guns in hand, guns with bullets in them, facing other men with guns filled with bullets? What glamour in risking life to make a movie about their lives? What was admirable about any part of this cold, grim evening, or the ugly reality that underlay it? Iguado caught my stare.

"Not nice, tonight," he said. He shook his head.

"Not like *you're* used to," said someone out of the darkness.

"No—it's different," I replied. "I'm used to people destroying others with words. Here they use rifles."

"No good, no way," said Iguado. "No place."

"All vigilantes!" someone volunteered. "All the same!"

"Perhaps you're right," I said. I hadn't thought of it that way.

"Tell us how it was there, in Hollywood."

"That's a... well, it's a long story."

"Tonight, maybe... be a long night."

And they waited.

Part Two

HOLLYWOOD
1953

I

It was bitter cold in the shack. And raw. The men peered out through the windows, and waited.

The opening lines of narration in the film, spoken by Esperanza, occurred to me. I reminded the men of them: "Who can say where it began, my story? I do not know. But this day I remember as the beginning of an end." And I recalled for them such a day in our lives.

A subpoena to appear before the Un-American Activities Committee of the House of Representatives of the Congress of the United States. I became one of a special group of nineteen selected from vocal opponents of the committee.

At that time thousands of persons in Hollywood alone opposed it for riding herd on the people of the country, for telling them what kind of life the committee would allow them to build for themselves. Like the vigilantes out...

"But you know all this," I said. "Better than I."

"We like to know the battles of our friends."

"I get some coffee," said a miner.

While the coffee was poured, I picked up the story with our trip across country to Washington. Plane fare and six dollars a day expenses provided by the government for what was called "an investigation into the infiltration of subversive propaganda into motion pictures." The producers declared they made pictures for public approval. That was the error, the committee's representatives intimated.

"Some investigation!" one of the men said. "All over five months before it begins."

"But not the tactics," I explained. "The hearings began with witnesses against the producers. They gave the producers a chance to save themselves. They could have their jobs in exchange for our creative lives."

The door to the shack opened. The man posted outside brought a report from the scouting party. There was considerable vigilante activity about half-way back toward the mine. They might be aiming to attack the sets on the other side of the gully. If they did, the scouting party would take after them. The men in the hut were not to be drawn into it. If the attack broke toward the hut, then the scouting party would stay out. Did they agree? They agreed. The men inside fixed their eyes on the windows, fitted their bodies into the walls, and collectively created a silence that invited continuation of the story.

A voice in the room cried, "Hold it!" Everyone went stiff. Every eye was on the windows. A second of deathly silence. We heard the sound of running feet. The rifles at the window were ready. Then came some flashes of light, two short and two long. Our signal. A figure ran past the window toward the gully. The rifles lowered again.

"So y'all went to jail, eh?"

"No. The committee lost the battle. The hearings received a bad press. The country didn't like what was going on. And suddenly, on a Friday afternoon, after only ten of the nineteen had been called to the stand, the 'investigation' was called off."

I told of our short period of seeming success. Eric Johnston, president of the Motion Picture Producers Association, had said the industry would not submit to censorship, and that he would never be party to anything as un-American as a blacklist.

There were several snorts.

"But he changed his tune—or maybe his fiddle!"

"Not for some little time. We went back to Hollywood and to work," I replied. "And then the floor was cut out from under Hollywood. Eric Johnston called the producers to an emergency meeting at the Waldorf–Astoria Hotel in New York."

There was a long pause. The men standing at the windows were stretching the long string. A meeting, held five years before in a hotel in New York, might conceivably deprive their families of a father and husband in the next six hours.

"Big men!" one of them said quietly. "What are they big for? Only to serve someone bigger. Their bigness ain't worth a damn."

Another picked up the string.

"How many people in this country? Hun'erd 'n' fifty million? And six guys in a committee whip 'em into line. We ain't cowards. Don't go round shakin' before people we put in office. But they got us all staked out like mine claims, with fences between us. That's how!" Then he turned to me. "How'd *you* figure yours?"

"We didn't have to. Man named Ed Sullivan, columnist for the New York *Daily News*, a paper that backed the committee from the beginning, laid the answer on the printed line. He wrote: 'Wall Street jiggled the strings, that's all.'"

"And that's all there was to it. Before we could look around, Hollywood gave in. We were fired. Congress cited us for contempt. Then the producers went to work on us. Wanted us to turn tail with them. 'Be loyal to us,' they said. And because we remained loyal to the First Amendment instead, we became 'subversives.' A feat of magic, accomplished in a couple of weeks."

"'N' then you went to jail?"

"Not for almost three years. We battled through all the courts. When Justices Rutledge and Murphy died just as we reached the Supreme Court we received only two votes. Then we went to jail. The best ones in the country, from Texas to Connecticut."

"Fer not lettin' vigilantes bust yer skulls open."

"We're tryin' to stop the same thing tonight! Maybe we go, too?"

"First, we make picture," Iguado said.

Automobile headlights showed outside. We stopped and waited. One of the officers had arrived from the union hall. He reported that a large group of vigilantes had assembled in the little town of Central, some two miles away. They had just gone into meeting. Probably take them a couple of hours to get lickered up. Get started about eleven o'clock. The union would have people at the hall all night. If anything happened, it was to be relayed to the hall right away. He asked if the men were okay. He looked at Iguado and at Bostick. He waited. The men all looked out past the windows. He left.

I passed some chocolate bars around. And ate one. Iguado's phrase kept running around in my mind: "All vigilantes." But was there no difference at all between brutality and reluctant surrender to it?

"Did y'all start the movie soon's you got out of jail?"

"No. A few weeks before the last of the Ten were released, the committee announced a second investigation of Hollywood and the issuance of some seventy subpoenas. The studios welcomed the 'investigation' and officially promised full cooperation. Then the dam broke—and the flood swept out across the country."

A Mexican-American who had not spoken previously asked: "When was that?"

"In—1951."

"But when did they begin?" he asked again.

"In 1947," I replied.

"They didn't come back for all those years?"

"No."

"Then you Brothers in Hollywood held 'em back fer two and a half years!"

"The strength of America held them back. We were kind of a symbol, that's all. The committee was in a terrible hurry to spread blacklist all over the country in 1947. Announced they were going to. But they were afraid to move too fast. They have a healthy respect for America—all those 'vigilantes' as you call them."

The Mexican-American Brother spoke again.

"Sure, they got respect. Their hatred is only respect. They conquer one town, one industry, one profession like yours. But never the country, never for long, never enough of it. They try to beat us down. They jail us too. They try to beat you down. What happens? They bring us together."

He looked out of the window a long moment.

"Vigilantes put things together with spit. They unstick easy. Even your year in jail."

"I was only six months in jail. Dmytryk and I. The others got a year."

"How come?"

"We didn't know then. We still don't. Dmytryk and I were before another judge. We thought it was that judge's independence. But when we got out, Dmytryk became an informer. So? Not that that matters any more."

"Yes, it matters," the same man continued. "Informers' words against you turn into vigilante guns across the gully—pointing at *us*. It matters. *You* are blacklisted. *We* have to fight with guns in our hands to make a movie of ourselves. That is what informers do to our country. It will not last. Not in this country! But this is what they do."

He turned sharply toward me.

"I am angry only with him. Not with you. You are a Brother. You stood. But what he did *matters!* What your movie producers did, too! I say, don't forgive them! They know what they're doing! Like Ramón says in the picture, 'Fight 'em all!'"

"But in one thing you're wrong. We didn't stand. We held, yes. But we didn't stand. Standing is different. They knocked us over. If it weren't for people like you—who are still standing where you stood—as a union, as a people, as a culture—we couldn't even make a movie today."

"Okay. But we *never* made one, until you came. So for us, you're standing on movie ground! That matters too!"

In the full warmth of his emotion—a man I had never seen until that evening—I was suddenly struck by a staggering thought. To stand in that hut waiting for attack was no way to demonstrate faith in America. It was tantamount to accepting vigilantism as the way of our life. And it wasn't! Faith in America demanded unceasing struggle for its law, and for its application by those charged with giving protection under it. It had to be insisted upon, and fought for, and never surrendered. The attack had struck us all so suddenly, it had immobilized us. But it was not too late.

A sudden, small noise was heard, indistinct, but seemingly from across the gully. Then the low grinding sounds of a car being rapidly gunned through its various gears to high. We could hear it bumping along the rough, dirt road. It sounded heavy—like a truck. Nothing could be seen. It was a good quarter-mile off. We listened hard—listened and almost saw with our ears. The volume of sound did not increase because the road around our sets was an arc described around the hut. No one spoke. It was obvious the truck was making for the mine shaft set. Our bodies tensed—waiting—waiting for the sound of a crash. Our instructions were to stay put. We must not allow them to draw us all to a single point. The Roos ranch was only a few yards from our hut, and we had been warned they meant to burn it to the ground. The guard outside our hut had his eyes on it. A rifle shot would bring us all out toward it.

From the other side of the ranch house a shot was fired. But it was not our guard; it was too far away. We waited. Another shot was heard coming from what seemed our side of the gully. Whose shot? It was almost beyond endurance to wait inside. But as we listened, the motor seemed now to be moving off toward our right. If that were true then the truck had passed the set and was moving out toward the road that led to the highway. We became more certain of it. The sound was fading.

If we could only be certain that all the shots had been ours. The miners would have fired over the truck, avoiding any hits, merely to frighten the driver off.

The shots introduced a new level of reality. I was profoundly frightened. And as I looked at the men around me I was more frightened. Because they weren't. A sense of utter unreality then possessed me. This was the United States of America! The lives of these men dare not be lost—must not be risked. This was the state of New Mexico! There were law enforcement agencies somewhere within it. They had to be found. The *union* guard was all wrong. It must be replaced with proper agencies of law. I had to get to the union hall.

Two of the men of the scouting party came into the hut. They confirmed what we had supposed. The truck had started from the point back toward the mine and it had meant to ram the set. The first two shots had been fired onto the ground ahead of the truck to warn it off. The third one had cut the air between the truck and the set as the truck neared it. The truck never left the road. It continued on, past the set, and made for the highway.

Did this attempt herald others? Would this frighten them away for the evening? No one could hazard a guess. I suggested that word ought to be taken to the union hall—and I volunteered for it.

At the union hall the local's officers were in meeting. They had themselves come to the conclusion that the law must be called into the developing situation. They had telephoned the sheriff some time ago. He again stated his helplessness—with only seven men in the county. The union officers had asked him to join them in telephoning the state police chief in Santa Fe, four hundred miles away. The sheriff had come. They had telephoned. The chief was familiar with this area from the period of the long strike. Fifteen minutes after they had spoken with him, he had left Santa Fe with thirty-five cars of state police, headed for Silver City—half the police force of the state of New Mexico. There were six or seven hours of waiting before us.

When I returned to the lodge, I discovered the proprietor standing in the shadows, rifle in hand, protecting those who were asleep against any sudden change of mind on the part of the vigilantes. He knew our film was stored in the lodge. He meant for it still to be there in the morning.

The second group of the crew's volunteers had already left the lodge to join the union members at the hut. Everyone else was asleep. I had yet to prepare the shooting schedule for the next day.

I sat down upon the bed in my room, pulled a blanket over myself, drew my script and various notebooks close to the light on the night table. Gale's face increasingly cross-dissolved itself upon the pages before me. I had talked to her only four hours before. And after we had talked it was worse. It always was after talking with her. I hadn't seen her or the children, now, in over two months. I brushed aside all that the night conjured up for evaluation: the people of Silver City, of Hollywood, the state police riding in from Santa Fe, Rosaura, Ben, Mike and Paul in El Paso, the Brothers at the hut, the individuals whose money, loaned to us, was already spent—and Gale and our children.

Poring over the list of unshot scenes, I selected those for the next day that were *the* most important, knowing that all had to be shot or there would be no picture, that a week's work was a minimum! And then?

As I lay upon my bed in Silver City, I remembered Gale's greeting when I announced that we were incorporated and in business. Her embrace was warm and long. And then:

"I hope that we—and the children—can enjoy some part of these years ahead—together. We're important, too, aren't we? Good luck, my darling."

I fell asleep, feeling again the oppressive heaviness in the chest that I had felt in prison.

II

At seven the next morning, the shop steward of the crew informed me that unless the crew had some sort of police protection it was not going to location. The reason was clear to me. One member of the crew had come on this job as a job. He now feared for his life. He refused to endanger it and called upon the others to join with him. That he had no special loyalty to the meaningfulness of this undertaking, no one held against him. He had brought valuable equipment with him. That he loved his equipment even more than himself was also his right. Indeed he and his gear were also invaluable to us. He had a right to protection against extraordinary risk for himself and his equipment. The crew extended it, although many of its members would have gone to work under any circumstances.

Time was more valuable by the minute. We had still a good five days of work until the film would be completed. I called the sheriff and asked if the state police had arrived. They had, an hour ago, after driving all night. The chief was taking a brief nap. Did he know where? No. Would he ask the chief to call me the moment he awoke? He would.

For four hours we paced the living room of the lodge. There was almost unbroken silence. At eleven o'clock the chief called. I described our situation and asked for an escort. He refused one. He was not in this area to protect anyone in particular. He was there to permit everyone to proceed with normal occupations. The roads to the ranch were thoroughly patrolled; had been since six that morning. No one need fear to go about his business. I reported the conversation to the crew verbatim. I had made the call in their presence. They agreed to leave for location.

It was four miles to the main road. Our line of cars took off. I led the way. As we came to the main road a state police car zoomed by going north. A second later another zoomed by going south. We turned into the main road and proceeded down its straight-as-a-die length for ten miles. Every five hundred yards a state police car passed us in one direction or another. As the fifth or sixth car passed, my sensation of relief made me raise an arm in greeting. It was not answered. The formality of the police indicated their seriousness. We proceeded to the ranch and went to work.

We discovered later that the union guard had indeed checked the vigilantes from attacking the ranch the previous night. The vigilantes had remained in meeting all through the night and when the first state police cars had been reported to them they decided that they must strike at once. As they left their meeting place and headed for the main road they passed an old battered car in which a man was asleep. They paid no attention to it. But that car signaled the state police, and when the vigilantes reached the main road some ten state police cars were stationed there. The vigilantes looked, paused, turned around and went back to their occupations, whatever they were. The police cars continued their patrolling hour after hour after hour.

During the morning news came to us that the Dean of the cathedral at Silver City and two of the priests of the area, joined by the Bishop of El Paso, had taken to the air and had urged the people of the entire area to conduct themselves in a brotherly, American fashion. To maintain order and in every way assist the agencies of law.

That day we shot thirty-five scenes. It was a good day.

In El Paso it was a bad day, although the law was ours. The immigration officer at the border had, in failing to stamp Rosaura's passport, committed what was known legally as a ministerial error, which did not invalidate the legality of Rosaura's presence in the United States. We had the law, but Rosaura remained in custody. In Washington the representatives of the state of New Mexico were most sympathetic and would look into the matter further. It would — take a little time. Paul had called earlier asking Mike to join him and Ben in El Paso. Mike left, unwillingly. He had infinitely more attachment to the shooting than to legal processes. His presence through the shooting and through the difficulties was helpful and heartening beyond all description.

At five o'clock that afternoon a police car entered the Roos ranch. An officer sought me out and asked that I be ready at the lodge at eight o'clock. A car would pick me up. Would I have our production manager accompany me? I asked who would pick me up and

where we would be going. He did not know. I told him, most respectfully, that I would not leave the lodge until I knew who had sent for
me, who was picking me up, and where we would be going. He
returned in half an hour and said that the sheriff would call for me. I
was not to advertise the fact. I stated my satisfaction and agreement.

At eight o'clock the sheriff arrived. The production manager and
I took seats in the rear of the car. I was interested that the car circled
in its tracks many times. The sheriff obviously did not wish to be
followed.

We finally pulled up at the rear entrance to the cathedral. The
sheriff, the production manager and I stepped out. His assistant
parked the car elsewhere and joined us later. We followed the sheriff
into the courtyard of the cathedral ground and through a door and
up a flight of stairs and we found ourselves finally in the Dean's
study. Gathered there were the Dean, the priest of Hanover, the chief
of the state police, his assistant, the saloonkeeper of Central, the
Mexican-American *politico* from Silver City, the sheriff, his assistant,
our production manager and I.

I found this the most fascinating assemblage of people of which I
had ever been a part. I looked forward to the discussion, although I
could not imagine its content.

The chief impressed me at once as a gentlemanly, peace-loving
peace officer. His speech was cultivated and reserved. He was
respected by the union. Eminently fair during the strike, he had actually prevented violence on the part of the local sheriff on many
occasions.

The chief's opening remarks were to the effect that a canvassing
of the area impelled him to the belief that a dangerous situation
existed. There were a body of men in the area, at that moment, who
had been brought there to kill. Though he had some seventy-five
officers with him, in an area as large and as open as Grant County, it
was utterly impossible for him to feel that absolute security could be
achieved. If one man were killed on either side, a very perilous situation might result. Before it could be controlled a good many bodies
might be lying on the roads and fields of the entire area. He had a
proposal. He suggested that we pack up the following morning and be

ready to leave by nightfall. If he could spread the word that this was going to take place, he felt certain that, for that length of time, things could be kept in hand.

The Dean exploded. In a speech rustling with the most delectable brogue he asked what decent man wanted to be run out of town for no fault of his. And what decent man would run out of town when he was a peaceful individual going about his peaceable business! And, furthermore, he would not permit such a thing. And he turned to me and told me to sit tight.

I thanked the Dean but said I wanted to reply to the friendly and honest statements of the chief. I admitted that I was an amateur in this matter even though my reputation for love of overthrowing governments should have made me a little more conversant with the subject of violence. However, I was stuck with reality. It occurred to me that the very worst thing we could do in this situation would be to leave town. Once these hoodlums got a sense of victory they would probably go hog-wild and really try to take over the town. I pointed to the fact that they had shot Clint Jencks's car full of bullets outside his house only the evening before, frightening his family almost out of their minds. If we left they might wish to fill more than Clint's car with their lead. Furthermore, if we left, the film would have to be junked. And I did not propose to junk it.

I wished to suggest another approach. We needed a week to finish the film. But I would do it in three days. I expressed my belief that not only must the police remain until we had gone, but that they should make it very clear that they intended to leave a contingent for a time after we had departed. The serious time, in my opinion, would begin immediately after our departure. It seemed to me the vigilantes were not primarily bent upon dispersing our film company. They wished to break up the new feeling that had begun to develop in the community. Only if they succeeded in that would they any longer have any place in the community. They would move toward any act of violence which would guarantee that place.

"Good for you," cried the Dean.

The priest of Hanover also agreed, but he had another comment. He asked me to undertake to convey to the union, and to Clint

Jencks, that Clint had outlived his usefulness in this area. He had done excellent work for the union. He had served the Mexican-American people selflessly and with great credit to himself. But because he was an Anglo, championing Mexican-Americans, he had become the symbol of everything the rabid, racist elements in the area feared and hated. The priest stated as his conviction that if the union could be persuaded to his view, and Clint assigned elsewhere, a distinct contribution would be made to the pacification of the community. I agreed to convey his message.

I sought Clint out immediately and reported the conversation to him. He asked me to discuss it with the officers of the union. They were the proper recipients of the point of view. He had his own conviction on the matter. But he preferred to present it only after the union officials of the local had discussed it.

As I related the conversation to the union officers, they nodded their heads as if they had heard it before. They held in high esteem the priest from whom this observation came. They discussed his idea with seriousness and respect. But the discussion didn't take long. Their entire experience had dictated to them that no one gained from appeasing vigilantes. The community, equally with the union, would suffer from it. The vigilantes didn't hate Clint Jencks but what he stood for. And what he stood for was decency in the community. If Clint were let out, the union would be forcing the community to fight the battle all over again. And from a weaker starting point. The battle was against racism and vigilantism. One had to be clear about that. It had to be fought. The vote was unanimous. Clint was to remain—unless, of course, Clint believed that the physical safety of his family and himself counseled otherwise.

Clint's reply, their reaction indicated, was exactly what they had expected from him. He said that they had been in the struggle together for six years. It was not over. There were thousands of families who could not leave the area, or the struggle. They could not—then he would not. That was the answer, although he asked for permission to discuss the question with his wife and children.

The state police remained and filming continued.

From El Paso we learned that the only possible next legal step for Rosaura would be an appeal to the appellate court in New Orleans. At the earliest, it could be filed only two days after our shooting had to be concluded. The die was cast. We all agreed Rosaura must accept voluntary deportation. She did so and returned to Mexico.

Two days before we left, the vigilantes secured a theater in Silver City. They also got a film from Metro-Goldwyn-Mayer. It was a documentary called *The Hoaxters,* made in Hollywood for just such occasions, presumably. A good, hot, cold-war piece of provocation. The vigilantes considered it just the article to heat up this still peaceful community against the "Reds." With this event the Hollywood syndrome had come full circle. It was now furnishing cultural artillery to vigilantes in a tiny mining town of New Mexico, to use against its citizens, to overthrow their peaceableness, their fraternity, and their deeply ingrained sense of fair play. Small wonder that we Hollywood people felt more shame than bitterness that day. And no wonder at all at the pride we felt in the people of that area who, in droves, stayed away from the hoax they knew *The Hoaxsters* to be. The theater was opened to the public, without charge. Every business in Silver City was ordered, by the vigilantes, to close down for the day, or suffer the consequences. Every business shut down. But only one hundred people entered the theater. And on that day one of the largest businessmen in Silver City made his biggest truck available to us. That saved us a half-day's shooting time. He refused any payment.

On the morning our cars left, the union had wished to organize a caravan to escort us some fifty miles outside the city. We had counseled against it. Our cars left in caravans of two. At our final farewell there was not a dry eye. Men and women, normally shy and reserved, embraced and kissed each other openly and unashamedly.

III

The caravans left the lodge that Saturday morning by two routes and at half-hour intervals. Because a *New York Times* reporter whom I had known for many years arrived just as I was about to leave, I was delayed an hour. The interview over, I took off alone. I had no more than cleared the populated section of Silver City than I noticed a car in my rear view mirror. It was driving down at me with speed. About the third look back revealed that it had no license plate. Alert by now to my congenital insensitivity to danger I decided there was nothing to lose by losing that car. I stepped on the gas. But the faster I went the faster the car behind me followed.

When I had first seen him he was perhaps seventy yards behind me. By the time I determined to lose him he was no more than thirty yards behind. My speedometer showed eighty but I had gained no more than twenty yards. I put my foot to the floor. I reached ninety miles an hour. And the car was still there. I began to calculate every curve, seeking by proper maneuvering to save yards. For twenty minutes we matched speed. I wondered why he didn't shoot my tires. Then I understood the danger involved in it for him. At the speed we were traveling, if my car were to roll on the road he himself might not be able to stop in time to avoid smashing into me.

I had to keep ahead of him. Therein lay my safety. I bent over the wheel seeking more sensitive control. Only twenty minutes to Lordsburg. Ten minutes outside that city I saw ahead the truck of one of our caravans. I slowed down just in time to slide into place behind it. The car behind swept by me. As it passed the driver raised his hand in salute and grinned broadly. Then I noticed a medical insignia on the rear of the car. I learned later that he was a friendly doctor who had tended to members of our crew.

He had been trying to catch up to wave goodbye. He was on his way to deliver a baby.

In Lordsburg I bought some papers and sat down with them over a cup of coffee. We were in headlines. It was like reading about some other group of people in some other place. They made our story pop as if it had been enacted by demons and demi-gods, participants who bore no resemblance to members of the human race.

RACISTS QUIT SILVER CITY

COMMUNIST FILM COMPANY FINALLY GIVES UP

Then the news:

> The racists from Hollywood who were discovered making a secret, communist film in Silver City, New Mexico, today gave up and quit the area. Exposed by Congressman Donald L. Jackson of the House Committee on Un-American Activities in a speech before Congress on February 28th, he called upon the government and the people to rally behind him. The racist group was finally driven out of Silver City today. Denounced by Roy M. Brewer, head AFL spokesman of the studio workers of Hollywood, repudiated by Walter Pidgeon, President of the Actors Guild, their leading actress discovered to have entered the country illegally, and deported, the Red racist company was given final notice to get out by the patriotic citizens of Silver City. The air of Grant County is once again, pure, American and free from the stench of racist propaganda. The film was financed by the Communist Mine, Mill and Smelters Union whose violence on the picket lines of the year-long strike against Empire Zinc brought jail sentences to many leaders of this Red-dominated Union. Good riddance to the racists and congratulations to Silver City.

I found myself overcome by a sudden nausea. I saw hundreds, nay thousands, of papers in every city in the country carrying this tale. I saw decent Americans sitting over radios, television sets, shaking their heads and wondering what these subversive racists wouldn't try next. Always sneaking off into corners! Always trying to stir up trouble among people of color! Never would come out in the open and say whatever they wanted to say like anybody else. And some of them Hollywood people, too. But just like all the rest. A red is a red is a red is a racist. A congressman said so; Hollywood said so; Silver City said so; the papers said so. What more proof could a decent person wish?

I left the restaurant and drove to a gas station. I debated whether to show my credit card to the attendant. If he recognized my name there might be trouble. Better pay cash. Incredible. One newspaper story and I was nauseated, numb, frightened. After all I had experienced! Why?

"You coming from Silver City?"

The attendant's question gave point to my speculations.

"Yes."

"You part of that film group?"

"Yes."

"What the hell went on up there?"

"Haven't you read the papers?"

"Yes. That's why I'm asking."

"We finished a film about the miners."

"Finished, huh? Papers said you'd been run out. See what I mean?"

I pulled the papers out from under my arm, and flipped my hand over the face of the top one.

"I've been wondering what people will think about all this."

"Well, I reckon it's about like my old man says. Says he reads every word in them things and when he gets through he cain't remember a damned thing he read. But the next day he goes ahead and reads it all over again. Been doin' it for forty years."

"Thank you, very much. And thank him for me."

"Why?"

"I haven't really read a paper for about three months. I'd forgotten just what people do with them."

The attendant laughed. "Well, in this part of the country you know what people mostly do with 'em, don't you?"

It didn't matter for the moment that his views were perhaps not typical, not representative. He had dissolved my nausea in the way one decent, witty human being can. He sent me on my way with at least the ability to see the road. And the eighteen hours of driving proved a godsend. By the time I had been on my own for several hours, had eaten and accustomed myself to the roll of the car and the swish-by of that incredibly monumental countryside, energies began to pour back into me. Energies necessary to face this complex place called America.

So we were racists! Stirring up the people!

Congressman Jackson, speaking to Congress about *Salt of the Earth* and the people who made it, said:

> The name of the picture is unknown to me at the present time.... The picture itself is being financed by the Communist-dominated United Mine, Mill and Smelter Works Union. [First inaccuracy: the union is dominated by its members. Second inaccuracy: it had contributed not one penny toward financing our film. Third inaccuracy: the name of the union is the International Union of Mine, Mill and Smelter Workers.]
>
> Herbert Biberman is the actual producer of this Communist-inspired film endeavor, while Gale Sondergaard is the co-producer. [Fourth inaccuracy: Herbert Biberman is the director. Fifth inaccuracy: Gale Sondergaard's only connection with the picture was that she did *not* play the leading role. Sixth inaccuracy: the film endeavor was not Communist-inspired. It was inspired by the House Un-American Activities Committee and its effect on two hundred creative film craftsmen.]
>
> Paul Jarrico is a writer working on the picture. [Only a slight inaccuracy: Paul Jarrico is a writer and an excellent one, but he acted as the producer of the film.]
>
> Michael Wilson and Will Geer are two more uncooperative witnesses said to be active in the production of the film. [Said to be? Are! Mike's name was listed on every script of *Salt of the Earth* as its author.]

So far, the congressman had not been a particularly reliable witness. But to read on:

> This picture is being made in the state of New Mexico not far from the Los Alamos atomic proving grounds and, as Mr. Riesel points out in his article, "Where you try to hide secret weapons, you find concentrations of Communist."
>
> Also in his article Mr. Riesel states that Silver City, New Mexico, the scene of the picture, is located near vital zinc concentrate mines, and that the band of movie people, and I quote from his article, "few of whom will ever find work again in Hollywood, is shooting a propaganda movie produced, managed, written, acted and edited by men and women who have been charged by congressional witnesses with being part of the secret pro-Soviet apparatus in this country."
>
> Mr. Speaker, I have received reports of the sequences filmed to date during the making of the picture and it depicts exactly what might be

expected from a group of Communists engaged in the making of a motion picture. The picture is deliberately designed to inflame racial hatreds and to depict the United States of America as the enemy of all colored peoples. If this picture is shown in Latin America, Asia and India, it will do incalculable harm not only to the United States but to the cause of free people everywhere. In effect this picture is a new weapon for Russia. For instance, in one sequence, two deputy sheriffs arrest a meek American miner of Mexican descent and proceed to pistol whip the miner's very young son. The production company of this picture also imported two auto carloads of colored people for the purpose of shooting a scene of mob violence.

The congressman had never heard of Negroes working as technicians in a Hollywood movie. Mr. Roy M. Brewer's unions did not permit it. Mr. Riesel, the labor expert, undoubtedly also knew of Hollywood's anti-Negro practices. When he heard that we had Negroes in our company apparently all Riesel could think of was violence. And that felt right to Jackson too.

Then the former publicity man placed the Congressional toga upon his shoulders and in his own name summed up the calumny:

"... after having lost Hollywood as a source of income, and this only recently, [they] have succeeded in acquiring another source of income, perhaps a more lucrative one."

"... I shall do everything in my power to prevent the showing of this Communist-made film in the theaters of America and I am confident that millions of Americans will join in that effort."

Thus it was that Donald L. Jackson told the legislative representatives of the American people, and, through them, the people of the entire world, that we, a group of American citizens, were a threat to the atomic installations at Los Alamos, to the zinc deposits of New Mexico, as part of a secret pro-Soviet apparatus, on the payroll of Moscow, inflaming racial hatreds. If he really believed this why did he not have us arrested? Why did he not subpoena our script?

Congressman Jackson had said that he would do everything in his power to prevent the showing of our film. To succeed he and the studios and Brewer would require one thing: to make the United States their monopoly.

IV

Two weeks later, Congressman Jackson received consent of the House to publish an exchange of letters with various Americans; private citizens and government officials.

From the *Congressional Record* of March 19, 1953:

SUBVERSIVE FILMS

MR. JACKSON. Mr. Speaker. I ask unanimous consent to address the House for 1 minute, to revise and extend my remarks, and to include letters.

THE SPEAKER. Is there objection to the request of the gentleman from California?

There was no objection.

MR. JACKSON. Mr. Speaker, there has been considerable interest in the House and throughout the country generally with respect to a moving picture being made in Silver City, N. Mex., under the auspices of a number of witnesses who have in the past refused under oath to affirm or deny their alleged membership in the Communist Party.

I have asked all major studios, the Hollywood A.F. of L. Film Council, the Secretaries of State and Commerce, and the Attorney General of the United States to submit suggestions as to what legal steps can be taken, following upon a proper finding that the picture is indeed designed to inflame racial hatreds, toward stopping the export of this picture abroad to the detriment of United States policy and interests abroad.

I wish I could have waited for all of the replies to these inquiries before inserting any in the RECORD.

However, as a member of the Committee on Un-American Activities I am leaving tomorrow for Los Angeles where the committee opens hearings on next Monday. I am inserting those answers which I have received to this time from Roy M. Brewer, chairman, Hollywood A.F. of L. Council, Mr. Howard Hughes, of RKO, the Secretary of Commerce and the in Assistant Secretary of State. I will insert other replies following my return to Washington.

I hope that a legal method can be found by which the completion of this picture in the United States and its export to foreign nations can be stopped pending a legal finding as to its contents and purposes.

(The letters referred to follow—in part.)

LOS ANGELES, CALIFORNIA
MARCH 18, 1953

DONALD L. JACKSON
HOUSE OF REPRESENTATIVES
WASHINGTON, D.C.

The Hollywood AFL Film Council assures you that everything which it can do to prevent the showing of the Mexican picture [sic] Salt of the Earth will be done.... The film council will solicit its fellow members in the theaters to assist in the prevention of showing of this picture in any American theaters, but the extent to which we can as a union take action such a matter is limited by reason of the restrictive features in the Taft-Hartley Act....

Sincerely,

ROY M. BREWER,
CHAIRMAN, HOLLYWOOD AFL COUNCIL

MARCH 18, 1953

CONGRESSMAN DONALD L. JACKSON
HOUSE OFFICE BUILDING
WASHINGTON, D.C.

DEAR CONGRESSMAN JACKSON:

In your telegram you asked the question, "Is there any action that industry and labor in motion picture field can take to stop completion and release of picture and to prevent showing of film here and abroad?"

My answer is "Yes."

... Before a motion picture can be completed or shown in theaters, an extensive application of certain technical skills and use of a great deal of specialized equipment is absolutely necessary.

Herbert Biberman, Paul Jarrico, and their associates working on this picture do not possess these skills or this equipment.

If the motion picture industry—not only in Hollywood, but throughout the United States—will refuse to apply these skills, will refuse to furnish this equipment, the picture cannot be completed in this country.

Biberman and Jarrico have already met with refusal where the industry was on its toes. The film processing was being done by the Pathe Laboratories, until the first news broke from Silver City.

But the minute Pathe learned the facts, this alert laboratory immediately refused to do any further work on this picture, even though it meant refunding cash paid in advance.

Investigation fails to disclose where the laboratory work is being done now. But it is being done somewhere, by someone, and a great deal more laboratory work will have to be done by someone, before the motion picture can be completed.

Biberman, Jarrico, and their associates cannot succeed in their scheme alone. Before they can complete the picture, they must have the help of the following:

1. Film laboratories.

2. Suppliers of film.

3. Musicians and recording technicians necessary to record music.

4. Technicians who make dissolves, fades, etc.

5. Owners and operators of sound recording equipment and dubbing rooms.

6. Positive and negative editors and cutters.

7. Laboratories that make release prints.

If the picture industry wants to prevent this motion picture from being completed and spread all over the world as a representative product of the United States, then the industry and particularly that segment of the industry listed above, needs only to do the following.

Be alert to the situation.

Investigate thoroughly each applicant for the use of services or equipment.

Refuse to assist the Bibermans and Jarricos in the making of this picture.

Be on guard against work submitted by dummy corporations or third parties.

Appeal to the Congress and the State Department to act immediately to prevent the export of this film to Mexico or anywhere else.

Sincerely,

HOWARD HUGHES

THE SECRETARY OF COMMERCE
WASHINGTON, MARCH 16, 1953
THE HONORABLE DONALD L. JACKSON,
HOUSE OF REPRESENTATIVES,
WASHINGTON, D.C.
DEAR MR. JACKSON:

This is in reply to your letter of February 26, 1953, in which you inquire whether effective legislation exists to prevent the exportation of finished prints of the motion picture Salt of the Earth, now in this country.... At the present time, exposed motion picture film is not on our list of controlled commodities.

... I am not expressing an opinion as to whether such action should be taken since, as you are aware, it would necessitate a foreign policy determination with respect to which I should have to obtain advice from the Secretary of State, and possibly the President. It is my understanding that you have already written to Secretary Dulles in this connection, and also that regarding the alien agent aspect of this matter, referred to in your letter, you have written to the Attorney General.

Sincerely yours,

SINCLAIR WEEKS
SECRETARY OF COMMERCE

DEPARTMENT OF STATE
WASHINGTON, MARCH 18, 1953
THE HONORABLE DONALD L. JACKSON
HOUSE OF REPRESENTATIVES
MY DEAR DON:

... Section 5b, of the Trading With the Enemy Act, would apparently offer control over the export of any item. The history of this legislation did not contemplate its use as a means of censorship. Its terms, however, are broad and general in nature.... The terms of the Export Control Act... does not indicate that it was designed to enter the field of censorship; but in view of the fact that it covers anything that might affect the foreign policy of the United States....

... In regard to your question relating to the provisions of the Foreign Agents Registration Act of 1938, as amended, it would appear that this is a matter of interpretation and ruling by the Attorney General. This act is administered by the Department of justice, and I am informed that it becomes applicable when it has been determined by the Attorney General that funds are being employed whose source can be traced to a foreign principal.

    ... I would like to discuss this with you.

Sincerely yours,

THRUSTON B. MORTON
ASSISTANT SECRETARY
(FOR THE SECRETARY OF STATE)

Part Three

UN-AMERICA
1954

I

Within several weeks the union hall in Bayard was set afire. The damage was slight. The union hall in Carlsbad was burned to the ground. The home of Floyd Bostick was set afire when Floyd and his wife were away. The children narrowly escaped being burned to death. The house was destroyed. The union announced it would build a better house for the Bosticks than the seven hundred dollar edifice they had formerly occupied. Floyd said, "I'm stayin'." No one accused Congressman Jackson of arson or of destroying property. How can anyone set fire to a union hall or to children with words? No one accused the motion picture financing institutions of arson. How can anyone commit arson through mere blacklisting?

A representative of the mine companies appeared before the Senate Committee on Labor and Education. He asked for stricter laws and harsher penalties against Taft-Hartley non-Communist affidavit falsifiers. He spoke of the lengths to which the Communists had gone in Silver City. They had made a film stirring up all the old violence.

Two weeks later, ten days before the statute of limitations would have come into play, Clinton Jencks was arrested for alleged falsification of his Taft-Hartley non-Communist affidavit. He faced the possibility of five years in jail if convicted. A journalist for an El Paso newspaper reported that he had asked several FBI agents why they had moved against Jencks at this particular moment. They replied that it was because of the ruckus kicked up over that film.

Three months later the price of zinc dropped a half-cent a pound. The mines closed down. Half the membership of Local 890 was unemployed. Many of the actors in the film packed their belongings (as the shot of the departing miners' families shows it in the film) and moved all over the southwest looking for employment.

Congressman Jackson and his committee came to Hollywood. They subpoenaed Simon Lazarus. They did not subpoena Michael Wilson, Paul Jarrico or me. Mr. Tavenner, the committee's counsel, interrogated Mr. Lazarus.

TAVENNER: Who are the investors in the company?

LAZARUS: I do not know.

TAVENNER: Aren't you the president?

LAZARUS: No. I was. But I resigned.

TAVENNER: When did you resign? Just before we got here?

LAZARUS: Yes sir.

TAVENNER: *Is* it possible you will again become president after we leave?

LAZARUS: It *is* possible. Now I would like to tell you the story of the film *Salt of the Earth.*

TAVENNER: I have no further questions, Mr. Chairman.

Although Congressman Jackson's contention was that the film was subversive, the committee refused to listen to any testimony about it. We arranged with a magazine, *The California Quarterly,* to have the screen play printed in full and we bought ten thousand copies and sent them all over the country; to newspapers, writers, columnists, magazines, leading educational leaders, clergymen, trade union leaders—and members of the committee.

The *New York Times* ran a column on the script and asked, "What was all the shooting about?" The Santa Fe *New Mexican,* leading daily paper of the capital city of New Mexico, stated editorially: "Despite Senator McCarthy and Congressman Jackson, it occurs to us that the union has every right to tell its side of the story…. The country is in no stronger position when it suppresses films than when it burns books."

The charge of "inflaming racial antagonisms" could not be discussed. Upon what were they waging war now? Upon an unassailable film? Why not? Now, *surely,* this film must be stopped. Otherwise people might ask, "What was all the burning about? What is this committee?"

Six weeks later our film was still undeveloped. Not one laboratory in Hollywood or apparently in any part of the United States would handle it.

The technique was flawless. Most laboratories derived their business from two sources: the motion picture industry, the government, or both. Mr. Howard Hughes, with the profound understanding of the business outlined in his letter to Congressman Jackson, had only to announce that the "industry" would look with disfavor upon anyone who serviced our films. Mr. Brewer's attitude passed like an order through the laboratory locals: this film was not to be serviced. The international union placed a box on the seventh page of its monthly bulletin advising all locals to contact the international office before doing any work on the film. But to make the conspiracy triply certain, Mr. Brewer spent some time around the country to keep it alive. He voyaged even to Mexico. He made a personal appearance before the Mexican film union's executive board, we were told. He asked their "fraternal" assistance in refusing to handle any of our work. They were polite to Mr. Brewer. They tabled his request.

In his letters to individuals in the movies and to departments of government, Mr. Jackson referred to *legal* steps that might be taken. Mr. Brewer referred to certain *legal* limitations. They had to be legal, *in print,* although, obviously, neither one of them gave a tinker's damn about legality, and did not resort to it. But Mr. Hughes didn't give a damn about legality, *in print* or *out* of it.

Mr. Hughes had declared that he and a few other people in the United States owned all the means of producing motion pictures. As owners, in combination, they would determine what ideas might be made into films. "Herbert Biberman [and] Paul Jarrico... do not possess... this equipment." Then he continued, "If the picture industry wants to prevent the picture from being completed and spread all over the world... refuse to assist the Bibermans and Jarricos in the making of this picture." Illegal censorship? Conspiracy?

The departments of government were something quite different. As departments they were somewhat stuck with the law.

> Complex uniformities which... are mere cases of simpler ones, and have, therefore, been virtually affirmed in affirming those, may with propriety be called *laws.*

—John Stuart Mill

It was Mill's definition that saved us. We were the simple uniformity, and if the government had wished to move against us, it would
first have had to institute licensing against all films, the complex
uniformity.

But law was not necessary to deal with us. Mr. Hughes, Mr.
Brewer and Mr. Jackson could handle us, alone. Their representatives
merely went to a laboratory, if they were not already within it, and
asked if we had petitioned to have our film processed. That's all there
was to it.

The curious aspect of the complex, "philosophical uniformity"
lay in this: we did not believe with Mr. Hughes that all film servicing
agencies were part of a cabal against freedom of expression. We
thought some of them were independent Americans. True, we
couldn't find one in Los Angeles. But, filmically, Los Angeles was,
after all, only a suburb of Hollywood.

Paul Jarrico and our editor took our precious negative onto one
of Mr. Hughes's commercial planes and undertook a city to city jun-
ket. They searched for a man who ran a laboratory for the development of film, not the suppression of it. It took them two weeks. But
they found him. He did work for the movie industry and for the government, but he still had a sweet tooth for what he called democracy.
He also had the old-fashioned quaintness which led him to believe
that he was in business to do business. He asked one question: was
there any legal, moral or patriotic reason why this film ought not be
developed? The answer was a categorical no. Being an intelligent
democrat he asked that the film be put through a few thousand feet
at a time. Just so that none of us pushed our democracy too far, too
fast. Paul agreed. It took ten days to put it through.

We also decided that we would have a fine grain made. From
this positive print, of superior quality stock, we would be able to
make a new negative, if anything "happened" to our original. To
make a hundred thousand feet of fine grain would be most costly. We
could ill afford it. We would store it, safely, against that fine day when
Congressman Jackson inspired new incendiaries, or Mr. Brewer
stumbled upon our film somewhere and someone accidentally
gummed up the works.

After all, Floyd Bostick's home was a charred ruin, as was a union hall. We thought discretion was, lamentably, the better part of American valor that year. It was pretty sad to have to move with such suspicion of the methods that might be used against us by government, industry, and a "labor" leader. But it was the United States in 1953—the year, despite the objections of President Eisenhower and such organizations as the American Library Association and the American Book Publishers Council, that Senator McCarthy (with the help of Schine and Cohn) forced the removal and burning of books on the shelves of the State Department's overseas libraries; that J. B. Matthews, the McCarthy committee executive director, attacked the Protestant clergy as the "largest single group supporting the communist apparatus"; that McCarthy arrogantly demanded access to the records of the Central Intelligence Agency and attacked former President Truman for giving aid to some people suspected of being Communists. The film finally arrived in Los Angeles, courtesy of T.W.A. We "stored" the fine grain in another city. We "buried" the negative in Los Angeles. The positive print was kept available for cutting.

But this was only our picture. Our sound track still was on tape. It had to be transferred to film. This was not possible to do in New York, because we had used a type of recorder—the only one available to us—that worked at an un-normal speed. The gentleman in Los Angeles who had rented us this equipment was now thoroughly petrified by the agitation against us and refused to permit one foot of film to enter his premises. We had to build equipment which gave us the proper speed. Then we required a sound studio in which to balance our track. Would we now have to transport the equipment to New York as well?

Once more Paul took up the trail, convinced that oases of decency and courage existed. And again he found one not in Los Angeles. This gentleman was a Republican. He called himself a "black" Republican. He didn't care what the hell was in the film. He didn't even want to look. All he wanted to know was, could we pay our bills in advance? When we said yes, he went to work. And when he went to work, the best he had was none too good for a cash-in-advance customer. He swore himself blue—at the lousy equipment on which we had had to record sound. That equipment had come to us from a man who had advertised himself to us as a liberal. Now we were forced to listen to a "black Republican" curse, and correct, a liberal's failures in a pro-labor film.

America's chances for a democratic future were indeed good. America possessed one very meaningful attribute. It was so diverse in the composition of its human inhabitants. Not alone the vast bodies of minorities, with their backs to the wall and no place to go but forward. It also possessed businessmen who believed business was a way of making a living and not a cider-press to squeeze sovereignty out of a people. And it had a few businessmen who were so independently individualist that you attempted to organize them into a conspiracy at the peril of your life.

What was charming about the "black Republican" was that he had been ours before Paul ever got to him. He had been called upon before he had so much as heard of us. He responded to the visit with a near apoplectic stroke. Somebody had dared to walk into his place and ask him if he were doing business with a given group of people. They had "asked" him. They had "ASKED" him! No nosy big-shot in the world was going to tell him what business he might take and might not take! Who the hell was Howard Hughes or Roy M. Brewer? Or Donald Jackson?

Sweet, rebellious, black Republican. He was unowned and a blessing to his land in days of tribulation. And—he was more than a black Republican. He was a "mad" American.

The sound track was now on film and we could begin to debate where we might set up a cutting-room and undertake the long process of editing *Salt of the Earth.*

But this was not a simple decision. Owing to the difficulties and setbacks we had encountered, we had, to that moment, already spent twenty thousand dollars more than was allotted by budget for the entire picture. We had the cutting still to do, the music, the re-recording, and all the various processes which Mr. Hughes had so accurately outlined for Congressman Jackson. In addition, we were all concerned about the safety of our editor. He wished to do the work in another city. Since we had no money and every additional expendi-

ture was serious and, especially because we meant to participate fully
in the cutting ourselves, we compromised. We found a secluded spot
twenty miles from the city and went to work. I was in the cutting-
room eight to twelve hours a day, and engaged in raising money several evenings each week. Paul spent a good part of the entire day raising money.

We could not afford to take small sums. It took too long. Most of
the money came in quite large sums and much of it from people
whom neither Paul nor I had ever seen before. We called upon men
and women known to be philanthropic. In most cases they would
send us to friends whose democratic sensibilities were equally
offended as they listened to our story and especially to Mr. Hughes's
letter to Congressman Jackson. That was the *pièce de résistance*. People
became angry. "I thought this was America!" "You men are doing a
good job." "Somebody has to take those people on, I can't. If you're
willing to, the least I can do is support you with money which isn't
very important to me anyway." Without Congressman Jackson's
intervention and Mr. Hughes's letter, the job would have been infinitely more difficult. It might even have been impossible. But then,
also, it wouldn't have been necessary. They did, however, provide us
with documents that dramatized an America that was anathema to
every American concerned for the future of popular sovereignty in
our land.

But a film, unfortunately, is not made with money alone. It is
the most highly complex of all arts. In that vast complex of skills, it is
difficult to place one or another in first rank. No matter how excellent the script and the organization of its enactment by the director,
its final assemblage by the editor is crucial. He either brings out the
values of writer and director, synthesizes them and sharpens them, or
he can take off on a tack of his own and come up with a film which
bears little resemblance to the original intention.

There are skilled hacks in this profession, brilliant creative artists
and "art for art's sake" craftsmen. There are editors who put it
together out of habit. We, unfortunately, had no choice among these
various attitudes. There were few cutters in the United States who
would come to work for us.

Our editor had never cut a feature film before. He was a documentary man. For each new sequence he assembled all the film, on reels, in continuity, and then chose those sections which appealed to him as "film." These he would assemble as a scene. His theory was that one put "film" together rather than the line and emotion of the story. Developed film, in his view, became something independent of the script.

At the end of two months about one-third of the film was together. And it was unrecognizable.

The dilemma which faced us was almost insoluble. We asked for a deadline of six weeks for a rough cut of the entire film. He replied that he could not guarantee to have a rough cut in less than twelve additional weeks. This, he informed us, was about what it would take at Metro-Goldwyn-Mayer.

The cutting-room, which was located in a one-story building with a tin roof, was so brutally hot that the film, dried out by the intense heat, curled and rose like living snakes from the bins in which it hung. When we tried to work with it, it cracked. It was intolerable. We would have to move. And we decided that we had better risk everything with one fell swoop. We dismissed the cutter. And we moved.

Choosing a new location for the cutting-room was an anxious task. We knew from Brewer's statement that he believed the negative was in Mexico and was being cut there. But we could not be certain that this was not a ruse designed to encourage our recklessness. We had therefore, again, to find a remote place. The noises of the moviolas and of our improvised 35 mm. projection machines were easily identifiable. Simon Lazarus gave us one of his empty theaters in a small town near Los Angeles. We took this over as our cutting-room. The only area in the theater possible to use, with space for the easy storage of film, some accessibility to it in working, and by location capable of muffling the sounds of our moviolas, was the ladies' toilet. We moved in.

Because I was assigned to supervise the cutting, with the constant collaboration of Mike and Paul as sequences were completed, we were content to accept any cutter who was a fairly efficient craftsman. Our standards were not high, but we could not find anyone. Many of our friends in the industry, even those long unemployed, refused to take the risk. We again attempted to find someone in New York. That as well proved impossible.

But Paul, with his indomitable optimism, stayed with the task. And one day, through a suggestion based upon a suggestion based upon a suggestion, he found a cutter. This man read the script and said he saw no reason to object to its contents and would go to work. He would give us a rough cut in four weeks.

He had been a cutter for fifteen years. He had put together hundreds of films. He was a skilled craftsman, a hard worker, and a man with no philosophy regarding either film or life. We went to work.

The toilet-room in which we worked was suffocating. There was no ventilation whatsoever. We improvised a series of fans to stir the fetid air. We worked stripped to the waist. From four in the morning until noon. Beyond noon our wits would not serve us in that place.

During all these many months of nervous editing, the finished reels, especially as we neared completion of the rough cut, were dearer to us than the apples of our eyes. They represented an investment of almost six months of work, tens of thousands of dollars and that invaluable item; our maturing film. Each day I would pack all the cut film, load it into my car and take it home. There I would store it safely away from the eyes of visitors. In the morning it would be lugged down, packed into the car, taken to the theater, lugged up a long flight of stairs, unpacked, opened, assembled and made ready for work again. By the time we had finished the rough cut this was a formidable quantity of film. No mother ever guarded her child more constantly. No offspring, not even quintuplets, ever weighed so much. But I had some of my jail-muscles left and they began to harden up again.

And then one morning, suddenly, there was loud knocking on the theater door. We had two visitors. The chief of the fire department of that community and a member of the police department. They wished to know whether we had a license to operate a cutting-room in that area. We did not have and did not know that one was required in a theater. He asked us what the film was. I told him it was an experimental assemblage of old footage. And as I said so I believed that I was speaking only the whole truth. The film was old. It was battered. And it was as experimental as any film ever put together.

He had been in our "cutting-room" for only five minutes when the stifling air began to offend him. He wouldn't work in such a place for all the money in the world! I quickly agreed with him. I told him the man we worked for was the most inhuman of all humans. He didn't care whether we lived or died. All he wanted was a finished film. Then the chief told us to take it easy. It was pretty hard to make a living and sometimes people didn't really know what their employees had to go through. Well—he didn't like to interfere with anybody trying to make a dollar, but this was no place to cut film and he would give us a week to find another place and get out. I thanked him profusely, as employer and as worker.

The next day Paul began to look for a new cutting-room. And we began to pack up the enormous quantity of film and supplies and machines for our next move. Within a few days Paul found a new location for us. It was much nearer home. An old G.I. film school. It was spacious, insulated and, although without ventilation, was so large and so high-ceilinged that it promised comfort beyond anything we had previously known. We took our cutter with us. He approved. We made arrangements to move.

That evening we learned that our cutter was reporting to the FBI.

II

I stood shaking my head, that evening, as the news came to us. We were not floored. We were actually relieved. We had had our government-man with us all the time. He had proved by his presence that sabotage was not in the FBI plan. So what if they knew where we were now moving?

A new cutter was required and Paul Jarrico yet again left for the fields of Hollywood craftsmen to find a cutter. And, again, he found one. A young man, with not too much experience, but enough. He had a mature conscience. He had respect for us, for our struggles, for our purpose. But he had a wife and children. He was young and just beginning in this field. And he was sorely troubled. His wife was even more troubled. He wrestled with his conscience for two weeks and then became ill. He left us. And again we required a cutter, our fourth. Paul took off again and came back with our fourth editor.

The discovery that we were so carefully watched and need no longer scurry into and out of our cutting-room was a very great relief in many ways. Perhaps the most important, in a personal sense, was related to my children. Children love to know, have to know, where their parents are working. They have to see them in their mind's eye, settled in a job, in a place. They require this for stability and emotional security. We had been cutting the film for six months or more. When the children asked where and why they could not come, I would have to invent stories. Each day they saw box after box unloaded and each morning taken away again. I often wondered what they thought of this itinerant transporter of boxes who was their father. But now I could invite them to the cutting-room. On a Saturday I brought my son there. I taught him how to use the English automatic splicer, the moviola, and how to join film by hand. I will never forget the hugs that came to me from that ten-year-old boy, that Saturday afternoon. I knew the reasons for them and it brought tears to my eyes which I could not hold back. His father had not *lied* to him. His father *was* cutting a film. He *did* work. And in his work he did everything he had said.

III

Our fourth cutter proved to be the most creative we had yet had. He was not a member of the cutters' union. He had learned his craft at a university and his professional experience was limited. But he was a student of the philosophy as well as of the mechanics of his craft. He had not lost interest in learning. He brought to his work enthusiasm for the material, respect for his craft, and taste.

We proceeded to the polishing of our work print. It required, above all, the achievement of cinematographic pace through elimination of all the unnecessary interstices in the flow of the action. As this was achieved new flaws in arrangement of elements became visible. This necessitated many small adjustments in the actual weight of one scene against another. And as the smooth rise and fall of the action was achieved, the small pieces of repetition, of dead weight, of overstatement, raised their heads for elimination. Narrative section lost narration and became just moving picture. And slowly we became ready for the addition of music. This was more than mechanical. In many places scenes were lengthened to permit the music to play a more major part. In other places the music itself permitted the dropping of footage, sometimes of narration.

Sol Kaplan, gifted composer that he is, conceived his themes out of long familiarity with the film and in the final weeks was as constant in attendance at the long, long debates over final changes as Mike, Paul and I. These were very difficult weeks. Paul's was the eagle eye searching for solution by cutting. Mike's job was to insist on the values in the script. Sol's was more than to find every means of adding musical flesh to the bones and musical bones to the flesh. He fought against all sentimental attachments to things, concepts, performances. But a work print in which there were few sound effects, no music, and in which the film itself, so battered now, had almost as much blank leader as picture, was a difficult thing to judge.

Allowance had to be made for so many elements not yet there, but planned for. The film was not the full orchestration it eventually would be. And there was great danger in this moment. The inexperienced desire to make a half orchestra sing like a full one could

destroy the very framework which had been established for later fill-
ing. The debate over the film at this stage was fierce. So much had
been expended upon it, of love, of energy, of nerves. We fought the
various points of view out, mercilessly, night after night. Ours was
not studio procedure in which the writer was never present, the
director only perfunctorily and the executive producer did as he
pleased. Ours was collaboration, energetic and long drawn out.

Authority had to be earned in this debate. Invaluable suggestions
came from everyone and the film profited from each. Respect for
larger experience did not preclude the contribution of lesser.

Finally we were ready. We had to have a completely new sound
track for dubbing. The one with which we had been working was in
ribbons. This meant laboratory work. A great deal of it. Sound effects
were necessary; optical work: dissolves, fades, montage effects, the
main title, the end title. Everything Mr. Hughes had prophesied. Where
in God's name were we going to get all that done? We would require
some seven cutters, one for the music, one for sound effects, one for
special effects, one for negative cutting, one for laboratory work—these
in addition to our cutter and his assistant. Our new cutter found a few
necessary assistants and Paul found a few and they found others.
Within a week seven cutters were at work in that great barn.

How to get the film through the laboratories? Sending it to New
York was out of the question. At this stage of the game, with so large
a crew on our payroll, reprints had to be made overnight. Since this
involved our precious negative we could not have it in the air for
weeks at a time. This work had to be done in Los Angeles.

We selected a pseudonym for the film: *Vaya Con Dios*. This title
seemed "appropriate" for a film with many Mexican-American faces
and speech rhythms. We invented three fictitious names for three
"supposed" companies. And we selected three laboratories in Los
Angeles. Initially, we sent through sound track, because this was not
inspected in the laboratory early each morning before it was sent to
the shipping room for delivery. The first night we sent only a small
piece of negative film to each lab. I did not sleep an hour. It was not
primarily the fear of destruction of the negative sound film, for we
still had the original tape. It was rather the fear that it might be

detected and that we would find ourselves in Mr. Hughes's hands. But the film came back, developed and printed.

We sent our special effects cutter to the best special effects plant in the city. He found a man who agreed to take the work on and do it himself, but he could not send any of it through his own laboratory. He would photograph the effects. We would have to have them developed and printed elsewhere.

This meant that we now had to put the picture itself through. The problem was how to do so without its being run by the lab inspectors. We developed an approach. We sent the negative to one laboratory requesting that it make a positive copy but not develop it. This was then sent to another lab in the morning with instructions to develop it by afternoon. Since film was examined only in the morning we received ours without its having been looked at.

By using three laboratories and alternating this procedure among them frequently, we succeeded in obtaining picture reprints. By now, *Vaya Con Dios* was becoming known. It was important to discover whether any of the labs *knew* what they were working on. If one lab did there was at least the possibility that later it would take on the formidable job of making release prints.

For this purpose we sent some of the telltale main title in for printing, but assigned another man to order this piece of film. We had to protect our "established" underground procedure. The lab recognized it immediately and ordered our representative to take it "the hell out" and "bring no more back." We tried a second lab. Here the processing technician looked up from the printed film knowingly, and casually asked our representative how soon we expected to have the picture completed. We had found our man.

We did not rush the matter. But we began to funnel the great majority of our work to that lab. Within three weeks it had developed and printed forty thousand feet of track, perhaps ten thousand feet of picture and some three thousand feet of special effects.

We had, now, to prepare for sound dubbing. There is no more difficult, tedious, laborious step in making a film than combining the dozens of separate sound tracks—dialogue, narration, music, effects—into one perfected whole. And no earthly way of sneaking it

in and out. It would require many days of continuous work; of projecting the picture with the tracks, over and over and over again.

But before we came to that we had to have our music recorded.
Where? And how? And with whom? Paul took this touchy task
under his confident wing.

This could not be done in Hollywood. The number of studios in
New York capable of handling the size of orchestra for which Sol had
written was limited. Our New York attorney called them. They
refused categorically. We cudgeled our brains in vain. We thought of
attempting to score the themes for a small combination. But the more
we contemplated this solution, the less tolerable it became. The music
Sol had written demanded the orchestra of thirty-two pieces for
which he had planned. It was essential to the film's effectiveness. The
film had been edited specifically to give such music its maximum
role. We had to find a way.

When in New York, earlier, Paul had encountered an acquain-
tance who believed he had a solution. The best sound studio in that
city was owned by one of his close friends. He would talk with him.
But the mere mention of the title of our film brought an emphatic
refusal, as it had earlier to our attorney.

Paul insisted that only the most daring solution promised success. He telephoned that very studio in New York, introduced himself
under a pseudonym, and asked for time to record music for *Vaya Con
Dios*. They were "utterly" at our disposal. Delighted to be of service!
The date was made for four consecutive days.

Sol and Paul left for New York. They hired a union crew under the
actual name of our company. On the given day, the orchestra appeared
at the studio and scoring of the music began. Within an hour word
spread through the studio that magnificent music was being scored in
the large room. The musicians playing Sol's compositions indicated
their own pleasure while rehearsing by the expressions on their faces.
When the lunch break came, one of them approached Sol and asked
what this picture was. Sol, prepared, told a story offhandedly of a Mexican boy who was lost in the Arizona desert and was found by some
cowboys and became a sort of mascot. Then with a shrug, he said, "A
picture!" The musicians said nothing more and left.

During the recording, several executives of the studio entered. The following day they were back. The musician who had asked about the picture the previous day said to Sol, "I don't know what this picture is, but you're not kiddin' anybody. You like these people... whoever they are."

For four days, not knowing at what moment our luck might be up, struggling for quality, fighting for time, praying his good fortune would hold, Sol conducted. When the entire score was completed, one of the listening executives said to Sol, "That was one of the best scores ever recorded here."

We were yet a long way from home. And we were weary. And we were out of money again. And the special effects were held up through a machine breakdown. And we had no sound studio in which to make a composite track. And we still had no idea of where we would get a finished print. Before us as far as we could see lay a maze of endless connivings. The earlier sense of triumph in successful subterfuge was turning into disgust with it, as a total way of life.

At that moment I, for one, was tempted to surrender my interest in "Whither America." How appealing seemed normalcy and time with my family, such as a husband and father owed, and I had not vouchsafed mine for years and years. My temper grew short. My patience was all but exhausted. But sorely as I was tempted to decamp, there was one impossible hurdle—to face the miners of Silver City and their families and say, "I'm sick of it." As a middle-class person with a little money I knew I always had a paltry alternative. Mrs. Molano had said, "When you are discouraged, come to us. We have always our backs to the wall." But I didn't have time to go back to Silver City. And I didn't have to. Remembering her made me disrespect myself, the middle-class person with ability to escape problems.

I went back to work with Paul to raise more money. But I no longer had any inner propulsion. I was tired of aliases, tired of anonymity, tired of philosophy, of questioning, of Hollywood, tired of Hughes and of Jackson. But I raised some money and came home. I went to bed exhausted and got up exhausted and went back to work.

Perhaps fortunately, we did not, any of us, know how far we still had to go.

IV

Paul found a man who had a sound studio. Someone with whom the "black Republican" could work. But the sound man was worried. And the "black Republican" was disgusted with him. With curses he beat this man into metal. Like a Vulcan, tempering soft ore into steel with the alloy of imprecations, he forged. The sound man said yes. And then for weeks he said no and then yes. He was frightened and brave and terrified and abject. Tomorrow became next week and next week became the week after and finally there was a showdown. And tomorrow meant tomorrow and tomorrow came and it was finally today.

We thought that Brewer's men watched the place on double shifts. But we crawled in through alleys—we started work at one o'clock in the morning and left at seven. And the sound man slept from seven until nine, came back and did his day's work so that his business was "as usual." Then he slept for two hours, if he were lucky, and began with us again. We worked for six days and his eyes were slits and what one saw within them was a red, grainy mass. He had promised that on Saturday evening we could begin at eight. He believed it would be safe to begin earlier on Saturday. But when we arrived he was asleep on a sofa in his office and although we tried for an hour we could not rouse him. He was "unwakeable." We left. But we returned at eight Sunday morning and we shook and shook him and did finally manage to raise him to his feet. We fed him coffee and gave him food and within an hour he could see. And he worked from ten that Sunday morning until four Monday morning; the last three hours on alcohol. And we were half through our dubbing.

When the track came back from the lab it was poor and half of it had to be done again. We were spending a fortune and the work went slowly because after two weeks men cannot function without sight and a modicum of consciousness. But we went on. And that weekend we began at eight on Saturday evening and with but four hours sleep we worked until two o'clock Monday. And we were finished—until the tracks came back. And it was necessary to enact all our goodbyes and embraces again after two more sessions beginning at one in the morning and lasting until seven.

This was the moment for a large try. I went to the owner of the laboratory to which we had sent the majority of our work. I introduced myself to him. He knew my name and immediately told me of his respect for the battle of the Hollywood Ten. He was a liberal Democrat, he said. And he assured me that in 1956 when the Democrats were back in office all would be well. I told him we couldn't wait that long. What did we wish? Patiently I informed him that we had put many thousands of feet of film through his laboratory and that the film was *Salt of the Earth.* We now wished to finish the picture there. However, we could not do that surreptitiously. Our negative was involved. We had to have maximum security for it. He said he understood, and asked me to return the following day. When I arrived, he called in his superintendent. The superintendent called in the chief lab man. They informed the owner that they had recently become aware of what they were handling. They told him that some of the lab workers had begun to suspect what was going through their hands. There was no possibility of taking the picture now without its becoming known. The superintendent said they could certainly use the business. It would amount to quite a sum. But....

When they left, the owner told his story. He was for us and he was against Hughes *et al.* But he couldn't take this on, It would mean the end of his business. He wanted me to know how sorry he was.

"My heart bleeds for you," he said.

"And mine for you," I replied.

"Me? Why should anybody's heart bleed for me?"

. "You thought you owned your business. I think you have just found out you don't. Hughes owns it, and Donald Jackson. Brewer owns it. They haven't put a cent into it, or sweated over it. But they own it. You can run it, but only as long as you do what they wish. Now we, on the other hand, own our business. It's a hell of a good feeling."

The special effects work had started again and was two-thirds completed when the top brass of the company discovered that it was ours. The man working on it was ordered to throw us out, and he had no recourse but to do so.

A week later, our cut negative, our composite sound track, our work print, and the fine grain for the incomplete special effects and all the necessary logs and count sheets and cue sheets were packed in cases, loaded on to a plane, and I accompanied the cargo to New York. Still to be done: complete our special effects, cut them in, have a composite print made, check it, balance it, turn out a fine grain, a dupe negative and then with the dupe negative begin to make prints for theater showing. For this I required a cutter and a laboratory.

Within twelve hours after arriving in New York I was ensconced in a laboratory, the one that had developed almost half of our total negative after we left Silver City. The arrangements were that the name of the company was Plymouth Productions; the name of the film was *Vaya Con Dios*; my name was Herbert Joseph; my address was a hotel where I established the name; all transactions were on a strictly cash basis. The owners of the laboratory were familiar with all the realities and agreed to accept the pseudonyms. Through Paul's long arm reaching from Hollywood I found a cutter.

For four weeks the cutter, Irving Fajans, and I labored in the Brewer-Walsh-enemy-territory of the I.A.T.S.E. (union) jurisdiction. And in the totality of the experience of making the film I had never enjoyed collaboration such as was granted by our new cutter. He possessed no nerves, which is to say that his nerves were his possession, not he, theirs. No day was too long. No situation was beyond solution.

The men and women in the laboratory were most curious about the film as they saw bits and pieces of it. What was it? It seemed a pro-union film! Who had made it? And how come?

We replied casually and obliquely that it had been sent on to New York for us to put through. It was just a job.

But wasn't it a pro-union film? And who had directed it? And what was the name of the company? Was it planning to make others?

The sense that the film was pro-union inspired the men and women in the lab to give it the most preferred treatment. Our relationships were excellent although we made no close friendships, keeping very much to ourselves. We saw the workers in a group only at lunch time. An open space near the freight elevators, where a coffee and sandwich machine and some tables and benches had been set up, was their improvised lunch room. Here we would listen to hours of union talk. There seemed to be considerable antipathy to Richard F. Walsh, the union's International president. Some of the individuals talked of secession.

One day one of the more volatile of the "secessionists" looked at me, pointed his finger violently, and said, "Now there's a fellow. He wants me to do some work for him! Dick Walsh hates his guts and won't let us work for him! I get a crew together! We secede from the union! You mean to tell me we can't go to work for him and make up our own union?"

"Where you gonna do the work?"

"Whad'ya mean where? Right here."

"The boss here won't let you."

"Why not? He makes the same profit."

"But he can't let you. He's got a contract with Walsh."

"So we go to some other lab."

"They got contracts with Walsh, too."

"How do you like that!"

He looked around the room. He shook his head mournfully.

"We're dead, huh? And that guy..." His finger flipped straight at me. "He's dead—*and buried!*"

Everyone laughed. I did too. But I flushed crimson. My heart was in my throat. His reference to me had been purely accidental, but accident so clairvoyant!

At midnight one evening, after we had okayed our first composite print and were ready to order our first fine grain, we invited a group of knowledgeable film persons to see the film. They were people working in the various New York advertising and publicity offices of the Hollywood motion picture industry. They were hardboiled, practical men, with many years of experience. They told us later that they had met at dinner before coming to the viewing. They had agreed on ways of letting us down easily. Aware of the difficulties we had experienced and even more aware of the problems of making a good film under the most propitious circumstances, they were convinced that our film simply couldn't be much of anything.

They told us this after the showing, as evidence of the extent of their respect for the film. It was they who first compared it to *Open City, The Grapes of Wrath* and other classics.

Paul had arrived in New York, opened an office for us, and had begun to build a staff to exploit the film. He was present that evening. It was also the first time he had seen the finished film.

Our friends asked a thousand questions. How had we been able to do this and that and achieve such values and such other values? And Paul and I sat and listened with disbelief. Had we actually finished the film? And

was it truly good? How was it possible? We answered the questions of our
friends, but it was our own upon which we floundered. When our friends
said that this was a heroic work, we guessed that they meant only that
each day we had done what was necessary and for as many days as were
necessary.

No one ever knows what may be necessary to accomplish necessary
cultural statement. Life can only be lived one day at a time. And man is
built to be able to take anything one day can throw at him. We had been
able to do one day's work each necessary day. And the film was completed.
And the less than satisfactory print and the less than satisfactory sound
even the experts had not noticed. They were carried by the film.

We could not yet react to reactions. For fourteen months the task had
been to complete it. That in itself had seemed the miracle. How many mir-
acles were possible?

The following morning I went to the lab ready to order the fine grain.
I was called to the office of the owner. He informed me that the union had
discovered that this was *Salt of the Earth* and had ordered its members not
to work on it. The projectionist who had run the film the night before had
met a union official on his way to work and excitedly told him of the
splendid film he had run the night before. "The first, real working man's
picture ever made in this country... and acted by just working people."
The official asked questions and finally said, "That's the picture our International is against. For Christ's sake, quit working on the thing."

The morning had been filled with conferences of lawyers—the lawyer
for the lab and the lawyer for the union and our lawyer. Work on the film
stopped.

The projectionist came to me and begged me to believe that he had
not wished to harm us. All he had said was that it was the first real working man's picture he had ever seen. I reassured him. The other members of
the union in the plant walked by us and did not wish to meet our eyes.
The owner of the plant said there was nothing for us to do but sue the
union. But we had to get the "stuff" out, and immediately. If it were not
out of the lab by noon, the union would pull its entire crew.

The "political" situation in the I.A.T.S.E. was "tight." Brewer was
ready to launch a campaign for the International presidency of the union
against the incumbent president, Richard Walsh. Walsh knew that unless

he supported Brewer's position on this film, Brewer would make it a plank in his election campaign. The men and women in the union had little to say in the matter. No one dared oppose Brewer's action, or Walsh's. Both had declared that this was a subversive film. To oppose the union brass, in a union not celebrated for its democracy, was at least as difficult for a rank and file trade union member as it was for the heads of departments of the government of the United States to oppose McCarthy. To oppose either was tantamount, in their eyes, to supporting a subversion.

We packed our film on to a hand truck and wheeled it to the freight elevator, which faced some benches where the I.A.T.S.E. crew was sitting during a coffee break. To close the elevator gates and start down, it was impossible not to turn around and face them. I would have to say something to them. All morning as we packed they had been unable to speak to us, even the rebellious individual who, in his exploration of secession, had pointed at me and said with accidental acumen, "He's dead and buried."

I got as far as, "Thanks, for..." And they leaned forward and almost with a single voice said, "Take it...." But "easy" didn't come. They swallowed the word and leaned back. The elevator doors closed upon a tableau like the one that ends Gogol's play, *The Inspector-General*. The stage directions read: general stupefaction! Everything was equally clear on both sides of the slowly closing elevator doors. But no one dared to speak. Silence. Un-American silence. General stupefaction!

We had one positive print without a main title. This could be shown to potential exhibitors. We could, with risk, undertake theater exhibition with it. And we meant to if it became necessary. But that was only a stopgap. We had to obtain prints. But who—and how? Paul and I together could only scratch the surface of the work ahead in New York. I could not now go traipsing over the country. Irving Fajans must take over that responsibility for us. Paul was worried about it. No one knew the film as well as I. But it had to be done. Taking the negative film into a plane, our cutter started out across country. Paul's "outrageous" optimism had found a lab.

Paul pressed for instituting suit against the union immediately. I was opposed. Our pro-union film was banned by a union and the unions of the country were silent. That was not a background for legal action.

Brewer never understood why we refrained from suing him and his union two years before when he had denied us a crew. One of his lieutenants admitted they had been prepared to lose and to pay a goodly sum in damages. "And then nobody would have had to ask where they'd gotten the dough for their picture. They'd have gotten it from the I.A.T.S.E. Why the hell didn't they sue us?"

We were not opposed to the suit on any romantic grounds. If we had sued we would have had to invoke the Taft-Hartley law, a "slave-labor" law as it was characterized by the entire American trade union movement. And we would have used it to liberate our pro-labor film. Brewer thought we were fearful of giving him an opportunity to attack us as "anti-labor" for suing a union. He would have spent any amount of his membership's money to make political hay of such a suit for himself. But the simple truth was that we had a film to make and to exhibit and we never permitted Brewer or anyone else to make us lose sight of that objective nor to maneuver us into minor engagements. Suit had not then been discarded, merely tabled. And we tabled it again.

The newspapers deluged us with inquiries. What were we going to do? We held our peace. We said nothing. We had no "news." We had a film to make, not a controversy to stir up.

From one-third the way across country our cutter called to say the lab was puny. The work would be poor. He had no idea how long it might take. It was an I.A.T.S.E. shop. Should he proceed? We said yes.

For the next two weeks Paul and I searched for a theater. Theater owners and distributors of art films looked at our picture. Overwhelmingly they were filled with praise for it. But, with the union situation as it was, and the industry antipathy as intense as it was, they regretfully...

We attempted to rent a closed theater. But when the owners discovered what the film was, they regretfully... By now the I.A.T.S.E. was stating that its projectionists would not run the film in any theater. We learned of someone who had a connection with a miserable theater on Eighth Avenue. It was what is known in the trade as a flea-bag. But, in our desperation, we were ready to take any piece of air surrounded by four walls, a roof, and containing projection equipment. We were asked an outlandish price. We accepted it.

One of the owners of the building, Mr. George Brussel, Jr., an attorney with whom the theater lessees had discussed our offer, wished to guarantee to himself that the film was "American." He asked for the privilege of inviting a distinguished group of citizens of New York to a showing. It was arranged. One of the leading Protestant clergy of New York City, then Dean James A. Pike of St. John the Divine, one of the city's leading rabbis, Edward Klein of the Stephen Wise Free Synagogue, members of a number of conservative organizations and their wives came. Without exception they found it moral, moving and in the finest tradition of entertainment. Mr. Brussel, and the lessees, agreed to write into the contract agreement to engage non-I.A.T.S.E. projectionists if that union refused to operate.

On the day contracts were to be signed the operators of the theater reneged. Mr. Brussel, who had been deeply impressed by the film, was outraged. He offered to relieve the operators of their contractual obligations in order that he might personally offer the theater to us. They refused. He offered them five thousand dollars to surrender their lease. Their tongues showed, but their fright was longer. They refused.

Word trickled through from our cutter that progress was being made. It was painfully slow. It was poor. But it was crawling through. In three weeks some prints, if he could remain undiscovered that long. The workers in the lab were making pointed inquiries, but fortunately there was only a handful employed there. He hoped…

A week later the wife of our cutter called to say that a number of cartons had arrived from Chicago. I went to their apartment at once. There were a number of prints of *Salt of the Earth*—theater prints. I called a storage company. I told the manager that I had a number of prints of our film, identified by its true name, and wished to know whether he would store it. He would indeed. It was a storage company whose employees were I.A.T.S.E. members.

On the floor of the warehouse and storage plant I opened the cartons. We checked the film out. I was given a receipt. The manager and I were engaged in animated small talk. Suddenly a man walked in.

"Get that shit out of here. We're not handling it."

A union official! The phones had buzzed.

The manager attempted to remonstrate. A worker standing nearby began to help me pack. The union official barked:

"I told you we're not handling..."

"Just to help him pack?"

The union official walked up to him and he dropped the can. It fell to the floor. The can opened. The reel fell out and caromed across the floor, unrolling as it went. It unwound under a table, turned, and rolled again. While the union official and the member watched, I crawled on my knees under the table, retrieved the reel, wound it, put it into its can, repacked all the film just unpacked, loaded it on to a truck, wheeled it into the elevator and took it down to a taxi.

For four hours refusal continued from one I.A.T.S.E.-serviced storage plant to another. Finally, the first *pro-union* feature film made in America was stored—in a non-union warehouse.

That evening, as Paul and I were rubbing our red-rimmed eyes, our telephone rang. A theater exhibitor asked if he might come up. He had seen the film several weeks before with his partner and for two weeks had attempted to bring a modicum of courage to his associate. He had failed. He came to express his regrets and chagrin but volunteered to aid us personally in solving our problem. He was visibly outraged at what he knew we were having to go through. He had one idea which might result in a Broadway opening. We must investigate it. But there was something, else which was of the very greatest importance to us. There existed in New York a rival union of projectionists. It was small and its members usually operated theaters in remote neighborhoods. But wherever we had to open this picture—we *had* to open it. We had "to show these people!" I told him I had just been made aware of the non-I.A.T.S.E. theaters and was ready to investigate them.

He called the owner of the Broadway theater and made an appointment for the next afternoon. But that evening we went through the list of theaters under the jurisdiction of the rival union, selected the most likely in the group, the Grande Theater on East 86th Street. The theater exhibitor and I took a cab and drove there immediately.

At the box office we asked the name of the owner. Philip Steinberg. Where was he? Standing on the curb talking to a lady. We approached him.

"Are you Mr. Steinberg?"

"And if I am?"

"We'd like to talk with you."

"Talk."

"Couldn't we go into your office?"

"You got a subpoena for me?"

"We would like to talk with you about a first-run picture for your theater."

"Uh-huh. So if you got a subpoena for me, give —it to me."

"We have no subpoena. We have a picture. Couldn't we adjourn where we might discuss it with you?"

"So discuss it. I'm here."

"We would prefer to do it more comfortably."

"So, you want comfort, too. Wait a minute."

Half an hour later he returned and led us into his office. It was the size of a closet. We sat down. The theater man with me inquired whether Mr. Steinberg's brother had not previously operated this theater. He had known him well. This caused Mr. Steinberg to glow. It was evident that his feelings for his deceased brother approached adoration.

"He was afraid for nobody. Smart—tough—terrific!"

I took over at this point and discussed the film. I presented our problems and the reasons we were seeking a theater not operated by the I.A. projectionists.

"Not interested," said Mr. Steinberg.

"We can make this theater known all over New York."

"For stink bombs?"

"For a very important picture."

"Important is what makes money. Stink bombs I had enough. I got a theater—the New Dyckman—in the Bronx. Finest theater in New York. I'm a tough guy. The I.A. want to put in their union. I said, 'I don't need your union.' They asked me once. They asked me twice. I said, 'Not interested!' Next day—Saturday—stink bombs. For three days nobody would come into the theatre. The I.A. came back. They asked me again, nicely. So I took the union."

Then Mr. Steinberg suddenly pounded his fist on the table. An idea had come to him. If we would like to open at the New Dyckman he'd give us a "terrific" deal. We protested that we could not go to 207th Street for a world premiere of a film.

"Don't go. Not interested."

But his pride in the New Dyckman had taken over. He insisted that we come to see it. He would drive us. We refused. Then another idea came to him. Why not open the picture in both theaters at the same time? We must accompany him. What a dream of a theater!

We drove to see it. It was all he had said. A beautifully appointed barn, obviously lacking an audience. But this was an I.A. house. It occurred to us that if we opened at the Grande, and followed at the Dyck-man two weeks later, we could be running in a non-I.A. house while bat-tling for an I.A. house. But we would open! It had much to offer. We began to dicker. Mr. Steinberg asked outrageous terms. I modified them ever so slightly.

"Not interested."

"Don't say that to me," I shouted back in tones meant to approximate his own. I had given him "vocabulary" long enough, now, to prove I was no pedant. "When I make you a counteroffer, you pay respect to it. I don't want your theater or any theater unless I'm dealing with a human being inside it. And if you're not a human being, I'm not interested in you or your theater. So calm down!"

"Oh ho! He's a tough guy too. Just like me! How do you like it! He yelled at me! Okay, okay, we'll make a deal."

And we made one. We left his theater with a deal agreed to, for two theaters, subject to forty-eight hours thought on both sides. Mr. Steinberg had not seen the film and was very unconcerned about that.

"I'll see the film. Main thing is the deal. We got a deal? And with me, you don't even need contracts. When Philip Steinberg shakes hands, that's better than a deal from the best lawyers."

The following morning, while a contract with Mr. Steinberg was being drawn by our attorney, we called on the owner of the Broadway the-ater. He was beside himself. He had been running "third-rate Hollywood product, first-run"—a fate worse than death —and he was literally gasp-ing. As fast as he took films in, he threw them out and facing him was exactly what he had just jettisoned. He listened to us and said, "Bring your film over and I'll run it here in the theater this afternoon." I explained that there was not yet a main title upon it. That didn't matter. It was a rainy day, there weren't fifty people in the whole house. "Bring it over and put it on."

Taxiing back to our office, Paul and I picked up the film, and drove back to the theater. We sent the film to the projection booth and suddenly it was on. The theater had a Cinemascope screen. On that screen was our picture. The outdoor scenes looked magnificent, but the close-ups were cut off just below the nose and speech was coming from a mouth which would have been approximately in the orchestra pit. It was horrendous. There were not twenty people in the theater. There was no reaction, only theater echo. The owner was leaping up from his seat and rushing to his office to telephone. He would be gone for ten minutes at a time. He missed the entire end of the film.

Finally we were again called into his office. He was looking over advertising copy for his next picture. Utterly beside himself with worry and indecision, he said he just had to make some money.

"Look at what I have next week. Victor Mature. Piper Laurie."

"That's a stinker. It'll die."

"I know. But... I... I'm stuck with it."

At eight o'clock that evening he called. Could we come to his theater immediately! We raced. With him again, he asked if we could put our film into his theater in four days. He had to do something. He had done $102 of business during the entire day. And the next film was a real turkey. We pleaded with him to let the turkey run for a week and give us time to build the potential audience that existed for our film. No. He could not wait. He had to get some money into his theater right away. We argued. We disagreed. We agreed. He would run the turkey and give us time to exploit our opening. We hammered out all the details of an agreement. We left and returned to our hotel and spent several hours typing it into contract form. We had agreed to drop the contracts at his theater at eleven the next morning. At ten we were at our own attorney's office. He approved what we had typed. At eleven we delivered the contract to the theater, our hearts in our throats. That day we might have a theater—on Broadway— in the heart of New York—in which to open. At noon his secretary called. Mr. Rose could not sign the contract. His lawyer had advised him against it. I called him several times. Finally he was there. Why? Why?

His voice was harassed. He had called his booker at R.K.O. to announce that he would not require any film after the next turkey. He was going to run *Salt of the Earth*. And the booker had told him flatly that if he ran our film he would never get another R.K.O. film and maybe no films from anybody. His voice became frantic. "You have only one film, Biberman. I've got to have product. I've got to keep in good with these guys or I'm cooked."

"What are you, now?" I asked. He hung up.

At this point, Mr. Steinberg seemed a man of mountainlike stability. The forty-eight hours were over. We called upon Mr. Steinberg. He boosted his asking price a full notch... just to warm the pot. "Share advertising with you?" A bellow of a laugh. "Are you kiddin'?" He'd give us the theater. Everything else that cost money was ours. We fought. We shouted. We embraced. We signed.

"I ain't afraid for nobody. You got a man, a human being, like you said. You should be the happiest man." *He* obviously was.

I asked when we might screen the picture for him. A very happy man, he waved aside such a meaningless formality. He'd see it. There was time. The picture was, after all, only a picture. "The main thing is the deal. Right?" We arranged a semi-forced showing for him for the following morning.

Throughout the past weeks we had had many private screenings, morning, noon and night. Whatever else we were doing, that went on religiously and without interruption. Since the film carried no main title, the projectionists may not have known—as they projected the film—what it was. If some of them knew, they kept quiet about it. All of them enjoyed it as much as the audiences. To these showings we invited the largest possible number of leaders of people and opinion in New York. Our purpose was to give such individuals an opportunity to come to their own conclusions. Beyond that we asked nothing. Not endorsement, public expression of opinion, or sponsorship.

Clifford McAvoy had joined us and had taken charge of these private showings. Whenever possible Paul and I attended. But they went on day after day. Often four times a day. We believed that in any crisis beyond our solution the knowledge of the film by such people would be a public rock upon which the film could rest. The audiences were most varied. They included persons and organizational representatives of almost the whole political spectrum. Only the rank reactionaries were absent and they not through lack of invitation. Of the two thousand men, women and children who attended these previews, only five, to our knowledge, left without showering the film with expressions of genuine appreciation.

A minister's wife said, "I believe you made this film believing it was good for working people. It's even better for ministers. They need it more." Her husband agreed.

A distinguished lawyer said, "It's legal. That's all I'm interested in."

His wife added, "Yes and it's a beautiful legality which many legalities are not." Her husband agreed.

For months our problems had been physical and technical, fought on the edges of precipices. Now suddenly the film was alive, moving people, inspiring them! And we, who could not confide this to anyone, were still on the edge of a precipice. Would we get any prints? Would we ever open?

Our private showings continued and in them one theme predominated. "It honors minorities." "It honors working people." "It honors women." "It honors America."

As word of the reactions of these hundreds of people reverberated around the corners of New York, the film's enemies moved toward stronger measures.

The morning we ran the film for Mr. Steinberg the papers carried an announcement of our contract with him and the date of the opening. A few of these journals presented the background of the film's difficulty in the most lurid terms. When the film was only half-run Mr. Steinberg was called to the telephone. It was urgent. His daughter was on the phone. She had read one of the most scurrilous accounts and was calling her father to determine whether he had gone out of his mind to be running such a film.

Mr. Steinberg got the paper immediately and did not return to the showing. His manager came to me and confided that he doubted Mr. Steinberg would go through with his contract. When the film ended I went into the lobby. Mr. Steinberg was there, paper in hand. He asked what I had to say about the article.

And then a planned "accident" occurred. Cliff McAvoy had invited some twenty people to the showing that morning. As I stood facing Mr. Steinberg, a woman spoke to me. She asked if I were the director of the film. She introduced herself as the wife of a New York motion picture director. She asked if she might kiss me. She did. And as she did she burst into tears. In a voice that was choked, not with sadness, but with exaltation, she described what the film had meant to her as a woman. And she promised that until the film opened she would devote every waking hour to bringing it to the attention of everyone she knew. I introduced her to Mr. Steinberg. She asked if he operated the theater. He nodded. She told him that no words of hers could express her admiration for his courage; that he was a hero. And she embraced him.

The other members of the audience were now huddled about us. And each in turn came to him and expressed gratitude, promised extraordinary efforts in making this film a very great success, assured him that this theater would become a mecca for decent people in the community.

When we were alone, Mr. Steinberg asked how it was possible that such "high class" people could love this film as they obviously did and the paper could be so vicious? We talked of the reasons, political, historical and theatrical. I told him of my having been in jail. I pictured Hollywood as it was. I appealed to his sense of showmanship, his understanding that honest controversy was good for any entertainment item.

"You call this honest controversy? They'll say that I want to overthrow the government."

We readjusted the contract and sweetened the pot for Mr. Steinberg. He was a good businessman and since all business is composed of the basic elements of a bargain I did not resent his attempt to make the increasingly best deal he could. He was breaking untrod ground and he deserved compensation. If he would only stand!

But now the boys on Film Row took after him. They threatened that he would never get another picture from Hollywood if he actually played this film. "You'll ruin yourself, Philip," they said. Mr. Steinberg, a splendid deal in his pocket, convinced of a large potential audience, of the possibility of a long run in his house which previously changed bills twice a week, and at prices double those he had ever before charged, replied with real gesture.

"I'll ruin myself? You fellows have ruined me already for years. I'm ruined now. How can a ruined man ruin himself?"

He was beginning to stand on ground of his own making, beginning to develop a sense of his importance. He referred constantly to what that score of people had said to him the morning we ran the film for him. "They said I'm a hero; I'm the bravest man in New York. I'm not afraid for nobody." He began to look like the film.

Two hours later a business agent of the projectionists' union called on Mr. Steinberg and then Mr. Steinberg was worried. He knew the kind of people he was dealing with in the I.A. I sat down with him for an hour. I exhibited the lists of distinguished, influential and respected New Yorkers who had seen the film and were ready to defend it. I urged him to recognize the I.A. visit as a bluff. As a "hero," as a man who was "afraid for nobody," and "his brother's brother," he had to stand. Steinberg responded, "You want to open in my theater? Give me four thousand dollars bonus! My theater is the only theater you got in all New York. Pay or no opening. You got to make me happy. You can sue me, but sue don't open theaters."

I compromised. I gave him two thousand dollars in cash. There remained only four days to our opening.

It was now almost unprofitable for us to run the film. But we shook hands for the third time. Mr. Steinberg was feeling very happy. Now the "deal" was "as beautiful as a work of art," he said, as beautiful as the film"—which he had yet to see.

The business agent returned—but Philip Steinberg stood fast. News of the I.A. attitude reached the newspapermen. They besieged us demanding stories and statements. We remained sphinx-like. We knew nothing.

The day before we had announced previews for the press. These were held in a private screening room and were scheduled for three consecutive days. As a group of critics entered the room for the second screening, the owner of the establishment announced that there would be no showing. The union had called him and stated that the projectionists had refused to screen the picture. The critics, being newspapermen themselves, immediately sought out the projectionists. What they heard from them was succinct and newsworthy. The projectionists had *not* refused to run the film. They had been *"ordered"* not to run it by the union officials. The order didn't make any sense to them. They had run the film a dozen times. "It was a damned sight better just as a film than most of the stuff they ran day after day and pro-union to boot."

We still had nothing to say to the reporters except that the remaining press previews would be held at the Grande Theater. And for the first time in the history of New York motion picture criticism, critics went "way up to 86th Street" for a preview. And they went in spite of the simultaneous running of several "big" Hollywood pictures scheduled for the same hours in the screening room on Broadway from which we had been forced to retreat. They not only went to the Grande but brought indignation with them. It was becoming a serious matter when some I.A. officials took it upon themselves to decide what pictures even the critics were permitted to see. Instead of intimidating and stampeding the critics, the I.A. officials turned these previews into a "must." They had badly miscalculated the working press of New York. And our long silence, our stubborn refusal to debate the right of a film to be judged by the public and the public only, our confidence that the mature and decent people of New York would guarantee the preservation of their rights and ours, bore fruit. We had impressed the newspapermen with the simple fact that we had only one purpose in making this film: to secure public judgment of our efforts in the most normal, modest fashion.

The day before we opened we received our final shipment of prints from our cutter. There remained nothing but the opening itself.

Shortly before Rosaura Revueltas accepted voluntary deportation, the McCarran Act was passed. It was obvious that any attempt to bring her to New York for the opening would meet with opposition, even though the immigration authorities had promised that she might enter the United States as a visitor whenever she wished. We had, therefore, most reluctantly, to forgo the pleasure of even requesting her presence. Johnny Chacon and Henrietta Williams were invited to attend the premiere as representatives of Local 890.

Part Four

THE WORLD
1955

I

The World Premiere was scheduled for 8:00 P.M., Sunday evening, March 14, 1954.

At three o'clock, the mobile television unit of the largest broadcasting system in New York telephoned the theater and asked permission to cover the opening. Mr. Steinberg agreed. I arrived at three-thirty and he told me of this call. My heart sank. I prepared myself for the worst. Had they been alerted? Would there be a picket line? Had physical disturbance, even violence, been organized against this premiere? Would the papers of the country tomorrow be filled with gory accounts of our opening?

The theater was in that area of New York known as Yorkville. Before the war it had been a notorious concentration-place of pro-Nazi elements. Brutal acts of vandalism had taken place there. Since the War, however, many Negro and Puerto Rican families had moved into its outlying sections. We counted upon this change. Counted? What a feeble rationalization. The Grande was the only theater we were able to get in New York. We took it and hugged it to our hearts. It was *ours*, with whatever went with it. Many of our friends who knew the circumstances surrounding our "choice" of this theater expressed shock that we would open in Yorkville. They persisted in luxuriating in the illusion that we had choice. Our choice was to exhibit there or flee the scene. It was an easy choice. It remained so even at four o'clock the day of, and only four hours before, the first public exhibition of our film.

I occupied myself with setting lights on the curtain for the introductions to follow the opening, and checking the film sound level. An hour passed. The work was finished. Three hours remained. I did not wish to leave the theater. I sat down. As I did so a youngish man entered the auditorium and asked if I were connected with the picture. I introduced myself. He did also. He was Otis L. Guernsey, Jr., the film critic of the *New York Herald Tribune*. I expressed surprise that he had come at five. Our first performance began at eight. Had he been misinformed? No. He had stopped off on his way to dinner to inquire whether we expected any trouble that evening. I told him of the television unit call, of my apprehension. Beyond that I knew nothing. He explained the reason for his question. He wished me to know that his column and his paper were determined that this film be permitted the right of normal entry into the city. If anyone, no matter who, attempted to prevent it, his paper and his column would take the matter on as an issue of civic and national importance. He thought it might be helpful to us to know that in advance.

I attempted to express my gratitude.

"Now, wait a minute. Don't thank me. You haven't read my review. I think your film is loaded. I'm saying so."

I assured him it was not to his opinion of the film that I had spoken. I had wished to thank him only for his presence. It gave me hope that communication, without penalization, might again be possible in our country.

"Of course," he said. "Our country is growing healthier. We're *all* going to be able to express ourselves! Oh! I'll be back at eight. I want to be certain nothing goes awry. If anything does, I want to see it with my own eyes."

Six o'clock. All was serene. Seven o'clock. Nothing had happened. Seven-thirty. People began to enter the theater. Eight o'clock. Nothing had happened. And nothing did happen—except a most peaceful showing of the film, to a sold-out house, at five dollars a seat. When the audience left the theater at 10.15 P.M. it found almost a thousand people in line waiting to enter for the first showing at regular prices to begin at 10:30 P.M.

Throughout the evening we stood in the rear of the theater, feeling nothing. Inside ourselves, we had all been leaning against a mountain for a very long time, to prevent its falling upon us. And suddenly the mountain was gone. We had nothing to fend off. I didn't know what to do with my body and its energies. It was a little like being paralyzed, paralyzed by normalcy. At the end of the first performance we were all presented and made brief speeches. We went back to our hotel quarters, received a few guests, called our wives in California, read the early notices, and retired, exhausted.

For the first time in three years, we had experienced a moment of normal, peaceful living. But I had lost the technique for savoring it. The cup had reached the lips, the wine had touched the tongue and it had no taste. The brief moment of victory found us all emotionally impotent. But this we knew. We had called upon people to help us make a film. They had responded. The film had been made. It was being exhibited. We had created eight thousand feet of freedom in America. And if that much— then as much more as people would undertake to create.

For two weeks this brief moment of the illusion of full victory was repeated a number of times. The notices exceeded our timorous expectations. The critic who thought the film loaded did indeed say so. But he also wrote the most eloquent appreciation of the film written by anyone in New York.

New York Herald Tribune
Otis L. Guernsey

> With the majority of the characters played by non-professionals, it uses the semi-documentary technique very well indeed to dramatize human dignity and courage in harsh circumstances.
>
> At the same time it cannot be dignified with the word "controversial"… its conflict is so loaded in favor of the workers that its picture of conspiracy among bosses, police and the law is absurd as a sample of modern American justice.
>
> …The movie craftsmanship is excellent. There is a severe beauty in the location photography of a desperately poor community and enormous affection for these olive-skinned Americans.
>
> … In this bleak community of gray wooden shacks inhabited by people who carry their shoulders straight under work-stained clothing, there are many acute vignettes of character.
>
> … The work is capable throughout, and those who challenge the right of *Salt of the Earth* to be shown publicly are lending credence to its specious protest against a straw man of public evil.

New York Daily News
Kate Cameron

> Although the special pleading in this case may be exaggerated, it tells a story of injustice and inequality that arouses sympathy in the beholder. Of the professional members of the cast Mexican actress Rosaura Revueltas is outstanding as the wife of a leader of the local.

New York Times
Bosley Crowther

> Against the hard and gritty background of a mine workers' strike in a New Mexico town—a background bristling with resentment against the

working conditions imposed by the operators of the mine—a rugged and starkly poignant story of a Mexican-American miner and his wife is told in *Salt of the Earth*.

... This is the film which occasioned controversy and violence when it was being made near Silver City, New Mexico, just one year ago.

... In the light of this agitated history, it is somewhat surprising to find that *Salt of the Earth* is, in substance, simply a strong pro-labor film with a particularly sympathetic interest in the Mexican-Americans with whom it deals. True, it frankly implies that the mine operators have taken advantage of the Mexican-born or descended laborers, have forced a "speed-up" in their mining techniques and given them less respectable homes than provided the so-called "Anglo" laborers.

... But the real dramatic crux of the picture is the stern and bitter conflict within the membership of the union. It is the issue whether the women shall have equality of expression and of strike participation with the men. And it is along this line of contention that Michael Wilson's tautly muscled script develops considerable personal drama, raw emotion and power.

... Under Mr. Biberman's direction, an unusual company made up largely of actual miners and their families, plays the drama exceedingly well.

... The hard-focus, realistic quality of the picture's photography and style completes its characterization as a calculated social document.

TIME Magazine

... the film within the propagandistic limits it sets is a work of vigorous art. It is crowded with grindingly effective scenes, through which the passion of social anger hisses in a hot wind; and truth and lies are driven before it like sand.

... the passion carries the actors along too in its gale. The workers, actual miners of the New Mexico local, carry conviction in their savage setting as trained actors could never do. The best of the worker-players is Juan Chacon, real-life president of the local union. Ugly and cold as an Aztec amulet, his heavy face comes slowly to life and warmth as the picture advances and in the end seems almost radiant.

We had our scares as well. After the show had been running two or three days, one evening, at eleven o'clock, Mr. Steinberg called me at the hotel. His voice was loud and indistinct. He was saying, "They're lynching me! They're lynching me! Herbert, they are lynching me!"

My hair stood on end and I bellowed into the phone for some explanation. "Who?"

"The people. The people. They ask for me. They tell me I am the bravest man in New York. They kiss me. My face is full of lipstick. Men hug me. They tell me I am a hero. It is tremendous!"

At the beginning of the second week of the run, a man called Mr. Steinberg on the telephone. He had believed Mr. Steinberg to be a fine, patriotic citizen, he said. But now he had to change his opinion. If "that picture" were not canceled; if that "subversive, un-American propaganda" were not thrown out of his theater, picketing would begin at once by the American Legion and the Catholic War Veterans. Mr. Steinberg asked the man if he had seen the film. He said he didn't have to see the film. Mr. Steinberg agreed—he certainly did not have to see it—unless he wished to speak about it in the way he had to Mr. Steinberg! Then he *did* have to see it, or keep quiet. Would the gentleman come to the theater that evening as his guest? If he wanted to say just what he had said, *after* he had seen the film, Mr. Steinberg would listen to him with respect and attention. At the conclusion of the first evening show a gentleman walked into Philip Steinberg's office. He sat down. He spoke:

"I want you to know that I have just had a very good time. They told me this picture was anti-church. I have never seen the church treated more respectfully. They told me it was Socialistic and Communistic. The only 'istic' I found in the film was 'feministic.' And I never heard that was against the law. After all, what is this film? It's a story of poor people trying to solve their problems, and solving them, in America. That's a credit to the country. There will be no picketing of this film. Not by the Legion, or by the Catholic War Veterans. And if you have any trouble from any quarter, just send them to me."

But our opponents had a cozier opportunity when we opened at the New Dyckman Theater at 207th Street. It was an I.A. house. If they could stop us there, they would have a formula for the rest of the country. I called my established contact in the I.A.T.S.E.

This man was an official of a local union. When we had been ordered out of the laboratory Paul and I had determined that we must find someone inside that union with whom we could discuss our problems forthrightly. We had discovered who such a man might be. We had found out who his attorney was. Through him we had arranged a meeting for all of us. What Steve D'Inzillo told us was indeed unminced. Hollywood was out to prevent this film from hitting the American screen. The I.A.T.S.E. was working with them hand in glove. If we had any sense we'd pack up and get the bell out of town because we were not going to open there.

When we insisted that we had not come this far only to fold our tents on or off Broadway, he shrugged his shoulders. We had asked. He had told us. The blood was on our own heads.

Following our rejection by the lessees of Mr. Brussel's theater, I had called Steve D'Inzillo again. I told him of our dilemma. If we insisted on beating our heads against walls, he had said, why not at least try a softer wall. There were a few non-I.A.T.S.E. houses scattered around town. Why not try one of them. This had led us to the Grande Theater.

Since D'Inzillo was business agent for the projectionists' local, it was imperative that I confront him about our opening at the New Dyckman Theatre. We met again.

I never wanted to open this film at the New Dyckman," I told him. "It will die there. But I have to open there or Steinberg can cancel out the run at the Grande. So I'm going to open. Now, I want to know what you're going to do about your projectionist."

He looked at me strangely. How could I ask such a question? Of all people, I must know that he didn't make policy on the subject of this film. I knew that that was nationally made, straight from Walsh and even straighter from the coast. So what did I mean what was he going to do? He was going to do what he had to do—pull the man.

I then told him what I was going to do. Steinberg and I had engaged two projectionists from the small, rival union. They were going to be in the theater on opening day. If the I.A. projectionist walked out of the booth, these two other men were going to march in, and, Steinberg had stated, they would stay there from then on!

He thought a moment. "Maybe that'll make Walsh change his mind."

At twelve noon on the appointed day the film was screened. When the first run had been completed, the house lights went on. I went up to the booth and asked the operator why the film was not being projected. He said he was not going to project it. I asked him to wait, I was going to call his business agent.

When Steve D'Inzillo arrived, he talked to the projectionist. Then he approached Steinberg and me.

He told us that the operator had looked at the film and did not want to project it any longer. The showdown was at hand.

"Why doesn't he wish to run it?" I asked.

"I don't know. He just won't run it. He says it's Communist propaganda."

"You didn't by any chance order him not to run it?"

"No! I just walked in and he said he doesn't want to run it. I can't force him to."

"Do you have any ideas about what we might do?"

"Well, I just happen to have another operator with me. We could put him in the booth. Maybe he will run it."

I could not repress a smile. I asked the business agent whether the plan was to put a second man in the booth, who would also refuse to run it, and thus "establish" the fact that the union leadership couldn't find *one man* who would project this "subversive" film. Was that it? The business agent shook his head violently. Why—that—he—no. He *just* happened to have another man with him, and he *just* wanted to try to help us.

It was a ridiculous scene. My anger directed at a man who was sheepishly carrying out the bigoted' orders of a superior. But the fury was real. His attempt to put the "I have another man with me" maneuver over my head like a wool sack. And his shoulder-shrugging gestures of innocence. I calmed down. I asked him to listen carefully. I said that I wanted this film projected by an I.A. man. I would do everything I could to bring that about. Even my bringing two outside men in was an effort to force the I.A. to its senses and into projecting the film. But the film was going to be screened by somebody and within ten minutes. I suggested that he walk around the corner, find a telephone, and ask Mr. Walsh what he wished to do.

Five minutes later he returned. He spoke to the projectionist. Within a few minutes the film was being screened. The business agent shrugged his shoulders.

"You wanted an I.A. projectionist. You've got an I.A. projectionist."

After three years of refusals, we were running in New York with an I.A. crew. We were having a small, momentary victory at 207th and

Dyckman Streets. And, our jubilation to the contrary, we had accomplished exactly nothing.

I left New York for Hollywood and my family. I had not seen them in over four months. On my way home I stopped in Detroit and Chicago. In both cities I ran previews of the film for sizable audiences composed largely of trade unionists. Their enthusiastic reception of it was, by now, a foregone conclusion.

I was, however, especially interested in a new body of people in the unions in both cities, the new industrial worker—the Negro in basic industry. In each city they walked into the theater in large numbers. They were shop stewards, officers of local unions, they were educational diectors.

In Detroit, I had been especially attracted to three Negro men who walked into the theater together. I watched for them when the film was over. They came out side by side. One of them said, "Why doesn't our union make a picture like that? People with a little color in that one. Why don't we make one with people of a lot of color? Brother!" To which one of his companions replied, "Brother!"

I drew up a contract for the opening of the film at the Hyde Park Theater in Chicago, near the university, and made tentative arrangements for a theater in Detroit. The film had been submitted to the police censor boards of both cities and was immediately approved for exhibition. And we were running in New York!

With these prospects of success behind me, I was flying across country, on my way home! At the Los Angeles airport was my family—Gale, Joan, Dan, my brother Edward, Sonja and Rhea, my sister.

The sight and touch and sound of each wiped out the four and a half months of absence. Joan, Dan, Gale and I rode home with our hands constantly entwined, beaming at each other, chattering like four magpies. How sweet chatter was, rising out of happiness that was blowing its top!

I would be home only a week. But after the openings in Detroit and Chicago, the film would roll on its own. The future would be redolent of freedom to create, to earn a living, and to live unseparated from one's family.

II

After ten renewing days at home, I was again in Chicago. The fruits of two years of assiduous cultivation were about to become ours.

I made final arrangements with the Hyde Park Theater, opened an office, set dates, engaged a staff, and left for Detroit.

While I was in Detroit news came of the opening of *Salt of the Earth* in Silver City, New Mexico, where it had been made. It opened the newest drive-in theater in the area. It was scheduled for four nights. On opening day, the line formed three hours before the show began. Second in line was the Bayard banker and his wife, the gentleman who had been part of the vigilante group in front of the union hall in Bayard. The opening night was a triumph. And so was every other performance. The run was extended. In six days, a phenomenal run for any picture in Silver City, five thousand persons paid admission into the theater. The union people came, and the community people came. And people came from as far away as Texas and Arizona.

On the morning of the second day, we were told, the wife of the Bayard banker asked the wife of the theater owner to thank her husband for having played the picture. It was, she said, one of the most beautiful she had ever seen.

As I entered the theater that afternoon to sign a contract for the opening of the film in Detroit, I found the theater owner barely recognizable. His face was gray. His warm, confident manner was filled with gaps. He had been visited by a representative of the American Legion. He was told that the Legion wanted him to refuse to run our film. If he did not "cooperate" the Legion would picket not only that theater but every one of the dozen or more this gentleman owned.

A short while thereafter he had another visitor; a man had entered his office and asked politely whether he was native born. The theater man was so startled by this question, from a stranger, that he completely forgot to ask his name or business. He replied, impulsively, that he had been brought to this country when he was two years old. He was next asked from what country. His response, in spite of himself, took on an immediate defensive cast. He had come

from Russia, but he had been only two years old! The inquirer nodded politely and left. In the space of an hour he had been warned that
playing our film would risk attacks upon all his properties and he had
been reminded of the danger of being deported. He was a conservative man who had never in his entire life been associated with any
slightly liberal undertaking. He asked me to go to the Legion and get
this "straightened out." He was certain I could. I asked what the
Legion was that I must straighten myself out with it.

"You know, the veterans' group."

"Yes. I know. But who are they?"

"I mean—the patriotic organization."

"I understand very well. But do they pass on all business in the
city of Detroit?"

Every attempt to make him see the Legion in perspective failed. I
asked for a few days to show him what other elements in the community thought. I arranged a number of previews. On the evening of
a showing for educational directors of the CIO Auto Workers Union,
the theater owner asked if I would object to having representatives of
the American Legion present. Obviously, I did not. They were most
welcome. They came, six of them: the city commander, the county
commander, the head of the anti-subversive committee, two labor-
legionnaires, and one unidentified individual.

At the screening's completion, they heard the educational directors of the CIO entreat the theater owner to run the film. The theater
owner, much encouraged, asked if I would accompany him and the
legionnaires for a drink.

When we had ordered our drinks, a round robin got under way.
Each person present made his estimate of the film. There was not one
dissenter. They praised it for its reticence in dealing with, a labor–
management dispute. They held the film to be understatement. They
praised it for its beauty, for its entertainment value. One of the labor-
legionnaires insisted that any man or woman who worked for a living
and did not belong to a union would join or organize one the morning after seeing the film. It was the greatest boon to the labor movement in years. There was praise, praise, praise. And a second round of

drinks. And then the head of the anti-subversive committee said, "It's a great film. But we're not going to let you run it."

"What's the trouble?"

"You're the trouble."

"What's the matter with me?"

"You refused to cooperate with the Committee on Un-American Activities, and until you do, you can't run any film in the great city of Detroit."

It was only midnight and I had nothing to do until ten o'clock the next morning. Feeling in an investigative frame of mind, I determined to discover in leisurely, unprejudiced fashion whether reason could affect these praising legionnaires. I took one full hour to tell the story of Hollywood, 1947–1950, When I had finished, the anti-subversive chairman slapped my knee and said:

"Herb, you're a great guy. A great guy. Want you to know that. You're a great guy. But we're not gonna let you run the film."

"What's the trouble now?"

"The union, that Mine-Mill Union."

"What's the trouble with it?"

"Got kicked out of the CIO."

"You know, gentlemen, I find this rather puzzling. I don't understand where the Legion stands in the hierarchy of government. I thought yours was a private organization, with the rights and privileges of all private bodies. I didn't know your authority superseded that of the United States of America!"

"What do you mean?"

"You see, this union is recognized by the government of the United States of America. What does it have to do to get yours?"

The "anti-subversive" turned to the labor-legionnaires and demanded to know if this were true. He was assured that it was. The facilities of the National Labor Relations Board were at the disposal of that union equally with all others. This gave the gentleman only a moment's pause.

"Okay, Herb, the union's okay too. The union's okay. But, we're not gonna let you run this film."

"What's the trouble now?"

"Orders."

"What!"

"Orders," he repeated. "That's the way it is. But the thing I like is the way in this country people can sit down together and talk things over, like Americans."

I kept my rising temper in hand.

"If you have orders that you are going to follow blindly, why did you waste my time? I don't find it 'American' to discuss anything with people whose minds have somebody else's padlock on them. I thought that only went on in Russia. I thought we were all free Americans, especially legionnaires! I'm afraid I've been taken in. But by now I guess we all know we have nothing to talk about. So let's call it a night."

"Now, don't take it like that, Herb. Let's have a drink and I'll drive you to your hotel."

Reluctant to give up any possibility of solving the "problem," I lingered. Out came photostatic copies of newspaper columns of Howard Rushmore attacking those New York critics who had praised the film as "communist-fronters." Then followed copies of *Counter-Attack* and *Alert*, magazines devoted to outrages upon individuals after the fashion of the Rushmore columns. The legionnaires paraded those "documents" with the servility of men presenting credentials written in the hand of the Almighty.

At this point the unidentified man was identified for me by the anti-subversive. He was an FBI informant. He then took his moment of full stage, and proceeded to lavish his praise upon the film.

As we reached the door the "anti-subversive," who had a Welsh name but now said he was a Jew, asked to drive me to my hotel. I consented. I was eager to play the evening out to the full. We had driven only a block when he pulled to the curb. He turned and looked at me with eyes brimming with friendship.

"Herb. You're a great guy. Whatever your politics are. I don't know and I don't care. It's your business. But I want to appeal to you as a Jew. We Jews get everything thrown at us. We got to think of the Jews. Now, we're *not* gonna picket the theater! I'll tell you that. But if your picture plays we're gonna take out a half-page advertisement in the papers and expose you. What does that mean? We expose a Jew. Herb, I appeal to you."

"But you can't expose me in half a page of a newspaper. For heaven's sake, take at least a full page!"

"This is no joke. When we move, we move. Like we moved with Chaplin's picture *Limelight*. We had pickets in front of the theater... wait a minute. I got something in the back."

He walked around to the back of his car and opened the trunk compartment. Then he returned. After turning on the inside light in the car he held a leaflet under my nose.

"This is the leaflet we passed out by the thousands."

I found myself looking into a suspiciously anti-Semitic leaflet. Held by a Jew, before me, a Jew, as an appeal by a Jew, and a threat by a Jew to a Jew. I knew that if I sat there another minute I would become physically ill.

I stepped out of the car. "Look, you have orders? Carry them out! But do it as a vigilante! Don't pose as a Jew. You're about as Jewish as your leaflet."

I walked back to my hotel chilled to the bone. Not because of his threats. I had heard the story of their picketing of *Limelight*. It had been a total bust. After two weeks the pickets were withdrawn because they were bored—didn't know what they were doing there to begin with—and the picture ran for nine weeks to packed houses.

No. I was chilled to the bone by this Jewish-American "patriot." He was undoubtedly convinced he was serving his minority people. He, the anti-subversive of the patriots? I knew as I walked that if this were a patriot I wished to be a "subversive." And if I were not one yet, I intended to be, to the full limit of my ability. This collection of stunted witch-doctors, with their leaflet, and Rushmore, and *Alert*! These were the guardians of America? Even the charitable Almighty wouldn't help a country represented by them. They had orders. That was obvious. But the horror resided in that they could be decent human beings—decent Americans—were they but free and unordered. Who gave the orders? The I.A.T.S.E.? Brewer? Hoover? Johnston? Walsh? Jackson? It made very little difference.

The following day I spoke to my theater man and it was obvious that he was bewildered and incapable of making a decision. I called upon a number of booking offices. They were interested. I arranged to screen the film. Each time they canceled the appointment before a screening could be arranged. One finally told me that the League of Detroit Theaters had warned them to beware of this film. Why? He didn't know exactly. Something about the studios and Communism.

I went back to the theater man and attempted to revive his original ardor. It was impossible. He suggested I find an empty theater. Then I would have to be beholden to no one. He'd help me staff and operate such a theater. We found a theater and I made an appointment with its owner. He was most pleasant until he discovered the name of the film. Sorry.

At my hotel a call from New York. I must return there at once. Quite extraordinary developments with respect to distribution. I was on the plane within an hour.

The following day I found myself sitting in the office of a labor attorney, together with the man whose company had been engaged by us to check box office receipts at the Grande, where the film was in its sixth week and going very well. I listened to an uncomplicated, unbelievable story. Three conservative leaders of AF of L unions from Pennsylvania had wandered into the Grande.

They believed our film could be the most meaningful shot in the arm that workers in this country had had in a long time; it would give them a sense of who and what they were. And the film could make a fortune. Would we permit a number of trade unions of size and unquestioned position to take over the distribution of the film in Pennsylvania?

My voice choked and my eyes filled. Would we permit unions to assume responsibility for this film? We would grant such right upon the most generous terms! But did he know of the opposition to the film? Did the trade unionists? They knew, he replied. And they were not troubled by it. If they decided to take it over, *they would take it over.*

His confidence caused me to experience anew the sensation that had nibbled at me so often in the past years. Our country was within one large step of democratic self-realization, of peace, reasonableness and fraternity.

"Tell you something interesting", he volunteered, through a spreading smile. "When I first heard of this film I thought to myself—this making of a film by blacklisted film-makers and a union for theatrical exhibition—pretty suspicious business! What did working people have to do with acting? Film makers with unions? Workers becoming intellectuals? It sounded pretty subversive. Then I saw the film. I bought it."

He grinned.

"But—I thought maybe I'd been taken in. Maybe I'd been brainwashed. I took a tough V.I.P. trade union leader to see your film. He bought it too. Then I felt better. Because if you could brainwash him—you deserve to get away with it. So," the attorney continued, "I think you can understand that I have given this matter some thought. It will take a little time; work with trade unions always does. But I want you to know that the more I heard about the gang-up on this film, the angrier I have become. I mean to put this through. I'm a fan and a partisan. Any questions now?"

I left Mr. Seymour Baskind's office with an unabashed sense of triumph for us all. This had taken place of itself. No pressuring, no salesmanship. The film itself had made its way. I rushed across town to get to our office, and to telephone to California. But another call was waiting for me from our office in Chicago. The message was that the Hyde Park Theater had canceled its contract. I decided to call my colleagues later from Chicago. I left to catch a plane immediately.

In making my contract in Chicago I had dealt with the general manager of the Schoenstadt chain of theaters, of which the Hyde Park was one. Upon first viewing, his superlatives reflected his genuine enjoyment of the film, and his estimate of the amount of business he expected to do.

From the Chicago airport I proceeded directly to the manager's office. He talked about his health, his bad cold and his suspicion that something was wrong with his heart. He was chatty, pleasant and ingratiatingly eager for my sympathies. They just couldn't run the film. These things happened. He knew we had gone to some expense and he would gladly pay a part of it. Wouldn't I be a good fellow and let him off the hook? I offered to—if I could let him off alone. But not cheek by jowl with the pressures! I might meet them elsewhere. What were they? He smiled sweetly and held his heart. It was evident that the manager also had "orders." From his squirmings it was obvious that he did not like them. But business was business, and he was, alas, only an employee.

I sought out Mandel Terman who operated the Cinema Annex theater.

Mandel Terman! Businessman, theater operator, son of a former sheriff of Iroquois County. Six feet two and gentle as a lamb. Fighter, amateur painter, lover of humanity, with a piece of himself in every hard battle for people's rights in the city and the country.

When I had first arrived in Chicago he sought me out. The film must play his theater! I had refused. I wished a more *representative* theater, in geographical location, in the public's knowledge of it. He suggested that the most representative theater in Chicago might well be the one that would still present this film in difficulty! He wished me luck. I was not certain that he was certain that I would have it.

When the Hyde Park theater defected, I went to the most representative theater in Chicago: Mandel Terman's Cinema Annex. In the testing moment, the only theater in Chicago where people might see what they chose to see, was the theater I had turned down as not sufficiently representative, geographically.

As we were discussing opening the film at the Cinema Annex, a letter arrived for Mr. Terman. He read it and then handed it to me.

THE AMERICAN LEGION

DEPARTMENT OF ILLINOIS

MAY 12, 1954

CINEMA ANNEX
3210 W. MADISON ST.
CHICAGO, ILLINOIS
GENTLEMEN:

Like other loyal citizens, we of the American Legion have known from the inception of the making of the motion picture, Salt of the Earth, that it was thoroughly, through and through, an endeavor on the part of the Communistic elements to produce the greatest Communist propaganda picture ever developed in the United States of America.

The Communistic background of the International Union of Mine Mill Smelters Workers, prominently known as such along with the writers and producers, actors, and actresses all identified with the Communistic movement, have developed the picture with the sinister intent of lowering the prestige of the American way of life and in a most noted manner attempting to sell Totalitarianism.

We note that the Salt of the Earth is scheduled for the Hyde Park Theater, 5310 So. Lake Park Avenue, for May 14, 1954, and at your theater for Friday, May 21, 1954, We have discussed the picture scheduled for the Hyde Park with Mr. Schoenstadt, one of the owners, who is very much chagrined that unknowingly, this Communistic picture has been scheduled for his theatre. We were assured that if there is a possible chance for him to cancel this picture, he intends to do it. If this is accomplished, your theater will be the only one in the great city of Chicago to show Salt of the Earth. While it is your prerogative to show any picture you decide to sell to your customers, we, however, do not believe it is becoming the dignity of your house to indicate cooperation with the Communistic elements of our city and nation. We trust there is sufficient time available to replace Salt of the Earth with one whose complexion is not identified with a foreign nation that has the objective of conquest in accordance with their way of life, regardless of bloodshed, be it the soldiers on the battlefield or the women and children unfortunately caught in a war torn area.

I remain

Sincerely yours,
EDWARD CLAMAGE, CHAIRMAN
ANTI-SUBVERSIVE COMMITTEE
Dept of Illinois

Mr. Clamage held the same post as my anti-subversive friend in Detroit. But Chicago was not Detroit. In Chicago there was Mandel Terman. We signed a contract. We had a theater. We printed new

leaflets, new tickets, new trailers and began our exploitation campaign all over again.

Our previews began at the Cinema Annex in Chicago. One of
our most vocal enthusiasts was the projectionist. He labored to make
each showing as perfect as possible, cleaned and cared for the film
with affection beyond the call of duty. At the end of a preview, he
would hasten to the auditorium to listen to the comments of our
guests. He was delighted by their delight.

News began to come about the preparations to open in Los
Angeles. It had very special significance for us in Chicago.

Immediately following the opening in New York, Simon Lazarus
had called Charles Skouras, top man in the Fox West Coast theater
chain. They had known each other, dealt with each other, actually
had joint interests in theaters together over the years.

"Charley, we opened *Salt of the Earth* in New York. We're doing
well. I want to screen the picture for you. I want you to see it."

"I don't want to see it."

"Charley, I want a theater from you. I want you to see for yourself, so you will know."

"I know. I know all about it. They already told me what it is. I
don't want to see it. I have no theaters for that picture."

Simon tried dozens of theaters, to no avail. It was a trying experience for him to be turned down by friends and business associates
of many years. When finally he had been forced to lease a closed theater, he called upon his booker to rent some short subjects to fill out
the program. None were available from any of the major distributors.
He called the exchanges himself. Some of the salesmen told him quite
frankly that no shorts would be given to him.

The theater Simon finally obtained for the picture was in Hollywood. It had no parking facilities, which, in Los Angeles, is a crippling
handicap. The theater had to be leased on a fourwall basis at an exor-
bitant two thousand dollars per month. The minimum lease was four
months, all rent payable in advance. Eight thousand dollars was paid
over to the theater owner.

Advertising copy was submitted to the newspapers. All those
with large circulation refused to carry the ads. The press had been

added to what Mr. Howard Hughes had listed as the facilities we did not own and therefore could not use. There was considerable public reaction to this refusal. Delegations of important persons called upon the heads of the papers. Like the legionaires in Detroit, they agreed to see the film. And like them, after enjoying the film, they persisted in refusing to sell us any space. *The Daily News* demurred. It was a Democratic paper, the smallest in the community and on the verge of bankruptcy. Approximately one person in a hundred in Los Angeles would discover where we were playing, or that we were playing at all.

No such problem in Chicago, we thought. Chicago was in hand!

However, the afternoon before we were to open, the projectionist asked Mr. Terman and me to come into the projection room. He told us that Mr. Jalas, an officer of the projectionists' union, had called him on the telephone and asked if he had run previews of *Salt of the Earth*. When the projectionist informed him that he had, Mr. Jalas rebuked him and ordered him to report to the union office first thing in the morning.

The projectionist assured us that he would not crawl before Mr. Jalas. He would insist that he liked the film, wished to project it, and would say so publicly. If there was any "nonsense" suggested to him, he would resign from the union and retire. He was a man of advanced years. He was not too well. He was too old, he said, to turn his back upon the old established principles of working people and become party to a racketeering operation parading as trade unionism. He didn't know what had happened to this country anyway. He didn't recognize it. And if he were too old to fight for it, he certainly wouldn't betray it in his ultimate moments of life.

We arranged a preview for two o'clock the next afternoon. He was given a call to be at the theater at one-thirty P.M. If he could not make it for any reason he was to notify us.

At two o'clock the next afternoon he had neither appeared nor called us. We telephoned his home. His wife had not heard from him. We telephoned the union and were informed that he had been there that morning, but had left. We tried to find Mr. Jalas. He was not in. At fifteen-minute intervals we called the union, and the projectionist's home. Finally, Mr. Jalas was in. The theater manager informed him that the projectionist had failed to appear and demanded a substitute. Mr. Jalas said he would send one. At five o'clock, no relief man having arrived, the manager again spoke to Mr. Jalas. Mr. Jalas told him not to worry, a man would be there. At seven o'clock no man had arrived, nor at seven-thirty, nor at all. And Mr. Jalas was "gone" for the weekend.

That was Friday evening of the long Memorial Day weekend. Two thousand outraged persons were turned away from the theater on that Friday evening, and some seven thousand over the following weekend. Thousands of dollars of exploitation, staff salaries and advertising were also "down the drain." Again, most climactically timed.

Mr. Jalas was not to be found; the projectionist was not to be found. Mr. Terman went to his home. The projectionist's wife was there. As Mr. Terman walked into the living room he saw the telephone receiver off the hook and he heard a moaning voice coming out of it. He picked it up and said "Hello." He thought he heard low sobs in what seemed to be the voice of Louie, the projectionist. He turned to the man's wife, told her what he had heard, and gave her the receiver. She promptly hung it up and said the call had not been from her husband. She had no idea where he was. Perhaps he had gone fishing.

"This late in the day?"

"He's a funny man."

"But he's never done this in three years!"

"He's funny that way."

The following morning Mr. Terman, his associate in the theater and I proceeded to Mr. Terman's lawyer's office. It was located in the same building as the projectionists' union office. We were about to turn into the building, when we saw our missing Louie! He was standing at the curb, outside the building, apparently waiting for the union office to open. It was not strange that we almost passed him. It was difficult to recognize in him the formerly pleasant man of the theater. He was sunken, sallow and jittery. Mandel approached him and asked what in the world had happened to him.

"Oh, don't ask. Don't drag me into this. Leave me out of it."

"But why didn't you come or call?"

"They locked me in that office last night." Then he turned to me.

"You been in Hollywood. You know these people. You know what they're like." Mandel took hold of him. He reminded him of his promises, of his volunteered assurance that he would take no nonsense from them. Why didn't he do as he had promised?

"You don't know what it's like. I can't do anything. Just leave me out of it."

"But I can't leave you out of it. You're in this whether I like it or you like it. You're just in it. Now tell us what happened."

"They sent me out on another job."

"But you just said they locked you into the office."

"I didn't know what was in the picture."

"But you ran it half a dozen times. You said you loved the picture."

"I know. But I'm no critic. I don't know what it's supposed to mean."

"Who told you what was in it and what it was supposed to mean? Jalas?"

"Yeah. Jalas."

"Has he seen it?"

"No."

"Then how does he know?"

"I don't know. Somebody told him. How do I know? I—I don't know. Hollywood told them."

"Listen to me, Louie. Thousands of people are being turned away from the theater. You can run that film. You can, because they can't do what they're doing without your help. If you love that film..."

"I don't want to run the film."

"Why not?"

"I just don't want to, that's all. I won't run it. God, don't you people understand?"

The projected three or four weeks away from home had stretched into seven. And now I must dig in for a long stretch. As Chicago went, so would go the entire Midwest.

III

Chicago.

The most corrupt, the healthiest, the most violent and degraded, the most folksy, the ugliest, the most beautiful, the most savage, the most enlightened, the most benighted—Chicago could be described in only one way: Chicago was Chicago. Anything one might say of the United States of America was *doubly* true of this undigested Goliath community.

In five weeks I had run scores of previews for as many organizations. Hundreds of letters had been written to the newspapers calling upon them to intervene. Editorials had appeared in the *Chicago Daily News* and The *Sun-Times* castigating Mr. Jalas' unmitigated arrogance. Hundreds of letters had been sent to Mr. Jalas, with and without accompanying delegations. But Mr. Jalas, "patriot," intimated confidently that our film would never play in Chicago.

Undoubtedly he, and those for whom he acted, thought themselves victorious. Our film was not running! But their triumph was not over us alone. It was over the inhabitants of the second largest American city, showing contempt for the judgment of its people and for their rights. Their victorious "patriotism" was a padlock upon a population. It ghettoed Chicagoans. It decreed that they might see a film they admired only in 16 mm., and only in underground, democratic storm-cellars. Public communication was the private property of the motion picture industry, of Mr. Jalas and his associates.

An eloquent and impassioned minister took to the air on our behalf. The university newspapers printed stirring reviews. From one of them the community picked a phrase and the word in Chicago was "Pass the Salt." I "rode" the film day and night—into the offices of professionals, into the homes of influential citizens, into the universities, into the studies of ministers and rabbis, into the offices of businessmen. Everywhere anger, decency and fraternity. Yet nothing happened.

With reluctance, and some chagrin—but necessarily—I acceded to the popular advice. After twelve weeks of battle, I engaged an attorney and a suit was prepared. But before I could permit it to be filed, I made one last, stubborn gesture toward people, organized people who could win this battle for themselves. I telephoned the labor attorney in New York. I asked how the AF of L negotiations were progressing. He reported encouraging results. Beyond his most optimistic hopes. Sue? We dare not! A very little patience, and we'd have it made. Once the AF of L moved, they would take Chicago in stride.

Letters came to me from Mr. Baskind and his associate, reporting that Mr. James McDevitt, director of L.L.P.E. (Labor's League for Political Education) and Mrs. McDevitt, together with other officials of the national AF of L and their wives, had seen the film. They were solidly behind the plan for national distribution with AF of L backing. The print was being shipped to Washington for Mr. George Meany and other officials to see. The wives of those officials who had seen the film were as moved by its being pro-woman as the men were by its being pro-working man. I was not to be concerned about Mr. Walsh. Brewer was opposing him for President of the union and was accusing Walsh of being soft on *Salt of the Earth*. Brewer was going to be defeated. Then Walsh would no longer be under the gun. And, when the Washington labor people talked with him, all our problems would be at an end. No suit now! I was to do whatever I could... but I was not to rock the ark that was being built as a national showcase for this film.

I telephoned my colleagues. They debated my optimism with respect to this developing project. They doubted that the cabal would permit these negotiations to come to fruition. They urged suit. I argued passionately against it. Even if they failed, the negotiations had to be given full, patient flight. We had to know we had tried. Reluctantly, they agreed to my urgings.

Now, again, I was free to return to Hollywood and my family. The few weeks away which were to have seen successful openings in Detroit and Chicago, to be followed by our family reunited against any further cleavage, had turned into an absence of almost four months and failure. And I was somewhat guiltily undismayed. A battle as old as America was raging in Chicago! It was a battle that could be won— would be won! I had come to know an American community more intimately that I had ever known one. I believed in it.

I had written in this vein to Gale—day after day. Often twice a day. Extolling people. I wrote of a stockbroker who said, "Don't tell me about your Americans! There isn't one in a hundred, who, if he thought he could escape being caught, wouldn't murder his mother for a quarter." I countered by saying that I believed that there were ninety-nine in a hundred, who, if they were not afraid of the consequences, would do the most heroically fraternal things. He thought for a moment, and then, quite happily, said, "You know —that's true, too!"

But one cannot bring up a family upon enthusiasm alone. Our company was broke. And the members of it on the ragged edges of financial precipices. Like Mike and Paul and their wives, Gale and I would have to dig into this rudely. What could I offer reality's queries as they would come from her? Only faith in the New York negotiations, faith in the foreign openings, faith in—Faith!

As we broke out of our embrace at the airport, Gale looked harder at me, even, than I at her. My eyes bespoke nothing to report for four months but total failure. But she shook her head sharply. "No, no, no! It was a magnificent fight. Come what may, we are staying with it. A family must be stronger than any individual within it. We're not defeated. And we're proud. No bitterness, now—and no guilt!"

When I could reply, I asked, "What does a man do to earn such a woman?"

"Just join your family in a two-weeks vacation, like every other good American."

As we rode home, a vast inner amusement shone from her. The mood of my flight home ill-prepared me for its cause. I probed. And it burst forth.

"With all the foreign openings ahead, I've had the most comforting thought," she said, so gaily.

Brimming with a resurrected faith, I said, "We'll finally pull out of our stalemate, you mean?"

"No. Just, how wonderful that with all those openings all over the world, the government won't give you a passport! That's the first contribution it has made to our happiness—in seven years."

I wasn't brightly responsive. And she threw firmer foundation under my feet. "Because you must go, wherever you can go. Do you understand? I'm a fan. Like Esperanza in the film. I don't want to go down fighting! I want to win!"'

IV

The film opened in Canada. Because most of the theaters there are operated by or controlled by chains in the U.S.A. and dependent upon their exchanges, we were relegated to a miserable theater in Toronto, its equipment so poor that it was almost impossible to understand the dialogue. But the film reviewer for the Canadian Broadcasting System devoted a full fifteen minutes to it in a coast-to-coast broadcast:

> *Salt of the Earth is* an American movie about workers, which fact alone makes it unusual. The idea that workers are people, and have conflicts and problems worthy of attention, has never impressed the American film industry.... Not that workers are ignored altogether. Sometimes they are used as comic relief, or as background figures in an industrial epic, a pliable, anonymous mob streaming into plants early in the morning and from them late in the afternoon.... Quite often, too, we run across workers in crime stories, as the victims or pawns of racketeers in control of their union. But the notion, so commonplace in European and English films, and in the entire world literature, that the lives and struggles of ordinary people are of dramatic interest seems too exotic for American consumption.... According to this philosophy, to be a worker carries with it a stigma of degradation and inferiority. It is something that cannot be helped, but about which—like the skeleton in the family closet—a decent silence should be kept.
>
> ... Cinematically, *Salt of the Earth is* an exciting experience, a deeply human drama in the documentary manner perfected by the Italians in such masterpieces as *Open City, Bicycle Thief* and *Shoe Shine*... it's strongly pro-labor.... If it plays in your town, by all means see it.

The film was invited to the Edinburgh Film Festival. A warm reception there accelerated its London opening. No sooner was that announced than the "cabal" in the United States sought out ways to prevent it.

A trade union leader was approached. He was asked to go to London, and to involve London technicians in stopping the opening. The reply was, "Why should I go? You can do it as well as I. Just have the theater bombed." But neither went. It opened in London.

The Times:

> American films as a whole proclaim that all is well with the American citizen and the American way of life; that both, indeed, come as near to perfection as is possible in this mortal world. it is natural that they should do so, but there is much value in a minority report—and it is a minority report that *Salt of the Earth* draws up....

Sunday Dispatch:

> A picture that touches greatness.

Sunday Graphic:

> ... you will be impressed by this film's integrity, its insight into the tribulations of the poor, and its power to move.

Sunday Times:

> *Salt of the Earth* is a good film, well written, persuasive, played with humor, sympathy and infectious enthusiasm.

Catholic Herald:

> ... *Salt of the Earth* is a different, challenging film that first and foremost is a human document in which the people are real—and likeable.

But following this opening, no major theater chain in the land of Magna Carta would book the film. No doubt they are too closely allied with Hollywood.

The film was entered in the International Film Festival at Karlovy Vary, Czechoslovakia. Films of twenty-nine nations were entered. The judges were hard put to decide between *Salt of the Earth* and a Soviet film for the grand prize. They voted one to each. Rosaura Revueltas was awarded the prize for the best acting performance by a woman.

Under the auspices of the Miners' Union of Czechoslovakia, the film was exhibited in a great outdoor auditorium seating thirty-five thousand people. Rosaura Revueltas was present and reported to us. In discussion that followed the showing of the film, the president of the Miners' Union addressed the Czech film artists on the podium. "Study this film well. Why do you not create films of the stature of this one from the United States?"

Europe, west and east, greeted the film as a reflection of "the other America," which, if it could make a film, must be livelier than they had thought. The "other" America. Not the McCarthy America increasingly feared by the peoples of the world, but the America of friendly, neighborly people with whom living in and sharing the peace and fruits of the world would be a rapturous experience.

While the film was traveling throughout Europe and winning approbation, reports came from New York that most conservative trade union leaders were viewing the film with growing interest and were discussing ways to support its exhibition.

Thus, in August 1954, conservative leaders of American unions, and the people of western Europe, the Communists of Prague and Moscow and the conservative *Times* of London were at the same time enjoying and praising an American film that described the dignity and stature of American working people.

As if to bring final punctuation to this phenomenon, the New York attorney telephoned. I must come east immediately. I arrived, to be told of the plan that had been devised to distribute the film nationally. A new company would be organized. The film would carry its name. As a neutral, commercial, third party, it would call upon all interested unions and other public bodies for support.

The plan was satisfactory. The attorney flew to the coast. In consultation with Mike, Paul and our attorneys, Ben Margolis and Charles Katz, a contract was drawn up and signed by us. It would be taken back to New York for signature and returned to us within two weeks. He had also a detailed plan of operation. A new premiere would take place in Philadelphia shortly thereafter. I met Mr. McDevitt and heard his comments on the film's conservatism and pro-Unionism.

We were as controlledly jubilant as our various temperaments permitted. I could now go to Mexico City for our imminent opening there. There was a most important test. Congressman Jackson had made a dire prophesy: our film would gravely injure the United States if shown in Mexico and Latin America. We believed that if the film were successful—if the stamp of approval of Mexico were placed upon it before our new opening in Philadelphia—the long struggle would be at an end. There was little sadness in parting now. Faith might well be wedded to reality in Mexico. And the fruit of their union might, thereafter, utter its first cry of life and independence in Philadelphia.

V

Six months before I arrived in Mexico City for the premiere, our representative had screened the film for an officer of Mexico's largest distributing company, who had expressed high hopes for the film's commercial success. Yet within twenty-four hours that company's door had slammed shut. Its top man had sent word down that the film was not to be exhibited in any part of the Republic.

The other large company was already "in tow" when we addressed it. We finally found a small distributor who operated a single theater in Mexico City. We signed a contract. There followed month after month of stalemate.

Without a Mexican government seal, it was impossible to hold even private showings. To get a seal it was necessary to fill in the Spanish titling. Since there was fear that the picture would never be shown, there was intelligent hesitation in spending the money necessary to complete the titling. We undertook to pay this cost ourselves and advanced money for it. Delay fell upon delay. It was too costly—too difficult—it would be undertaken very soon—it was in work. And then we discovered that the film we had shipped for titling was still at the Mexican customs. It had not even been picked up. Unless it was within three days, it would be returned.

The contest in Mexico was clearly to be of inordinate interest!

To investigate the stalemate we had sent a young American trained in America to love justice and his neighbors. He was energetic—tended to be impatient—was in love with the film, and eager to prove his mettle.

He found all the Mexican principals charged with furthering the opening of the film in a state of suspended animation. Each was fearful of moving alone. The young American had one quality that was invaluable. He was a Mexican-loving arrogant American. And without being aware of it himself he was what the doctor ordered.

He picked up the film and took it to a lab. He negotiated the work and the money to complete it. He arranged to have the completed film taken to the Department of the Interior. He made a date for a premiere, according to the existing contract. He arranged for proper exploitation of the film, also according to contract.

It was only after this was accomplished that I arrived.

The premiere was unlike any I had ever attended. The film's humor was greeted by salvos of laughter. Its dramatic moments drew round after round of applause, often overlapping like waves upon a shore. At the end of the showing no one rose to leave the theater. Rosaura was picked out by a spotlight and near pandemonium broke out. An anthem was begun and sung lustily by the entire audience. Rosaura was escorted to her car in the fashion of a great star in the early days of this century.

The following day the newspaper reviews began to appear. For a week the reviews came, from a dozen, two dozen journals; daily papers, weeklies, sport papers, film magazines, the Spanish edition of *Time*; some reviewing it once, some twice, some three times. It was not possible to distinguish between a paper of the left, the right, the center.

Tiempo (Spanish edition of Time):

> ... a picture has been produced which for its realism, its social content, and its human stature rivals such great international films as *Grapes of Wrath* and *Open City*....

El Nacional (Government news organ):

> ... To ask equal treatment for American citizens of a different race is not a communist demand, but simply a demand for one of the rights guaranteed in the American Constitution. To believe the former is to accept Washington and Lincoln as the precursors of communism—nonsense which could not occur to any sensible person...

Novedades:

> ... *Salt of the Earth* is a film of exceptional character and worthy of all the superlatives... a fortunate antithesis to those false and shoddy films which are made in Hollywood with no thought except for dividends.

El Universal:

> The picture has a tremendous impact, like when Super-Mouse hits the spectator in the solar plexus... takes one's breath at moments with the strength of the story.

K.O. (Weekly sports magazine):

> Rosaura Revueltas comes back to the screen in *Salt of the Earth*, a picture full of action which all workers of the continent ought to see.

In groups and singly people came to me to explain their country. I must understand that every man, woman and child in Mexico was indebted to us. A Mexican journalist said:

"I will tell you, my friend, what I have learned in my life, here in Mexico, looking at our pyramids, at our ruins, at our ancient sculpture and at our ancient people so many of whom cannot read or write. In life there is a law. Every people must have a chance to express itself. Many have been suppressed. Many have been prevented. But that has nothing to do with destruction. Their chance is postponed, held in abeyance. Destruction comes only to those who are free to choose. And for them it is self-destruction—suicide.

"Those who are free may choose a path without constraint. They have only to perform one deed and the whole world would flow to them. The deed? Invitation to others to grow. And for us, this film gives hope for your country's future—and ours."

We did not suspect then that, despite such acclaim, this third- or fourth-rate theater would be the only one in which the film would be permitted exhibition in Mexico City.

Because I could not imagine such a circumscribed life for the film in Mexico, I flew back to Hollywood. *Salt of the Earth* was playing in Mexico. It had been embraced as a deed of North American friendship. Congressman Jackson's "fears" were dissolved. Surely, now, in our own country, supported by representative organizations of its people, this work would be permitted to earn its own way.

VI

The days following my return to Hollywood were anxious ones. No contract, and no word from the attorney in New York about the Philadelphia opening. While our company was meeting to discuss procedure, our representative in Chicago telephoned. He wished permission to re-address Mr. Jalas of the projectionists' union there. This was a most propitious moment, he believed—following upon the film's splendid reception in Mexico. He proposed only to submit evidence to Mr. Jalas of the growing appreciation for the film in increasing areas of the world, and to respectfully solicit the union's re-examination of its position. My colleagues supported his plan.

Scarcely was that conversation completed than the eagerly awaited letter from the attorney in New York arrived. My fingers trembled as I opened it. The attorney acknowledged receipt of the reviews from Mexico. They were magnificent! Heartiest congratulations! Most deserved! But—he was desolated to have to report that efforts to secure national trade union support would have to be abandoned. A very important person had threatened it into the ground. The plan was dead.

The day following the receipt of that crisp bit of news, an equally succinct communication arrived about Mr. Jalas of Chicago. He had let it be known that our film would *never* play there.

Our company met again. My earlier pleas for subordination of all of our plans to patient fostering of national trade union support had ended as my colleagues had anticipated. They were not unhappy that we had tried. But it had cost us six full months and thousands of dollars. Now there was no alternative but to take the union to court, however reluctant we were.

We instructed our attorney in Chicago to prepare a complaint naming the union officers, the individual projectionists who had failed to run the film, and the union, as defendants. He was to seek both injunctive relief and damages. The American Civil Liberties Union of Chicago filed a supportive brief, *amicus curiae,* in the federal district court of judge Philip N. Sullivan. We awaited legal decision.

But an infinitely more momentous decision was nearing in Washington. The Senate of the United States was debating a resolution. Though the debate related only to censure of Senator Joseph McCarthy, the kernel of the question before the Senate was: shall reason be declared subversive in the United States of America?

McCarthy had staked his fate upon an affirmative decision. Relentlessly he had arrogated "absolute rights" to himself. He demanded that the Senate confirm them. His charge of "twenty years of treason" against the Democratic party had been a glove slapped across the face of the entire political center of the United States.

Having tasted the alum of "absolute rights," of rule by threat and ruin, our nation had lost its popular physiognomy. It was on the brink of disaster. McCarthy was jettisoned. Following that action, the United States of America was again able to find its political feet, to reassert respect for its origins and for the opinions of mankind.

Within a few weeks our tiny office registered immediate vibrations of the changing nation, within a changing world. From student bodies and faculty advisors in almost every part of the country came requests to exhibit *Salt of the Earth* on university campuses. Northwestern University requested it for Constitutional Liberties Week. It was sought by the Governmental Research Center of the University of Kansas, by the students of the University of Chicago, by Antioch College, Oberlin; by small colleges: Bard, in New York, Goddard, in Vermont, where it was proposed that the showing be sponsored jointly with the Central Labor Council of that small community. It was requested by the Cinema Club of the law school of Yale Unversity.

The film was sent. Everywhere capacity houses and reports of reception ranging from "warmly received" to "ovation." Ten thousand students, in seats of learning from Kansas to Vermont, were applauding the film's democratic inspiration, drawing sustenance from it for future living—three thousand of them in Chicago. And the film was barred from commerce there.

Before the showing of the film at Yale, the Cinema Club became aware of some discomfiture at the prospect among members of the Conservative Club. They were invited to preview the film for themselves. The offer was appreciatively accepted. At the conclusion of the screening, the Conservative Club members applauded lustily. Then, in the best tradition of conservatism, they attended the general showing. And, by their own loud applause, built public approbation to a near ovation!

But in the federal court in Chicago, the union moved to have our case thrown out of court. It denied any conspiracy among the defendants, or any prohibition by the union officers of the running of the film. The individual members, the motion stated, had refused to run it upon their own patriotic initiative. For them to run the film:

... would be in furtherance of the communist conspiracy to overthrow the government by force and violence.

... bring the United States and its institutions into disrepute....

... [the film] degraded the American worker in the eyes of the world.

That evening, from Berlin, East Germany, the following cablegram: "SALT OF THE EARTH OPENED WITH THE GREATEST SUCCESS."

A few days later, from Paris, the following radiogram: "FILM OPENED SATURDAY. PUBLIC AND PRESS RECEPTION UNANIMOUSLY ENTHUSIASTIC."

The press reviews arrived a few days thereafter:

L'Aurore: ... it earns the right to be called a classic.

Paris-Soir: Zola would have loved it.

France Tireur: ... it resounds profoundly in our hearts.

Combat: ... it is a masterpiece.

Le Parisien Libre: A great social film... of an extreme loyalty.

Le Monde: ... it is a long time since we have seen such a forthright American film.

Paris-Presse   ... it is certainly the most forthright work of

L'Intransigeant: American cinema. It is also one of its masterpieces.

La Croix: ... it is an ardent plea for the dignity of man.

L'Observateur: ... a film most American... truth brought to the screen with a gratifying courage.

Les Lettres Françaises:Salt of the Earth will make you discover America.

L'Humanité: ... it will convince you that... in... America the flame of
                 mankind still burns.

Upon the desk in our office, side by side, lay the union motion to
quash our complaint, and the press reviews from Paris, Berlin, London, Prague and Mexico City. As we studied the documents it seemed
to us that, for the world, our film confirmed the existence of reason
in the United States. For the "cabal," it confirmed reason as
subversion.

In Chicago, judge Sullivan handed down his opinion upon the
union's motion to strike our complaint. He dismissed the union's
motion on every count, and added: "... the public has the same interest in being able to see motion pictures of their choice as it has to be
able to read books and newspapers and see plays and attend meetings
of its choice."

He ordered the union to reply to our complaint. Immediately,
our attorney addressed the union through its counsel. He stated that
we were prepared to waive all claim to damages if it would permit the
film to be projected. If any face-saving were involved, we would be
pleased to import a projectionist from out of town, provided the
union would grant him a card and permit him to project. Beyond
that, we would refrain from any advertisements or public statements
that might redound to the union's discredit.

Reply to this offer never came directly. Indirectly we were told
again that we would *never* open in Chicago. Through interrogatories,
directed to Paul and to me, they tried to get answers to some hundred
questions of the kind we had refused to deliver to the Un-American
Activities Committee. The questions were the same gross invasions of
our private affairs, entrance into which, the Supreme Court had just
declared, was precluded, even to Congress. The union's interrogatories were objected to.

We determined to hasten the court decision in Chicago by seeking an immediate temporary injunction against the union defendants. Judge Sullivan's ruling presaged success. The "time" seemed
propitious.

VII

On the day I arrived in Chicago, and just before calling upon our attorney to accompany him to judge Sullivan's court, I passed two theaters in the very heart of downtown Chicago. One was running *Five Fingers* by Michael Wilson, author of *Salt of the Earth*. It had been written by Mike for Twentieth Century Fox before Mike was blacklisted. In the other theater, not three blocks away, a double bill was playing. Both films had been written by Dalton Trumbo, one of the Hollywood Ten. They were made by Metro-Goldwyn-Mayer from Dalton's scripts before he had been blacklisted. All three films were playing in top-flight theaters and were being projected by *union projectionists*.

Further down the street, billboards announced a concert by the Soviet pianist, Emil Gilels, to be played in Orchestra Hall, where the entire crew belonged to the same international union as did the projectionists. The morning paper I read in the courtroom listed a Soviet film, *Russian Holiday*, current at the Cinema Annex—the theater where the projectionist had refused to run *Salt of the Earth*. It was being projected by union projectionists. And the paper announced yet another Soviet film, *Boris Godunov*, to be premiered at Orchestra Hall. This one was not only projected by the union projectionists, but portable projection equipment was brought to the hall by a company owned by Mr. Jalas, and installed by union men.

What added whipped cream to these excellent cups of morning coffee was the *New York Times*, of even date. It carried a large advertisement announcing the re-opening of a ten-year-old film, *The Life of Emile Zola*, featuring the distinguished blacklisted American actress, Gale Sondergaard. That film was to play in a leading New York art theater and would be projected by union projectionists. It had been made prior to the blacklisting of Miss Sondergaard.

But Mike Wilson's *Salt of the Earth* had not been projected in any theater in the United States for a year and a half!

We appeared in judge Sullivan's court only to be faced with a distressing turn of events. Fearing judge Sullivan, the union had changed counsel. The new attorney introduced himself as a nephew of judge Sullivan, and he told us before the court opened that he would seek an immediate transfer of the case out of his uncle's court. Our attorney assured judge Sullivan that we were content to remain there. But judge Sullivan, after some thought, exercising discretion wholly within his authority, had the case transferred.

The case was assigned to judge Sam Perry. Our motion for a temporary injunction was presented to the court. The union's legal staff objected. Two basic grounds were advanced. First: Some of the makers of this film had been named as Communists and had refused to affirm or deny the allegations. Therefore, the union members in refusing to project the film had exercised an "absolute right!" (No cases cited in support.)

"Absolute right!" I was not a lawyer and my head spun. But, it turned out, our attorney's spun as rapidly. We attempted to unravel the pronunciamento.

This "absolute right" was a little hard to square with the fact that the union, at that very moment, was projecting a film of Mike Wilson and two of Dalton Trumbo. And not three blocks from the courthouse.

We searched for the subtle distinction between the Mike Wilson a union would project, and the Mike Wilson they refused to project. Their position seemed to comprise two opposite absolute rights—to play and project a man, and not to play and project a man. But under what logic could the same man be projected, and not be projected, *at the same moment?* And then, suddenly—light!

If a film was owned by Warner Brothers, Twentieth Century-Fox, or Metro-Goldwyn-Mayer, then, apparently, the union would permit audiences to see it. For in that case Mike Wilson was not Mike Wilson. He was Mike "Studio" Wilson.

This cleared up the subtlety. And pinpointed the crime. Two private bodies, the industry and the union, not only were determining who might have access to the American market, but which of their works, and when.

Laboratories all over the country were happily making prints of the films of Mike "Studio" Wilson, Dalton "Studio" Trumbo and hundreds of the "Studio" blacklisted. Huge theater circuits were advertising their films as outstanding entertainment. Prints in 16 mm. were being sold to television networks. A number of my films, of Gale's, of others of the many hundreds who were now not permitted to work in films or in television were, at that very moment, playing on millions of TV screens.

But one film made by these artists could not find a laboratory, a theater, a network among all those profitably exhibiting scores of their films. And this was so because an American industry had written "NOT FOR EXHIBITION" upon property not theirs; "TO BE SILENCED" upon men and women they did not own; and "RESTRICTED" upon the eyes and ears of 151,000,000 people who had never consciously surrendered their sovereignty.

These were curious "rights." Curious for the United States! For they were private rights *to destroy*. Under them living, communicating, self-respecting Americans could be canceled out at the whim of others. This could be done in part, in whole, even in perpetuity. Some Americans could treat others as if they were hydrants. Turn them off at will. Separate them from their work. To begin this process with ten men; to extend it to thousands. To include the Fund for the Republic. And the *New York Times*. And the Negro people. And the Supreme Court of the United States. Even the Union! And to do it in the name of the "nation."

The union lawyers then produced their second objection to our motion for a temporary injunction. They stated that our film had been made with a non-union crew. The union projectionists therefore were possessed of an absolute right not to project it.

Under such extraordinary "rights" court proceedings surely would be shorter. No cases need be cited. What arguments can prevail against absolute rights? Congressman Jackson had said of us that we were racists! The industry had said that we were subversive! The union now accused us of being anti-union!

The logic of the unions' "legal" argument was that, when Mr. Brewer refused us a crew, we should have honored his "right" to break the law. We should have willingly severed our creative jugular veins. We should have been happy to sell television sets, instead of creating for them, or to engage in black market writing for the studios at bargain rates instead of publicly undertaking a production of our own. Why had we refused to conform, to adjust, to accommodate to the way things were, and to the "times"' representatives, Mr. Clarence Jalas, Mr. Howard Hughes, Mr. Donald Jackson?

Having failed to pay Mr. Jalas such honor, having dared to be creatively independent, we became "anti-union." In spite of the fact that every member of the crew that shot *Salt of the Earth* was a member of a recognized union—and some even of Mr. Jalas' as Mr. Jalas well knew. Every foot of film had been developed in a union laboratory. Every note of music had been performed by a union musician. Every cutter had been a union member. It had taken enormous pains and dedication to accomplish this. It had been meticulously and scrupulously achieved on the basis of conscience. And we had turned out a pro-union picture, honored as such in every part of the world where it had been seen—even in America—even by the American Legion in Detroit, even by an FBI informant who had accompanied the legionnaires to a showing and by the FBI plant who had been cutter on the film.

But the union lawyers for Mr. Jalas felt unobliged to deal with reality. They believed they required neither law nor facts. They still trod the emptying road toward McCarthyism and "absolute rights to destroy."

Judge Perry asked for briefs from both sides. He would render his decision upon them.

I had not been in Chicago for over a year. I remained for a few days to renew acquaintanceships. Friends asked what we had been doing since I was last there. Had we made another film? What a pleasant—aye, a lovely thought!

I asked my friends under what logic we could have made another film when we had failed to establish our ability to play the present one. Under what logic could we have asked for money for another film while we still owed a quarter of a million dollars on the one we had not been able to show? For three years and a half we had received no payment for our work—no support for ourselves and our families. We were now also utterly without personal funds. We had had to spend upon this film, and our joint livings in the years of making and attempting to distribute it, over a hundred and fifty thousand dollars of our own funds. The Hollywood Ten had spent a quarter of a million dollars in its three years in the courts. I had not earned a penny for eight years. Hearing this, my friends were aghast. When I suggested that, nevertheless, in our opinions, for the sake of our country it had been worth every dollar it had taken and every atom of energy, they did not reply. Perhaps they were not certain.

Then came judge Perry's decision. He ordered Paul and me to reply to the interrogatories of the union! Overruling judge Sullivan, in itself an unusual action, he ordered us to disrobe in public at the command of Jalas. It was a late date for us to perform in this dying circus. We chose rather to withdraw our complaint. Judge Perry was startled. But, upon reflection, he said he chose to believe that we were seeking to test his ruling in a higher court, and acceded to our request. Our action was dismissed!

For a year and a half we had sought to separate the partners in conspiracy, and had addressed ourselves to the union, alone. In Chicago that long drawn-out effort failed.

In 1703 Daniel Defoe wrote from the jail into which he had been thrown for non-conformism:

> Actions take their tincture from the Times,
> And as they change are Virtues made, or Crimes.

"The Times" had come for us to lock horns with the *whole* body of the cabal.

VIII

For many months Paul Jarrico had been at work upon a compendium of illegal actions against the film. Completed, it covered forty pages of single-spaced typing.

Within a week of its delivery to our attorney, Ben Margolis, for examination, the magazine *The New Yorker* carried a story to the effect that *Salt of the Earth* had been selected by the motion picture critics of Paris as one of the seven best films of 1955. Jules Dassin's film *Rififi* was selected as well. In the opinion of the critics of Paris, artists black-listed in Hollywood had accounted for two of the world's seven best films that year. The Hollywood motion picture industry also won two nominations: *On the Waterfront* and *This Is Cinerama*. Three of the four were doing very well commercially. *Salt of the Earth* was in black mothballs, with nothing to show for almost four years of embattled existence in the United States, except Paul's compendium of forty pages of alleged violations of anti-trust laws.

As the complaint was drawn up by Ben Margolis, the list of defendants and co-conspirators grew. At a minimum they would number sixty—all the major producing companies, the distributing companies, the laboratories in Hollywood, in New York; sound studios, special effects establishments; Howard Hughes, as an individual, Congressman Donald L. Jackson, as an individual—for illegal activity outside his Congressional immunity; Roy Brewer, Richard F. Walsh, international president of the union, and several members of his staff; theaters throughout the country for having broken written contracts or verbal agreements; and one member of the investigating staff of the Un-American Activities Committee for extracurricular conspiracy.

As the darkness continued to give way to what the *Chicago Sun-Times* called "the dawn of the post-McCarthy age of re-Enlightenment," it was rewarding to remember that the Hollywood Ten and some of the two hundred blacklisted men and women of Hollywood had been among the first resisters. It was rewarding to remember that among others, the Hollywood Ten had slowed McCarthyite violence and moral delinquency at its very inception, and for a period of three years! Our American faith of 1947 was being cast into the simple American truths of 1956.

Simple truths? To us—it seemed so. Was it not, now, self-evident, that over even a short spread of time, an injury to one is an injury to all? It is never too difficult to detach for attack and punishment, just a few, whoever they are. But those so selected, if they fight back, do not suffer the major injury. They escape the degradation of conformity. The true injury is suffered by those who tolerate the attack upon another, for it is they who succumb to the attack and are crippled by it.

This we had feared from the beginning, and this fear had motivated our resistance. Even when we knew that our resistance had been rendered pitifully weak, we persisted, to prevent the total obliteration of resistance. What gave us hope in this formative, present moment of change was what seemed to be the recognition by the nation of the fact of injury to *itself.* How well we knew that the reappraisal was not for our sakes, and that we would be the very last to benefit from it. What made the battle into the future profoundly and freshly compelling was that the nation was moving oblivious of us, and increasingly concerned for its own hurt. How deep that hurt had been, as yet, was unsuspected by anyone.

Though our happiness in the beginning of national self-assertion was profound, our fears were not abated. For the progress seemed painfully slow. The truth of the decade behind us was indeed simple, and not new. It had been very well stated by John Stuart Mill a hundred years ago:

> A State which dwarfs its men, in order that they may be more
> docile instruments in its hands even for beneficial purposes, will find
> that with small men no great thing can really be accomplished.

That truth was now so palpable. How long, until... Patience. Patience!

As Ben continued to work upon our complaint, our film was leased for exhibition to Belgium, Holland, Israel and Australia. It was sold to Romania and Czechoslovakia.

When the complaint was completed, we met with Ben. He was then able to volunteer an estimate of the fantastic cost of the litigation to break the conspiracy. If it had to go all the way to the Supreme Court, it might take six to seven years! In addition, the case should be brought to trial in New York, and a top-notch anti-trust attorney must be found.

We responded to that information with numbness.

Neither our company, nor we personally, possessed a penny. The years of conspiracy against us had ground us down to our bones. It was unfortunate, but a fact that must be reckoned with. Was this to be the writing of *finis* to our efforts?

How curious that this latest crisis, in a *promising* climate, approached panic. Not our wills, by now, but rather the ungainsayable obligation to find an anti-trust lawyer with a fighting bent for justice, moved us back into battle.

I left for New York, where I was to search for a skilled, indefatigable attorney, independent and devoid of ordinary fears, who, in addition, would take on this case without fee, without even the guarantee of payment of ordinary, minimal court costs.

After several weeks—unmitigated failure. Sympathy on every hand but: "Good Lord, man, this case would take one-third the time of an entire office, for perhaps several years, and at a cost of several hundred thousand dollars. You must understand that *no office* can afford that." And with the speech, the look in the eyes that suggested that by now I must be a little soft in the head.

Chin in hands, in my hotel room one afternoon, I ransacked memory for an attorney—an attorney—one I had surely met somewhere along the way. A name flashed! George Brussel, Jr.! He it was who owned the theater on Eighth Avenue we had almost leased for our opening in New York. He it was who had called a number of church and lay leaders to see the film and to obtain their opinion of its character. And he it was I remembered with delight, who, after they had endorsed it without qualification, had become majestically enraged when the men who had the theater under lease succumbed to pressure and refused to sign the sub-lease to us. What was pleasurable in that sudden recollection was his sculptured anger at those intimidated lessees. I leaped for the phone. Finally, he was there.

"Mr. Brussel?"

"Yes."

"This is Herbert Biberman. Do you remember me?"

"Yes, Mr. Biberman."

"May I call upon you this afternoon?"

"What do you have in mind, Mr. Biberman?"

"It's difficult to recite into a telephone."

"Try."

I paused, knowing how much depended upon the next sentence.

"Mr. Brussel, I remember you as a man with a profound sense of social justice."

"And, Mr. Biberman, you have had nothing but social injustice visited upon you." A pause on his part, and then, "Come in to see me at four."

That visit was followed by another in his home. There I met Mrs. Brussel, and two infant children. At first glance I took them to be grandchildren. Mrs. Brussel, soft-spoken, delicate of movement and, as I was to discover, with bottomless love of all living beings, told me these were their children, recently adopted. They each had grown-up children by former marriages. These children were to be the product of their own union. Clearly, these were individuals who were not seeking to escape responsibility. Life, for them, was obviously composed of ever-enlarging areas of moral commitment. Mrs. Brussel was an ardent partisan of our cause from the beginning. She volunteered to act as archivist for our case, if her husband took it. Little did we suspect then that, by the time we had been into it for a few months, Mrs. Brussel would be the most informed part of our team.

After a number of visits we came to tentative agreement. George Brussel, if he took the case, was to have full authority for its direction. Every officer of the company must individually subscribe to it. I returned home. Some days later Ben Margolis flew east. Few men in America had fought more diligently, more selflessly and with more success for civil and constitutional liberties. George had devoted his career to corporation law. These two lawyers, with such dissimilar histories, were to meet for the first time. If common confidence in the issues and in each other developed and their collaboration followed, we would have a team, and once again, a crisis would be resolved.

Their meeting lasted several days. It was thorough and frank. And it built confidence. They left as friends and co-counsel. George Brussel guaranteed to carry our case through trial without respect to the cost. Two Americans, Mr. and Mrs. George Brussel, Jr., with a taste for social justice, kept the battle alive!

Then, without previous warning, we were notified that we of *Salt of the Earth* had been awarded the International Grand Prize for the best film, made anywhere in the world, to have been exhibited in France in 1955. The awards had been made by the Académie du Cinéma de Paris (The Paris Academy of Film). Crystal stars would be awarded to Rosaura Revueltas, Michael Wilson and myself and other winners at a dinner to be held in Paris late in June.

Rosaura was in Europe at that moment and would unquestionably remain for this happy event. Michael Wilson applied for a passport and, although he anticipated rejection, he was sent one immediately. Since I had been denied a passport some time before, I had, perforce, to savor the occasion vicariously through Mike's letter from France:

> The awards dinner was at Maxim's. Rosaura got back from Frankfurt and Lausanne to attend. Très élegant. Awards were: Simone Signoret, best French actress 1955; Rosaura best foreign actress; Jean Servais (of Dassin's *Rififi*) best French actor; James Dean (of America —posthumous) best foreign actor; Jean Renoir, best French direction; best picture of 1955 *SALT OF THE EARTH* with crystal stars to Herbert and myself. American Embassy was there. We chatted together, were photographed together, after my speech. Herbert's *étoile* award was turned over to the attache to send to him via diplomatic channels. Amusing, *non*?
>
> This afternoon, Simone Signoret, Rosaura and I were presented before Le Président et Les Membres du Bureau du Conseil Municipal de Paris (The Mayor of Paris to you) and in the ornate l'Hôtel de Ville he gave us a little speech of welcome, in the manner of mayors, and the keys to the city were symbolized in champagne. By now you should be giggling.

At that moment Paul and I felt free, finally, to take a most difficult step. We offered our resignations to the company. Legal process, which was the film's future, was in excellent hands. We dared now to seek to secure our personal and family livelihoods. On June 1, 1956, after five years of total and uninterrupted devotion to the affairs of Independent Productions Corporation and I.P.C. Distributors, Inc., our resignations as president and secretary-treasurer were accepted. Simon Lazarus was elected to his former position as president and Mr. David Grutman, who had supported the company financially from its very inception, was elected vice-president.

It was a lonely moment for us. And the loneliness did not soon evaporate. Those had been exuberant years, to which we said farewell. They had been the most American years of our lives. We suspected that those ahead would be as much harder to live through as they would be seemingly easier. Our loneliness did not derive from mere separation. It had a profounder origin. Time is not sufficient unto itself. A decade such as the one through which we had fought required resolution. And there was none. There was unfinished business behind us, around us, and ahead of us. The unfinished business was the question of freedom of communication in the United States of America for the sake of the United States of America! That question was now in the courts. Resolution was yet years away.

Part Five

AMERICA
1964

I

Life, in its normal and familial aspects, now could be lived. It was
nine years since we had attempted it. Money had to be earned, debts
repaid, children had to be brought up and helped to mature, our
interests in life had to be reconstituted. Whatever the realities were,
we had to act like fully viable individuals.

In the months of June and July of that year, 1956, I bought with
borrowed money several by-passed, steep, slope lots adjacent to our
house. Bought from maps at high prices in 1924, before the roads
leading to them had been engineered, they had turned out to be
unusable holes in the landscape. For thirty years taxes had been paid
without any increment in value. During World War II machinery had
been developed which, it occurred to me, might make these sites
available to current engineering practices. In the fall of that year a
company was formed to construct cantilevered houses on those sites.
I was given the title of "land-procurer," made a junior partner, and
given a modest drawing account against a share of the profits. I was
instructed to buy my head off at those prices.

I tendered fourteen working hours a day to financial survival.
And, for the first time in many years, I felt a sense of guilt for absence
from meaningful struggle in those McCarthyite years.

At the age of fifty-six, that early summer of 1956, I celebrated
the thirtieth anniversary of quitting my father's business to enter the
field of communication. Now, welcomed back into the fraternity of
commercial money-making, where there was apparently always
room, I was barred only from the field of communication, where participants had become subject to screening.

I bought heavy boots, heavy trousers, heavy shirts and made my
way to the hilltops of Hollywood to cut those pleasant hills down to
ugly and saleable size. At the same time Paul and Mike were working
their way through the black market in motion picture scripts. If occasionally I stopped to cast a glance eastward, it was toward the federal
courthouse, Southern District of New York, where George Brussel, Jr.
was slowly moving the case of *Independent Productions Corporation and
I.P.C. Distributors, Inc.* vs. *Loew's Inc., et al.* through the intricate mazes

of an anti-trust action. There, at least, vicariously, we were still in the battle for our way into the future.

From the exalted physical posture of my hilltop world of bulldozers, cascading rivers of decomposed granite, sewer lines and storm drains carved out of the freshly compacted dirt, I peered out at the men and women deigned safe to communicate in the mass media. Everywhere Henry Luce was winning hands down.

In the forties, in one of his *Life-Time-Fortune* journals, he had announced the American Century. This was followed by a fervent plea to the artists and communicators of the United States to abandon the little, lost causes they served and to come boldly to the side of American business.

McCarthyism, which drove many American artists into neutrality if not into Mr. Luce's mink-lined stalls, helped his call immeasurably. So did the mass exodus of Americans into the limitless jaws of TV. The sponsor became master of America's free time, of its relaxed hours and of its unsuspecting cat-naps. TV was free to all Americans—and, lamentably, vice versa.

In the swirling dust where we powdered the ancient hills behind Hollywood, contractor attempted to devour sub-contractor while sub-contractor attempted to devour the sub-sub-contractor or materials man. And the Savings and Loan Associations devoured all—with their interest rate of 7.2 per cent plus four or five points (loan fee payable in advance). In the mass media, competition raged in defaming man, in portraying him as a clown or a son of a bitch. We were living in the eye of a manic-depressive fifty billion dollar military program within which lay all the eggs of our industry-government-culture psychosis: man was absurd, evil. Only the weapons with which he might obliterate himself held promise *for* the future. So long as the market held and the inflationary spiral continued under control!

Negation was not of the fissures and shortings in our society and culture, only of life and man. McCarthy had been jettisoned, but McCarthyism persisted in the basic assumptions under which we lived. One was free to attack our mores, institutions, personages without limit or fear, so long as one also despaired and offered no alternatives.

In this context, how could we contemplate a reversal of "the times" in court? Was it not errant folly to try—to face a jury selected from this seemingly pummeled, self-centered population? Was it a delusion to feel that the country needed dissidents willing to fight upstream carrying a soaked placard reading, as General Stillwell put it, *"Illegitimati non carborundum"?*[*] There were enough patriots to ride the swift, careless current. Did we not have a duty to our country *as we saw it?* To fulfill this duty, we had to overcome fear of failure. Winning the case was not the only consideration. But this view was not widely shared. A friend's reaction was not comforting. "Do you know what happens to anyone who carries a struggle on too long? The hero turns into a jerk."

---

[*]Don't let the bastards grind you down.

II

The bulldozing gave way to caisson drillers, and caissons to foundations. Then, the frames of houses began to rise into the sky.

Not far away, in the motion picture studios, the work of other blacklisted men—writers—was also making its way, albeit clandestinely. They were writing scripts which were being produced. The prices for scripts were mounting for those who had been working assiduously in the black market. It was again possible to make a living, even as a blacklisted writer.

The first public incident relating to the blacklisted revolved about Michael Wilson. Some years before, at Paramount, he had written the screenplay of *Friendly Persuasion* for William Wyler. Now it was announced that Wyler was about to make the film at Allied Artists with Gary Cooper starring. Wilson asked Wyler for assurance that his name would appear on the screen. He was told that it would not. Wilson appealed to the Screen Writers Guild's arbitration committee dealing with credits. The Writers Guild had previously amended its agreement with the producers to permit them to eliminate from the screen the names of any writers who refused to doff their hats to the Un-American Activities Committee but had kept its arbitration committee intact. Although the committee awarded sole screen credit to Michael Wilson, the producers, nevertheless, exercised their right under the Guild contract to withhold credit, and no credit appeared on the film. Then the membership of the Screen Writers Guild, in secret ballot, nominated Wilson's script for an Academy Award. In order to "defend" the industry against his winning the award, the board of the Academy of Motion Picture Arts and Sciences eliminated Wilson's name from the final list from which the award winner could be chosen. Subsequently the film entered the Cannes festival to represent the American motion picture industry, where it won the award for the best picture made anywhere in the world in the year 1956, even though, according to its credits, it had never been written.

Hypocrisy in the film capital of the world received a further undressing when *The Brave One* won the Academy Award as the best original screen play of the year. But Robert Rich, its "author," did not walk up the steps of the theater, jauntily, to receive his Oscar. No one walked up at all. The Oscar, to the chagrin of the industry, was unclaimed. The trail to the possible author ended at the door of Dalton Trumbo, one of the Hollywood Ten. Trumbo at that time refused to say whether he was or was not Robert Rich, but, with a mynah bird propped on his shoulder for the TV cameras, he stated, with glinting eyes, that he had won more than one and less than four Oscars in the ten years of his blacklisting. One would have thought that the blacklist would have been hooted out of its bombed cellars by then. But it continued. And the cracks in it continued to appear.

Although Jules Dassin was turned down as a director for an American film, he built a routine French film, *Rififi*, into a fantastic technical accomplishment and a tremendous box-office success. Rumor, later confirmed, had it that Mike Wilson was writing *The Bridge on the River Kwai*. Other rumors indicated that Carl Foreman had collaborated with him. In the United States rumor brought news that Dalton Trumbo was writing *Spartacus*—and even more important news that he was to receive screen credit. Stanley Kramer had purchased an original screen play by two writers, one of them named Nathan Douglas. *The Defiant Ones*, however, was written not by Nathan Douglas, who was unknown, but by Nedrick Young, blacklisted. And rumor had it that at the appropriate time Ned Young would identify himself, with Mr. Kramer's knowledge. Guy Endore's novel, *King of Paris*, published by Simon and Schuster, was taken by the Book-of-the-Month Club. Albert Maltz was writing a black market screenplay in Mexico. And half a dozen blacklisted writers were turning out product in Europe.

The report of each new crack in the self-righteous mask of Hollywood filled us with expectation of momentary change. How long would an American industry continue to deny work, and to deny credit for work used? How much needed to be done for them by those they suppressed before they turned a finger in their own behalf? Apparently a great deal. For while the industry was gladly counting the profits from films the blacklisted had helped to create for it, both new films and hundreds of old ones sold to TV, it was sending emissaries to the American Legion to swear upon a stack of industry Bibles that the blacklist was in force and that over two hundred individuals were excluded from the industry.

III

When the deposition of the plaintiff corporations through Simon Laz-arus, as their president, had finally been completed by the defen-dants' counsel, they informed George Brussel that they now wished to examine the plaintiffs through Herbert Biberman and Paul Jarrico as *managing agents*. This was precisely the event that George had pre-pared affidavits to preclude. He presented a motion before judge Sug-arman to debar the defendants from examining us as managing agents since we had formally and legally resigned two and a half years before.

Judge Sugarman acknowledged that our resignations had been tendered and accepted and that we were, in fact, no longer officers of the corporations. But he found that, nevertheless, "it is inconceivable on the evidence presented that if a situation arose requiring action by Biberman and Jarrico in furtherance of plaintiff's interests, they would not gladly take such action."

Subsequent events proved judge Sugarman wrong, for we both refused to obey his order and would have persisted in our refusal even if the case had been permanently dismissed. But our later dis-proof of the judge's prophecy did not wash away his finding. We were deemed by his decision to be permanently indentured officers of the corporations, incapable of divorcement by will of either. We were ordered to appear for deposition as managing agents for the plaintiffs. This meant that we had been set up for limitless political questioning to which we were legally ordered to accede. Declared to be corporate instruments, we were deprived of all individual rights to constitu-tional privileges. I was notified by George Brussel of the ruling and asked to submit myself for deposition as managing agent for the plaintiffs.

I arrived in New York, engaged my own counsel, told George Brussel that I was ready to appear as a voluntary witness in order to aid in moving the case forward, but that under no circumstances, however punishing it might be to the plaintiffs, would I appear as managing agent. I was not a managing agent, I had not lifted a finger with respect to the corporations' affairs for several years, and I would not accept the loss of my personal rights and privileges.

I appeared for the deposition with my personal attorney, Mr. Leonard Boudin. When Mr. Myles Lane, chief counsel for the producer–distributor defendants and the two motion picture producer associations, heard that Mr. Brussel had failed to produce me as managing agent, and that I had produced myself as a voluntary witness, he stated that he was proceeding to examine me in the guise in which the judge had ordered me to appear. Mr. Brussel stated that no matter what Mr. Lane wished to do, the plaintiffs did not recognize me as their managing agent; I was there as a voluntary witness.

Mr. Lane proceeded. He asked not one question that related to *Salt of the Earth.* He asked the question concerning membership in the Communist party, which I had refused to answer before the Un-American Activities Committee, and hundreds of other questions about my associations, the periodicals I read or wrote for, my friends and their lives, views, reading habits, associations and affiliations. I refused to answer all but a few—one of those being whether I believed in the overthrow of the government by force and violence. I stated that I did not.

When I would not answer the stock questions, on the grounds that they were irrelevant and destructive of my individual constitutional rights and privileges, Mr. Lane appeared before judge Sugarman, stating that I had refused the court's order to appear as a managing agent in order not to answer questions, and requesting that I be compelled to answer.

In an unusual action, the judge asked Mr. Lane if he would move that our case be dismissed. Mr. Lane moved for dismissal and judge Sugarman granted the motion. We were thrown out of court. The order was dated September 25, 1959. It took a year and a half until a ruling came down from the appellate court which held that the lower court, in not granting a hearing, had been erroneous. A hearing was ordered, intimating that dismissal was too severe.

Some six months later, under judge Dimock, the hearing was held. The judge stated that since Mr. Biberman had refused to answer certain questions in any forum that had been made available to him through fourteen years, it was doubtful that he would choose the federal court, Southern District of New York, in which to break the precedent. He also believed that the defendants did not require proof of their allegations that Jarrico and I were or had been Communists. It was sufficient for their purposes if they could allege that such was the common, prevalent belief in the community, and the trial judge could make such belief available to the defendants to use in the trial for whatever purposes he might deem it valid.

This seemed like a total victory for the plaintiffs, as dismissal had been reversed, but it was in fact a victory that was also a setback. It did not *introduce* the question of communism, Communists and subversives into the case. We had done that when we alleged in our complaint that the Waldorf Declaration's commitment to "eliminate Communists, and alleged Communists and subversives from the motion picture industry" was the beginning of the conspiracy under which we had suffered. However, now the defendants had the right conclusively to label as Communists certain individuals associated with *Salt of the Earth*, specifically Paul Jarrico and myself. Thus the defendants had a good handle with which to exploit the issue. They might now pose as patriots who had sought to combat these subversives.

At this very time, a young anti-trust lawyer, David Shapiro, of the firm of Dickstein, Shapiro and Galligan of Washington and New York, was asked by a number of the blacklisted in Hollywood to meet with them to discuss a new turn in anti-trust law following the Supreme Court decision in the Klors case the previous spring. Prior to Klors, the court had demanded more than concerted action in restraint of trade. It had required proof of public injury stemming from the conspiracy. In Klors it ruled that if two or more persons entered into an agreement in restraint of trade, that agreement was in and of itself a violation, a *per se* violation, the restraint residing in the agreeing parties' restraining of themselves from competing. The court was not required to look to any injury beyond the agreement itself.

Following the discussion the Hollywood group asked Shapiro if he would represent them in an anti-trust suit against the major studios, a suit against the agreement to blacklist.

In the fall of 1961, the Emergency Civil Liberties Committee, founded by Corliss Lamont, arranged a meeting at Carnegie Hall in New York to describe the issues in this case, known as *Young* vs. *M.P.A.A. et al.* Ned Young, Gale and I had agreed to speak at the meeting. I arrived in New York early to assist in arranging the meeting and, as had become my pleasant habit by then, I accepted George and Eleanor Brussel's invitation to stay with them at their home in Elmsford.

George and I drove into town the morning after my arrival. We talked of the six years of prodigious labor which had been expended in attempting to bring the *Salt of the Earth* case to trial. I commented upon our more than profound appreciation of George's limitless gift of his office, his staff, his endless energy and dedication to the case. Not merely beyond duty—beyond credibility. George spoke in his characteristic low, measured voice of what the case had done to enlarge his own horizons, how very much it meant to him personally. He also made it clear that unless the heavy atmosphere of official repression and popular acceptance of it lifted, the case could well be lost. But he spoke of his own increasing awareness that certain cases needed to be fought without regard to victory or defeat. He described his enjoyment of the special kind of companionship that developed among those engaged in such efforts. He spoke of "moral compulsions"—the Sunday morning kind—which are, upon examination, so often merely ideals which tie us not at all to action. To transform them into ideas which ran in the current of reality took the kind of relentless battle in which we were engaged, a fight against what our opponents called "the nature of things." "Nature of things, indeed," George said. "That, as I have come to see it, is the lie consummate. People, not things, define nature. People in action against 'things as they are.'"

Then he said something for which, as lawyers use the language, there was no foundation laid. The $20,000 he had received from the corporations as fee, had, through his investing of it, grown to

$24,500. I couldn't imagine why he wished to discuss his personal investments with me and suggested as much.

"I have never had any doubt but that I have a legal right to that money," George said. "But I have never been satisfied that I had a moral right to it. And I worry about what would happen to this case if anything happened to me."

Two weeks later George Brussel was dead following a heart attack.

And $24,500 had been set aside by his estate to be returned to the corporations so that the litigation of *Salt of the Earth* might continue. Simon Lazarus, as president of the corporations, refused to accept the money. We discovered that George had not left a large estate and that such a sum of money was of importance to Eleanor, left with two small children. But Eleanor was adamant. George's wish in this matter was to be respected. Additionally, it was her own. She was not only George's wife and a co-sponsor of his having taken the case, she was also archivist of the records and a partisan in her own right.

After consultations, Eleanor and Ben Margolis determined that the firm of Dickstein, Shapiro and Galligan be engaged to handle the litigation.

Salt of the Earth was ending its sixth year of effort to reach trial. The blacklist was entering its fifteenth year. But the indomitable commitment of persons like George and Eleanor Brussel was of infinitely older vintage.

IV

This, then, was the posture of the case when the new attorneys pre-pared Paul Jarrico—"managing agent"—for his deposition by the defendants' counsel. Paul had just returned from two and a half years of work in Europe in his profession's black market.

Paul informed the attorneys that he would state that he was not a Communist, if the question were asked, but would refuse to answer any questions about the time before he left for Paris. His deposition proceeded and lasted for twenty-two days. When I read its several thousand pages just before trial began three years later, I understood why the attorneys had been excited about him and it. I understood why even the attorneys for the defendants had expressed their plea-sure in working with him. They had "made no bay" with him, but that was evidently beside the point, even for them. His demeanor, cooperativeness, openness had commanded absolute respect. *His memory!* Total recall barely describes his faculties. He had saved every scrap of paper upon which he had ever typed, written, scrawled, or fingerpainted since the age of eighteen months, each meticulously filed and cross-filed in absolute chronology and finally committed to memory. He had maintained an AGENDA, a gallic invention in the shape of an india paper pocket notebook which became famous dur-ing the trial. All the lawyers on both sides treated it with neo-Biblical reverence. For in these notebooks must have been inscribed what he had done every hour on the hour since his Bar-Mitzvah.

In preparation for trial, I suffered chagrin that brought me to the edge of a temptation to destroy myself. Biberman, the fileless, the unpapered soul, had only a run-of-the-mill memory and an incom-plete file with which to reconstruct in detail events that had occurred over ten years before. Valuable evidence was not available because I had no carbon copies of letters written by hand during the busy years of directing and attempting to distribute the film. When the lawyers addressed a query to both Paul and me regarding an event and we disagreed, I was always wrong. I walked the streets late at night after preparing for the next day's trial, contemplating the neat and orderly soul I had imagined I possessed now revealed as an uncentered, slovenly de-concentration camp.

At the end of *twenty-two days* of deposition, after Paul had refused to answer questions about his political life before 1959, Mr. Lane and his co-counsel again tried to compel answers. Such an order was entered. Paul still refused. A hearing was arranged by counsel for the defendants before judge Metzner asking to have the case dismissed. Judge Metzner, following the rulings of both the appellate court and judge Dimock, refused. But he issued a *Sanction Order* in the defendants' behalf. This was a sanction against the plaintiffs. It established, *for the purpose of this case only,* and to whatever use the trial judge would deem it appropriate, that everyone in the plaintiff corporations, and all those associated with them in the making of *Salt of the Earth,* could be deemed to have been Communists.

The plaintiffs had the alternative of giving up the case or carrying the burden. To have given up would have been to surrender their duty to the corporations' note-holders to attempt to expose the defendants through the winnowing process of a jury trial. It would have been to give up the opportunity to lead a jury through the calumnies to the injuries. It would have been to express no confidence in the American jury system. The plaintiff corporations accepted the burden in all soberness and moved toward trial—which was yet several years away.

For six-and-a-half years, in accordance with the procedures of the federal court in the Southern District of New York, day-to-day decisions were referred to the judge sitting for this purpose. In these years, the various lawyers had appeared before seven different judges for fairly major decisions. By now the documents upon which new decisions would have to be based, including complaint, pleadings, briefs, counterbriefs, motions, depositions, etc., occupied a seven-foot shelf. Swift decisions were well nigh impossible and the Siamese twins, time and money, were breathing heavily down the backs of the plaintiffs. A gambling decision was made—to ask Chief judge Sylvester J. Ryan for a permanent judge to be assigned to this case.

This meant facing the possibility of an unhappy throw of the judicial dice. Yet, better face the full facts now, the plaintiffs' lawyers concluded. In two years they would have the opportunity of attempting to win some accommodation by the judge to their theories, positions and arguments.

On January 4th, 1963, the case was assigned to judge Harold R. Tyler, Jr. for all purposes. Judge Tyler was a relatively new judge who had formerly been attorney for the Civil Rights Division of the Department of justice.

In the winter of the seventh year of litigation the delivery of all discovery documents and the taking of depositions had been completed by both sides. A deposition is to all intents and purposes a run-through of the trial with a witness without the judge and jury being present. The process is of course under total review by the judge. The purpose of the deposition is to eliminate, as much as possible, any element of surprise in the actual trial. Both sides enter trial aware of the facts to be presented and therefore able to deal with them knowledgeably. A proper deposition presumes meticulous preparation by the attorney conducting it. Every document, every piece of evidence which remotely relates to the deponent must have been studied, coordinated with all other associated elements and witnesses. For the plaintiffs this was the assignment given Arthur Galligan.

From the winter of 1961 through trial in the fall of 1964 he was archivist of this case and he conducted most of the depositions. Young, athletic, black-haired, handsome, vigorous, aye, indestructible, he shuffled the documents ten to twelve hours a day, seven days most weeks, for two years. They were indexed, cross-indexed, and arranged in referenced categories for reassortment when the case went from defendants to plaintiffs or plaintiffs to defendants. He controlled them as a splendid gambler controls a deck of cards. Arthur surrounded his work with a robust and inexhaustible humor. He was possessed of an utterly delicious vocabulary composed of two parts Yiddish, picked up in this Yiddish speech-loving city of New York, two parts straight, ugly New Yorkese, one part Shakespeare, and one part Irish profanity and belligerence. He blended them into a cradle of supporting language which rocked exasperation and fatigue out of himself and any fortunate enough to be near him.

David Shapiro was author of a constant flow of briefs to the judge. In physical form David is a lowering bullock, in emotion and dedicated intellect an incandescent talmudic scholar. The law is his passion. And if it is not precisely his love—the concept of love here is indistinct—then it is his daemon. Totally on the manic side, restless, adventurous, never satisfied that the ultimate case has been found, and himself found by dawn more often in his office library than in his bed, he pored, like an intellectually avaricious Faust, over his own kind of exotica. And if, at 3 A.M., the saving case were found, his client might well be called by David heralding the glad tidings with the naturalness of a parent handing a child a popsicle. David possessed two weather-vane phrases, indicating hot and cold. Before he had found "the" case it was, "I've got a problem." After "the" case was in hand, "I've got them *locked* on the law." A rigid civil libertarian, a passionate devotee of "one way for all men and free speech for everybody," he defended the Nazi Rockwell, and he continued to do so even after Rockwell had informed him that the fact that he was acting as his lawyer would not wipe out what was coming to him as a Jew when Rockwell's day came. David cursed him and continued to defend him, for from his point of view no one was so vile he had lost his right "to shoot his—face off."

As massive in body and in law-sense as was David, so lean and delicate and precise was Sidney Dickstein. He spoke sculptured English. His vocabulary, and his manner of speaking it, indicated a master craftsman. His speech to juries, judges and to friends alike retained that touch of formality which betokened an ingrained composure. To my observations, usually apologetic, about my concept of this or that point in the case, Arthur would be apt to say, "Don't *hock mir ah chainik,* you can't do that in a courtroom." David would tend to say, "Herbert, please—we haven't got all night—I'm talking cases." Sidney would smile and say, quietly, "Interesting—but not admissible."

When Ben Margolis arrived to take over chief-counselship of the case during trial, a team was created which won the respect and, I believe, even the affection of those in the courtroom. There were undoubtedly a few exceptions, but they were in the minority. The judge did not hesitate to express his appreciation of the memos which came regularly from David—and were expatiated upon orally by Sidney. Sidney's cross-examinations were concise and sharp. Arthur sat with his documents and rarely failed to produce precisely what the examining lawyers wished. And Ben Margolis, disciplined, organized, trained by the very toughest political cases over the hardest years of such litigation, had an utterly instinctual sense of the heart of a case and of an argument. Quiet, courteous, and always direct, he could lay a foundation for friend and for foe with equal power.

At nine o'clock in the morning of September 9th, as the lawyers for the plaintiffs prepared to leave for court from their headquarters in the Marcy Hotel, 95th Street and West End Avenue, the order of witnesses had been tentatively set. Paul Jarrico was to be first and I was to be last. We were well along in our preparation. Legal memoranda had been sent into the court. That morning the jury would be selected. Ben would then outline to them the facts to prove conspiracy. He was well aware that what could convince unbiased minds might fail to reach subconsciously biased ones. Therefore the jury must also be assisted in overcoming bias, labeling. Could this be accomplished? Our lawyers thought we had a 25 per cent chance. Our opponents, we learned later, did not think we had a 5 per cent chance of having the judge submit the case to the jury.

I did not go to court that first day. We needed money desperately—about fifteen thousand dollars—to guarantee that we would have a transcript of each day's session, indispensable for cross-examination. Our attorneys were willing, if they had to, to try the case with only occasional portions of the daily transcript made available to them. They prepared to cancel the order for the transcript until further notice. I asked them for several days in which to make a serious attempt to find some financial help. I tried. I failed. The issue was old. People had lost interest. I told the lawyers I had promising leads— when I had none whatsoever. I listed for myself names of persons in the theater whom I had known, some only slightly. I made my first call.

Behind the desk, in shirt sleeves, sat a man with massive shoulders, a strong neck and a head which at once reminded me of a sculpture of the head of Solon, the first Greek legislator, I had seen somewhere. I told my story.

He asked several questions to determine for himself whether our case would make a contribution to the general welfare or whether it was something of a private vendetta. I said that it appeared to me that we were fighting for the civil liberties of free enterprise—a free market for every American, and without exception.

"I'll give you five thousand dollars."

It was almost too quickly granted, one-third the sum the lawyers required. I wanted to say that he deserved to hear more before he committed himself. But he began to speak. "The only views that are dangerous are those that are bottled up. It's a duty to safety to encourage speech and to make it accessible. Under the Constitution your rights are my duty—and vice versa. Constitutional guarantees are more than moral obligations. They are open bank accounts for Americans to draw on freely. That's the bank that underwrites the security of the whole country. The only bank that does. Draw on it!"

That night I screened the film for him in our apartment. He found it a good film. "If you need another five thousand dollars, let me know. I don't want to underwrite the whole case, but I want to do my part."

We did require the additional sum. And we received it. A transcript was made available to our attorneys for the entire trial. By insisting on finding the money to wage the trial with some equality of means, we also found someone who reidentified us for ourselves.

V

It is not the purpose here to render a full and objective account of the trial, the transcript of which covered almost seven thousand pages. Nor to reveal the attorneys' technical or vocal brilliance, or to create courtroom drama. This was not a glamor trial. For the most part the trial was undramatic. Many days there was not a single spectator present. Not a word appeared in the press until the verdict was announced. An atmosphere of "relaxed tension" permitted the case to develop with minimum sensationalism.

Although I spent some six of the nine and a half weeks of the trial in the courtroom and almost every evening until midnight or beyond with the lawyers in their suite at the Marcy Hotel, I doubt my capacity to give a valid legal account of the proceedings. The law is a meticulous and exacting discipline.

What follows is my story of the trial, my selection of a few excerpts from the testimony that seem to me to illustrate what I consider the more important issues in this case.

In the city of New York there are perhaps a million Negroes and a half million Puerto Ricans. The panel of one hundred and fifty from which the jury was to be chosen included two Negroes and not one Puerto Rican, so far as the plaintiffs' attorneys could determine. The jury was all white. The foreman was a man who worked for an airline company. The rest were accountants, engineers, an ex-policeman, the president of an investment house and two women whose husbands worked for Con Edison and the water department. The lawyers returned from the selection of the jury concerned.

A jury of peers for a film dealing with embattled members of a minority might well have included a Negro, a Puerto Rican—persons who know the edges of poverty, of discrimination and who could have brought sensual understanding to the deliberations. It might have included a teacher or an artist—an individual who understands that the subject matter of art is as open to the pauper as the prince, to darkness as to light, to the storms of soul and nature as to sunlight and laughter. Such individuals were quickly weeded out by the lawyers for the defense. For them, a teacher was anathema. They clung to the skills which served big business. This was not difficult since this was the basic composition of the panel. Both sides knew that in the psychological areas of the jurors' psyches probably lay the clue to victory, that the matters of fact and law would all be washed, finally, in their capacity to grant equality before the law to dissidents. Not to alleged dissidents, but to sanctions—declared, court-designated dissidents: Communists, subversives. The jury had, each one, professed to the judge that he could render justice without bias even to Communists and subversives. All the fat was in the fire of the law for rendering. Trial could proceed. It had taken eight years—but we were in court.

The next morning Ben opened the trial with an address to the jury. He told the story presented in this book in brief, suggesting those major events plaintiffs would prove to indicate clear violation of the anti-trust laws by the defendants. Then he added:

MARGOLIS: Let me make one thing crystal clear. The three I have named... seek in this litigation to establish their right, as part of the right of any persons regardless of views and associations, to compete in the market place whether their ideas be popular or unpopular, Communists, anti-Communists, or don't care about it. They are here to protect their right to continue to offer their works to the public without accounting to a private group for their beliefs and associations, with the public of course free to accept or reject their product for any reason that it chooses.

You may hear the word "Communist" echo and re-echo from the mouths of defense counsel throughout this trial. You may be told that person after person who has been connected with the plaintiffs was a Communist or belonged to organizations listed as subversive or Communist-front organizations by various committees or various governmental and nongovernmental bodies. So be it. *For the purpose of this litigation, ladies and gentlemen, we do not intend to challenge these contentions.*

Mr. Myles Lane opened for the defense. He countered the specific charges of conspiracy made by Ben Margolis. Then he came to the very special nitty-gritty of the defendants' argument:

LANE: What was the climate of the time? You ladies and gentlemen remember the same as I do.

The "climate of the time"! Out of an English prison 262 years before, Daniel DeFoe lampooned this concept as noisome political palaver to validate crimes. The "climate of the time"! An argument later used to justify the gassing of human beings, an argument used to explain away the murder of innocents under Stalin. But in 1964, in New York City, in the United States of America, chief-counsel for defendants, Mr. Lane, still proceeded to string a necklace for the throat of the plaintiffs, with the beads of "the time."

LANE: First of all, there was a national feeling, as I recall it, of revulsion for the Communists. We had the Korean War just about that time when the Soviets went over to the side of the Chinese and the North Koreans. We had in this very building in that period the Alger Hiss case. We proved these things through witnesses. And we had the Rosenberg case right in this very room. And the two Smith Act cases, where these Communists, the first- and the second-string Communists, were convicted of a conspiracy to overthrow the United States by force and by violence, one before Judge Medina, you may recall, and the other before Judge Dimock. And in the same building we had the Remington case.

The necklace was strung. The jury would now require considerable help to come fresh to the real issues in this case.

LANE: They started out at that time with a Communistic background to the picture, with a picture that was produced, distributed, financed, acted all by members, persons who were identified as members of the Communist party. So I say they started out at that time I believe with two strikes on them.

There was the "sanction order" in full flower.

LANE: When a company is formed, if it is any kind of company, whether it is an independent or one of the majors, you usually do it through some reputable financing outfit. You do it through banks or you do it through some organization such as that. But the very fact that these people went out and on a shoestring tried to make a picture that was going to compete with all the product which the other companies had will give you some idea of the chance that picture had from the inception.

           … … … … … … … …

           They shot the picture in February of 1953, and in the picture itself they had five professionals, if you can imagine that, five professionals. Three of the professionals, I believe—and I think we will be able to prove it— were members of the Communist party…. And they brought a Mexican woman up from Mexico, a woman by the name of Revueltas. I don't know what she was. But the other actors, outside of Mrs. or Miss Revueltas, were on a wage scale. I think they got less than $100 a week for working on the project. The leading man in the picture was the head of the local Mine, Mill and Smelter Workers Union, which as I say again, was a Red-dominated union, a man by the name of Chakon or Chason, spelled C-h-a-c-o-n.

In the eight years of litigation Mr. Lane had not been able to learn to pronounce this single Spanish name, although tutored by a number of the plaintiffs' counsel. After having heard it during nine weeks of the trial he still made it sound like a firecracker that did not go off. He seemed slow at catching the beauties of foreign speech or people. "They brought a Mexican woman up from Mexico," he had said. Not even a Mexican actress. Nor even a Mexican national. A *Mexican woman*. Ignominy doubled in a female. God forbid Duse had been alive and we had imported her!

Well, there the jury had it from Mr. Lane. A few ousted Communists form a little Communist company and try to compete with the massive product of the giant movie corporations—and dare to share the film's main credit title with a Red-dominated union, The International Union of Mine, Mill and Smelter Workers, an incomprehensible effrontery to such august main titles as MGM's "Ars Gratia Artis," emblazoned above the roaring head of Leo the Lion.

But Mr. Lane had not yet totally interred us via the fatal malady of Red-dominated Don Quixotism. He measured our efforts against "normal practice."

Normal practice! Never for an instant during the entire five-year-long involvement with the film had we been permitted one breath of normalcy. Now to be chastised and ridiculed because we had not gone to banks for money, because we had not used Hollywood stars for our various roles, made a kind of helpless and debilitating anger paralyze me. Ah, those possessors of "normal" practices. The proud advocates of the normally affluent, normally blacklisting... whoops!

The word "blacklisting" had been denied us by the judge. Blacklisting meant conspiracy and we had not yet proved conspiracy. Paul Jarrico, testifying as to how he, Simon Lazarus and I came to form a company, had used the word for the second time, having been warned by the judge that it was an inadmissible word. At Ben's suggestion Paul found a typical Jarrico euphemism:

MARGOLIS: Suppose we find a phrase. You are referring to people who were unable to obtain work in Hollywood, is that who you are referring to?

JARRICO: I can find many synonyms, Mr. Margolis.

MARGOLIS: Let's use one that is less objectionable.

JARRICO: A large pool of talent had become available in Hollywood

Mr. Lane continued with his animadversions upon the theme of our flouting of normal practice.

LANE: For instance, as I said before, our companies have at least thirty, sometimes more than that, branch offices all over the United States, with a whole corps of salesmen, who go out and try to sell a picture. But here two people came into New York City, with no experience at all, to compete in New York City at that time, and try and get this picture, which was Red-dominated, Red-produced,

Red-directed, Red-financed and Red-acted—they tried
to get this picture distributed and they didn't even have
a distribution agency.

Mr. Lane then fell back into describing how *his* companies go
about the distribution of a film—the *normal* way to do this—the *professional* way:

LANE: Now in a road show the average amount they pay for
              exploitation in New York City—and sometimes, and
              very frequently, the picture fails even with this, it is
              $100,000 that is spent for exploitation, advertising, and
              so forth, on a road show before they open, and then it is
              $20,000 for the first two weeks and two thousand dol-
              lars a week thereafter.... At the same time that that hap-
              pens they must spend several million dollars in national
              advertising to even hope to have a successful picture.

The observation was, of course, sheer fantasy. Few pictures made
in Hollywood spend several million dollars in national advertising.
Mr. Lane had allowed his clients' necessary recourse to advertising
bombast in order to sell indifferent product to overexcite him.

LANE: And the print costs—these prints—you see, when you
              make a picture you must have so many prints to go
              around the country—there are 18,000 theaters or so
              they have around 300 to 350 prints, and those prints for
              black and white cost anywhere from $300 to $450
              apiece. Yet these people, as we will show, came into
              New York with a total of $25,000, nothing more, and
              eight prints. That is all they had at the time they made
              their first showing—eight prints and $25,000 to spend
              on advertising.

But eight prints were six too many for us. In the several years we
sought to break the barriers erected against us, we were never able to
get more than two into use at one time. Since storage facilities, simple
storage facilities—a bin in which to place our film for safekeeping—
were denied us anywhere in New York City, it would have been quite
a problem to store 350 prints in Mr. Irving Fajans' livingroom, where
we had just about enough room to store our precious negative and
the eight prints.

But Mr. Lane continued to elaborate his view of the matter:

LANE: Nationally it was also doomed. As I say, it had no distri-
               bution facilities, no branches, no salesmen, no money. It
               was sponsored by a Red union. It had Wilson and Jarrico
               identified as members of the Communist party before
               the House, and Biberman was one of the Hollywood Ten
               that gave such a disgraceful exhibition in 1947.... *

               ... We will show that this picture failed first because it
               violated what I deem to be the cardinal rule which you
               apply to all of our acts, to our business, to our negotia-
               tions, everything we do, and that is that you cannot
               insult the intelligence of the public; and by flouting [sic]
               communism at a time when there was a public revul-
               sion n against communism, in my opinion, and we will
               prove it from the witness box, was an attempt to insult
               the intelligence of the public....

---

*As I was typing this opening of Mr. Lane's, I stopped to look at that in-
stallment of President Truman's television program dealing with the Mc-
Carthy era. It was illustrated by the Un-American Activities Committee
hearing in 1947 and included clips of the appearances of Lawson, Trumbo and Biberman before that committee. With Mr. Lane's description of
my "disgraceful" appearance on my lap, I listened to Mr. Truman say, "I
made a statement at one time that that committee—the Committee on
Un-American Activities—was the most un-American activity in the
whole government." Mr. Truman also said, "One of my bitterest antago-
nists, Parnell Thomas, was found guilty of a crime, taking kickbacks from
his staff." I recalled that Mr. Thomas was sentenced to a year in jail and
reached there while the Hollywood Ten were still fighting for the First
Amendment in the courts.

VI

The derogation of our competence, while pursued throughout the case by the defense, was irrelevant to the main, issue, namely whether there had been an illegal conspiracy against the film. To prove their case, the plaintiffs built their testimony around two major pieces of evidence, the Waldorf Agreement and the organization of the MPIC. We charged that at a meeting of the motion picture industry at the Waldorf–Astoria Hotel in November 1947 a conspiracy had been initiated to "eliminate subversives from the motion picture industry," a per se illegal act. And that in implementation of this, and as an illustration of its continuity, the producers, with the talent guilds and the I.A.T.S.E. unions, had organized the Motion Picture Industry Council (MPIC) which in 1953 alerted the entire industry to intensify its boycott of *Salt of the Earth*.

The plaintiffs held that the declaration set up a climate of fear in the entire motion picture industry, set it up for the whole foreseeable future, and that for years after the declaration had been proclaimed, it aborted the attempts of the "eliminated" to purchase services and facilities with which to manufacture a product and to enter the market with that product.

In law, the wrong-doer is responsible for the foreseeable consequences of his act. Therefore anyone who knowingly joined in refusing to service those eliminated became a co-conspirator and a potential co-defendant, even if he never spoke to the originators concerning such refusal.

The anti-trust laws, to quote from Sidney Dickstein's summation in this case, are "the lubricant of the private enterprise system." They are the two-way street assuring individual Americans that they can enter a business if they choose to do so and that they have a fair chance to compete for public favor in this business. They assure every *individual* American the right *to refuse to deal* with another individual and also the right *to deal* with whomsoever he pleases, without restraint, without inhibitions, without duress, without the need for *industry-wide systems* and *industry-wide positions*. This choice for *individuals.**

But when we leave the field of *individual* action and enter the field of joint actions, the law sets up its legal restrictions, its interdictions "against." Then, suddenly, what was proper, legal, rightful for one man to do becomes illegal, subject to injunction and treble damages if two or more do it together. This simple rule is, for all its surface clarity, quite difficult to comprehend. I recall my own astonishment at the fantastically far-reaching decisions which stem from this law. In one of David Shapiro's legal memoranda to the judge I read that a group of fire insurance companies could be found guilty of violating the anti-trust laws because, in concert, together, they conspired to refuse to issue policies to known arsonists. What? This was too much even for me.

But the lawyers pointed out that I had misread the law. It did not provide for *giving* a policy to an arsonist. No company was commanded to do so. All that was proscribed was the banding together, in concert, in conspiracy, to *refuse* to do so. For, implicit in concerted action, in economic conspiracy, was that dangerous factor of control of the market— concerted error, concerted concealed purpose, the ending of competition among competitors, the discombobulation of the necessary push and shove of private enterprise, the prevention of the individual from exercising his own, individual right to initiate, terminate, explore, gain or lose based upon his individual entrepreneurship.

Mr. Howell, representing RKO Radio Pictures, now RKO General, Inc., seemed to be defending the industry's right to take such concerted action in his opening statement to the jury:

> ... the only thing he [Mr. Margolis] said... that bears any relationship whatsoever to any motion picture distribution company... was this famous Waldorf Declaration, in 1947. And the claim seems to be, if I understand him correctly, that if an American industry faces a critical industry problem, that can affect the earning abilities of everyone connected with it, it can't together stand up and say, "This is a bad thing which is happening to us and we should take affirmative measures to see that

---

*Insofar as refusals are based upon discrimination because of race, creed or color the public policy described and made into law in the new Civil Rights Act does limit the previous absolute right of refusal based upon any reason or no reason.

this—in this case infiltration of our industry—does not
proceed any further."

Here Mr. Howell touched the issue central to this case—the nature
of the anti-trust laws, and the relation to those laws of the Waldorf Declaration. The anti-trust laws! Can an American industry which faces a critical industry problem together stand up to use Mr. Howell's phrase—and
take affirmative action against it? May the motion picture *industry*, faced
with the accusation that it has been infiltrated by subversive influences,
undertake to "eliminate subversives from the industry"? He put it
squarely. And the legal answer is that it *may not*! Not as a combination of
individual —companies working together, in concert, as an *industry*.

Mr. Lane, more sagacious in these matters, ran—as if from the
plague—to get out from under Mr. Howell's phrase, "together stand up."
He insisted throughout that there was no joint action at Waldorf.

LANE: What was the result of the meeting? Each company,
                 after consultation with legal counsel, decided to issue a
                 press release reflecting their individual employment pol-
                 icies. And being members of this public relations com-
                 mittee that I spoke about, the industry organization, the
                 Motion Picture Association, it was decided to issue one
                 statement instead of 10 or 15 different statements....

                 In other words if you do have an association, such as the
                 Motion Picture Association, it wouldn't make much
                 sense for each company to issue on its own a statement
                 that each one of them was doing this thing separately.

No indeed! Ten or fifteen statements would have taken more
paper; ten or fifteen times as much. *But it would have prevented this
eight-year-long litigation.* It is precisely *to keep all the elements in line* that
such agreements in concert are undertaken. Had they not been
bound together to prevent each other from defection we might have
found leverage somewhere along the way.

Ben Margolis began the case proper with the reading of depositions given in previous litigation. He began with Eric Johnston's
description of the Waldorf meeting given in the case of *Cole* vs. *Loew's
Inc. et al.* in 1949. Lester Cole had sued MGM for breach of contract.
His firing was a result of the agreement that the studio had signed at
the Waldorf. In that case, anti-trust laws were not at issue. Mr.

Johnston, testifying on behalf of MGM, proclaimed that its action was justified. The industry had united itself under his determined leadership to save itself from a bad public relations situation. [*]

JOHNSTON: I felt from there on it was up to them to make a decision; that either they had a right to employ these 10 men... or, on the other hand, they could take action by not employing these 10 men....

Then Mr. James Byrnes, our counsel [ex-Associate Justice of the United States Supreme Court] spoke and spoke at considerable length, about what he felt they should do and he felt that the second action should be taken; that there were some legal risks involved in taking the second action but he thought, with all the circumstances involved, it was an action which should be taken and he recommended that it be taken....

There was so much discussion about it that I felt—and each one had a little different approach—that I felt a committee should be appointed to determine what action should be taken.

So much for Mr. Lane's statement that "each company, after consultation with legal counsel, decided to issue a press release reflecting their *individual* employment practices."

JOHNSTON: ... the next morning we met and Mr. Nicholas Schenck brought in a resolution which he said was satisfactory to the committee. Mr. James Byrnes, our legal counsel, read the resolution and he read it very carefully. He read it completely first and then he read it sentence by sentence and asked if there were any changes or corrections. There were objections to this or feeling that this should be strengthened or something else should be changed, and this took over a period of two or three hours in which the matter was discussed. And, finally, a resolution was prepared that seemingly all present could agree to. Then Mr. Mannix spoke up and said that he

---

[*] The jury in that case found no justification for breach of contract in the stories that Johnston and MGM told about the HUAC hearings and the resulting bad publicity. MGM lost the case and Cole collected damages.

didn't know whether this should be done because of the
California labor laws....

Then Mr. Goldwyn objected and said that he felt that he
didn't want any part of this; that he felt they shouldn't
go ahead with it. I then arose and said that, in my opinion, these men would have to make up their minds—I
think I used the expression "they would have to fish or
cut bait"—that I was sick and tired of presiding over a
meeting where there was so much vacillation: but I had
no authority to do anything; that I wasn't like the czar
of baseball who discharged people if their conduct
wasn't satisfactory and seemingly had that authority;
but I had no such authority; that either they adopt one
of two of these other alternatives, in my opinion, continue to employ men who are supposedly Communists
and justify that employment in the eyes of the American
public or they would have to take the other alternative
and not employ them. But for goodness' sake, to make
up their minds one way or another. There was some
discussion took place after that and finally it was agreed
they would adopt this resolution, which was finally
adopted. And the specific question was asked by me of
Mr. Donald Nelson, who was a representative of the
Society of Independent Producers, of which he was their
president, whether he agreed to this. He said he did.
And I believe one gentleman asked Mr. Goldwyn if he
agreed to it, and I think someone asked Mr. Wanger if
he did, and they said they did and they would go along.

To prove conclusively that the studios, working together as an
industry continued to enforce the Waldorf Agreement, the plaintiffs
introduced evidence of unabated *industry activity* twelve years later, in
1959. In that year Mr. B. B. Kahane of Columbia Pictures, and vice-
president of the Association of Motion Picture Producers, attended an
American Legion convention in Minneapolis.

Mr. Boren, head of the labor committee of that association, testified
via deposition which had been taken previously by Arthur Galligan.

GALLIGAN: Mr. Boren, was there a formal resolution adopted by the
              A.M.P.P. concerning Mr. Kahane going to Minneapolis

to present to the American Legion the concern of the
industry over the broadside attack?

BOREN: There was a resolution authorizing him to go to
              Minneapolis.

GALLIGAN: And to your knowledge, sir, were his expenses paid by
              the A.M.P.P.?

BOREN: They were.

Testimony as to Mr. Kahane's statements at the convention was
given in court by Mr. Edward Magnuson, an associate editor of *Time*
magazine. In 1959, he was a reporter for the Minneapolis *Tribune* and
he attended the meeting of the Americanism commission of the
American Legion.

GALLIGAN: Can you tell us what you recall, sir, generally, of what
              Mr. Kahane said to the commission at this time?

MAGNUSON: Yes. He was speaking on the subject of the problem of
              alleged Communists being at work in the industry, and
              what the industry was doing to get them out of those
              jobs.

              I remember he mentioned a list of some 200 names that
              he said the House Un-American Activities Committee
              had compiled and that also he had gotten —the industry
              had gotten—all but a very small number of those out of
              work; they were no longer at work. I don't remember
              the specifics he gave. It was a very small proportion....

              His general statement was that the majors, the big com-
              panies, were doing a good job of handling this problem,
              that if there was a problem it was with the small inde-
              pendent companies, over which there was no control.

Mr. Dore Schary, who had been present at Waldorf in his capacity as
vice-president in charge of production at RKO, was questioned about the
implementation of the agreement. In 1948, he had gone to MGM as head
of production, and Ben queried him about the so-called clearance program that had been initiated there as a result of the Waldorf Agreement.

MARGOLIS: And during that period of time was there a procedure at
MGM for checking the political background and activities of employees or prospective employees?

           ... ...

SCHARY: Yes. There was an executive at MGM, one Louis K. Sidney, who was appointed by the president of the company, Mr. Nicholas Schenck, to check the employment
of people. I know that when writers—when I, for
instance, wanted to employ writers, I would advise Kenneth McKenna, who was in charge of writers, that I
wanted that writer employed. Kenneth McKenna would
then go to Louis Sidney to check whether or not,
according to Louis Sidney's information, that man was
either a Communist or might be a Communist. I never
saw those lists, I never became involved in them,
because I felt, as I had felt originally, that the entire procedure was one I didn't approve of, so I stayed away
from it completely.

Defense counsel freely admitted all that Mr. Schary said, but
insisted that each studio did this separately, individually, with no contact with other studios, unions, guilds or the American Legion. This
was argued as evidence for no conspiracy.[*]

Testimony, however, suggested that this was not so. The studios
seemed to have become quite dependent on Mr. Roy M. Brewer, then
the international representative in Hollywood of the I.A.T.S.E., in carrying out the "message of Waldorf"—excommunicating or rehabili-
tating alleged "subversives."

A deposition had been taken by Arthur Galligan of Mr. E. Y. (Yip)
Harburg, author and librettist of many stage and screen musicals,
including The Wizard of Oz, and Finian's Rainbow. Harburg had been
blacklisted and MGM wanted him cleared. Mr. Arthur Freed, a producer at MGM in Hollywood suggested Harburg see Brewer. In the
deposition:

------

*Actually, individual implementation of an industry-wide conspiracy
does not escape the penalty of the law. It is the institution of the conspiracy, not the manner in which it is carried out, which constitutes the violation.

GALLIGAN: Now, what else did Mr. Freed say to you at that meeting;
              and, what else did you say to him?

HARBURG: He said, he would call Brewer, and ask him for an
              appointment for me, and that he, himself, had pleaded
              with Brewer—telling him that he knew me for a long
              time, and that he was sure that I was O.K. In other
              words, he was putting in every good word possible that
              he could, with Mr. Brewer to clear me.

              ... ...

GALLIGAN: Who asked you, Mr. Harburg, as best you can recall,
              whether you were a member of the various organiza-
              tions listed in Red Channels?

HARBURG: Mr. Brewer.

              ... ...

HARBURG: Specifically I recall his asking me why—

GALLIGAN: Who is "he," sir?

HARBURG: Brewer. Why did I join the committee—the Hollywood
              Committee for Arts and Sciences.

LANE: Well, what did he say?

HARBURG: And, he said, "Don't you know that this is a front of the
              Communist party?" And my answer to that in general, I
              believe, "I don't know that it's a front—never did know
              that it's a front"—and if it was a front—I don't see how
              it could be a front, when I, myself, helped to organize
              that thing, with some members—some other writers
              and artists, who were at that time trying to find some
              ways and means of reelecting Roosevelt.

              ... ...

GALLIGAN: Did you have a conversation with Mr. Freed at that time
              relative to your meeting with Mr. Brewer?

HARBURG: Yes, I did.

GALLIGAN: Will you tell us, as best you can recall, what you said to
              Mr. Freed, and what he said to you.

... ...

HARBURG: I told Mr. Freed what I had gone through—I said, "Also
            what I was incensed about was that it wasn't my mem-
            bership in the party that he accused me of, because he
            didn't. Brewer didn't accuse me of being a member of
            the party; he accused me of having thoughts leaning
            toward—at one point, what he called, being overbal-
            anced, so that I could become a member of the party;
            that I was predisposed to it." I said, "This made me a lit-
            tle angry, and I thought it was ignominious."

... ...

GALLIGAN: And what did Mr. Freed say to you, if anything?

HARBURG: I don't quite remember but, he did say, "Damn it; the
            hell! We can't get a clearance of any member, any artist
            we want around here to work for us, unless he O.K.'s it;
            and, he has got us all in a cul-de-sac, more or less"—he
            may have used the word "bottleneck." And that, "He
            has got us where he wants to," he says, "he is really put-
            ting the studio on the spot."

GALLIGAN: Did he ask you to go and see Mr. Brewer again, sir?

HARBURG: Yes. He said he was going to talk to Brewer, and he said,
            "By God! You go and see him again."

GALLIGAN: And did you, thereafter, go and see Mr. Brewer again?

HARBURG: Yes, I did.

... ...

GALLIGAN: If possible, we would like dialogue—if you can recall, sir.

... ...

HARBURG: "We know you are not a member of the Communist
            party; but, you have a big, bad record of having joined
            organizations, which you probably thought were liberal
            and reform, but, in essence, you were really a dupe of
            the Communist party, without knowing it. And if you
            want to save yourself—if you will do one thing for us —
            if you will do one thing for us, you will put yourself in

good with everybody. Write an article for the American
Legion magazine.

....

HARBURG: And they took out an American Legion magazine, and
               they said, "Now, here is an article by X" and, I think the
               article was entitled "I was a Dupe for the Communist
               party."*

....

HARBURG: And I said, "I was never a dupe for the Communist
               party; I was never a dupe for the Communist party; I
               was never a dupe for any party. I am a person who
               thinks for myself, and who tries to fight for some kind of
               justice. I have devoted my life to saying, in my works
               and deeds, things that I think are unjust, and fighting
               for a little better world—just a little better society; and
               that each of these organizations I joined, I joined not
               because I was a dupe for anybody—except in my own
               conscience—"

GALLIGAN: Did you tell them that you would not write such an arti-
               cle, sir?

HARBURG: And I said, "On top of that, I consider the American
               Legion magazine, from a literary point of view, a third-
               rate magazine; and, I try to write for first-class papers. I
               try to do first-class shows, and why should I write for
               one that, literarily, is not up to my standard."

....

   Mr. Harburg did not go to work at MGM. His lawyer, Mr. A. L.
Berman, suggested, he said, that the man to see was a Mr. O'Neil of
the American Legion.
   Here, the plaintiffs produced important pieces of the conspiracy
puzzle. An MGM producer had sent a writer to Brewer in the hope
that he, Brewer, would permit the studio to engage him. What if

---

*In order not to bring undue attention to individuals not connected with
the issues of the trial, the judge ordered names to be eliminated and letters used to identify them.

MGM refused to knuckle under to Brewer, and had hired the writer? Could Mr. Brewer then unleash the Legion upon MGM? If the Industry–MPIC–Brewer–Legion collaboration could be established, that, to quote David Shapiro, "was the ball-game."

The reading of the deposition continued:

GALLIGAN: Mr. Harburg, I show you exhibit 6 for identification and ask you if you wrote that letter to Mr. O'Neil.

HARBURG: Yes.

GALLIGAN: How did you come to write that letter?

HARBURG: It was the aftermath of the meeting with Mr. O'Neil in which he asked me whether I wouldn't send him a letter verifying our conversation.

GALLIGAN: Did he tell you why he wanted such a letter?

HARBURG: Just to have it on his files and his records for the American Legion.

GALLIGAN: Did he tell you what he intended to do with it once he got it?

HARBURG: No, he didn't.

GALLIGAN: Did he ask you to send him a copy of the letter that you had sent to Mr. Arthur Freed in October of 1962?

HARBURG: I don't think so.

GALLIGAN: Exhibit 6 refers to your enclosing a copy of a letter. I am asking whether you enclosed that of your own volition or whether Mr. O'Neil asked you to enclose it.

HARBURG: I don't recall. I told him I had written a letter to Arthur Freed. I told him I had seen Mr. Brewer and I said I would enclose a copy of that letter to him, which he thought would be very good.

GALLIGAN: And do you recall so enclosing it?

HARBURG: Yes, I did. I say so here. I say, "I am enclosing a copy of my letter to Arthur Freed." I remember enclosing a song I wrote, "Across Country." I also enclosed some songs that I had been writing for the Army, that the Army was at that time giving or presenting.

GALLIGAN: Did Mr. O'Neil ask you to enclose those, sir?

HARBURG: I think he did, yes. I told him. Because he knew the Army was doing my stuff. He knew the Army was performing my stuff. I said, "If the Army can perform my stuff, why can't MGM—why can't the studios be performing it?"

GALLIGAN: Was that part of your conversation with Mr. O'Neil at the time of this meeting?

HARBURG: I said so. I remember saying those things right along. I said, "If I am good enough for the Army, am I not good enough for MGM?"

Mr. Harburg did not yet go back to work for the studios.

But Mr. Harburg *was* "good enough" for MGM. They wanted him. He was "good enough" for the Army. They were using him. He was even good enough for Mr. O'Neil of the American Legion: apparently. But he was not good enough for Mr. Brewer, and he had his way—in palpable concert with others who conferred with him, who beseeched him, and who deferred to him. Membership in the Communist party was of little importance to Brewer. What he wanted was men and women of his stamp, and literature at his level, and for *his* publications. Quite a man!

When Brewer's name was called as next witness, summoned by the plaintiffs as an adverse party, I remembered Simon Lazarus coming back from his meeting with him saying, I have talked to a dictator. The man is like a dictator. He said he "would destroy me if I made a film with you." I remembered the phrase, "check it with Brewer" that ran through Hollywood for years.

The man who walked to the witness stand, however, looked nothing like the man my description suggests. Short, roly-poly, unimpressive in person and voice, he sat in the witness chair with a palpably faded present reality, like an ancient retainer being accorded security by those he had formerly dominated, to ransom their own image.

After identifying him and establishing his former position in Hollywood as international representative of I.A.T.S.E., under authority of the international president, Richard F. Walsh, Ben asked:

MARGOLIS: Mr. Brewer, there was an organization in Hollywood
              known as the AF of L Film Council?

BREWER: Yes.

MARGOLIS: About when was that organization formed?

BREWER: About 1948.

MARGOLIS: Were you one of the organizers?

BREWER: Yes.

              … … … … … … … …

MARGOLIS: What organizations constituted the membership of the
              AF of L Film Council?

BREWER: Well, all of the unions that held AF of L charters in the
              studios were eligible. Most of them belonged, but not all
              of them.

              … … … … … … … …

MARGOLIS: You became the first general chairman, did you not, of
              the AF of L Film Council.

BREWER: The chairman, yes, sir.

              … … … … … … … …

MARGOLIS: Was there an organization in Hollywood known as the
              Motion Picture Alliance?

              … … … … … … … …

BREWER: The Motion Picture Alliance for the Preservation of
              American Ideals. That was the official name of the orga-
              nization.

MARGOLIS: And one of the purposes of the Motion Picture Alliance
              to Preserve American Ideals was to combat communism
              in the Hollywood motion picture industry, isn't that cor-
              rect?

BREWER: Communist influence, yes.

              … … … … … … … …

MARGOLIS: Mr. Brewer, you were installed, were you not, as chair-
              man or president of the MPA early in June of 1953?

BREWER: Motion Picture Alliance, that is, yes, sir.

MARGOLIS: Yes. At that meeting, at which you were installed, was
              there any part of the program which was devoted in any
              way to the subject of *Salt of the Earth*?

BREWER: Yes.

MARGOLIS: Will you tell us whether or not that—well, tell us about
              it.

              ... ...

BREWER: Mr. Mark Armistead was the head of an equipment
              renting company in Hollywood, who rented cameras
              particularly, and he presented a check for, I think it was
              $1100, to Mr. C. B. DeMille, who accepted it on behalf
              of the Motion Picture Alliance as a contribution, and in
              the presentation it was announced that this was the
              amount of money that he had received for rental of
              some equipment to the company that had made *Salt of
              the Earth*.

MARGOLIS: Did he say that this was by way of atonement for having
              rented equipment to *Salt of the Earth?*

BREWER: No, I don't think he said that.

              ... ...

MARGOLIS: The Motion Picture Alliance, Mr. Brewer, published
              from time to time, did it not, a publication known as the
              Vigil?

BREWER: Yes.

              ... ...

MARGOLIS: In this May 1954 issue, it is a fact, is it not, that you
              signed a page "Roy M. Brewer, President" which was
              headed "President's Page"?

BREWER: Yes.

MARGOLIS: And it is a fact, is it not, that in that page you said, "In
              our own industry the producers of *Salt of the Earth* have
              been successful in launching their picture despite the
              unified opposition of the industry"? That is a fact, isn't
              it, sir?

BREWER: Yes.

This was damaging testimony. Brewer, the man of many hats, had
written, and now acknowledged that he had written that the film had
been launched *despite the unified efforts of the industry*. He would attempt to
pull away from this, his attorneys would seek to reconstruct and reinter-
pret this statement. It had been made in the year 1954, when Brewer,
like Johnston in 1949, thought he could wag the industry into the whole
foreseeable future. Ben was attempting to reveal the *labor man of 1954*—
their Gauleiter in the "command performance" into which they had been
bludgeoned—as the *producer's man of 1954*. This he became *in fact* shortly
thereafter when he resigned his union post to take employment with a
producing company, Allied Artists, of which Mr. Steve Broidy was president, the same Steve Broidy who had been president of MPIC when that
organization issued its statement on *Salt of the Earth*. From Allied Artists
Brewer resigned to contest for the international presidency of the
I.A.T.S.E. against Richard Walsh. When he lost the election he returned
to Allied Artists and was in that employment when he sat upon the witness chair. *Le plus ça change le plus ça reste le même.*

Ben Margolis was pinioning Brewer with his exuberances in his
heyday when he was doubling in brass as labor-man and producer-man.

MARGOLIS: I will ask you whether or not in the issue of the *Vigil*,
              dated May 1954, you saw the following statement in
              May of 1954: "It is believed that prints have already
              been shipped abroad for exhibition in Russia and Red
              colonies as an example of U.S. 'fascistic brutality.'
              Undoubtedly, the end will be changed to suit the Krem-
              lin's taste, for as the pic stands now, the strikers win, and
              who would dare tell that to the Soviet slaves."

Ben bit out each word of that quote, imitating what one felt had
been the writer's animus.

MARGOLIS: You saw that, didn't you?

Brewer's "yes" was a faint whisper. And well it might have been. Defense counsel had labeled the picture Communist propaganda of the worst sort. Now Brewer described the picture as so American its end would have to be changed before it could be exposed to "the Soviet slaves."

MARGOLIS: Did you have any information that when the picture
                    was shown in the Soviet Union the ending of the picture
                    was changed?

BREWER: No.

GOULD: I object to that, if your Honor please.

THE COURT: Overruled.

MARGOLIS: It is a fact, is it not, that this issue of the *Vigil* was pub-
                    lished in Los Angeles or Hollywood in May of 1954 just
                    before the motion picture *Salt of the Earth* opened up at
                    the Marcal Theater in Hollywood?

                    … … … … … … … …

BREWER: The only timing that I had any knowledge of was that it
                    was prepared subsequent to a meeting and published. If
                    it had any relationship to *Salt of the Earth* I did not know
                    it.

MARGOLIS: In July of 1953 did you issue a statement to the press
                    with respect to *Salt of the Earth,* as president of the AF of
                    L Film Council?

BREWER: Well, I may have. I don't recall specifically.

MARGOLIS: Let me ask you whether you recall issuing a statement
                    in which you said that *Salt* was "one of the most anti-
                    American documentaries ever attempted. Its aim is to
                    discredit the United States not only in the eyes of some
                    gullible Americans who might see it but in the eyes of
                    the natives of every country in the world." You did issue
                    such a statement, did you not?

BREWER: No. I did not issue such a statement as that. I know that
                    there was a story that appeared, but this is a reporter's
                    language, it is not my language.

MARGOLIS: You will notice that the language is in quotes.

BREWER: Yes, I remember that.

MARGOLIS: Did you take any steps to correct the "misquotation" of you in this paper?

LUDDY: Objected to as immaterial.

THE COURT: Overruled.

BREWER: I have no recollection of having done so.

MARGOLIS: What did you say?

                ... ...

BREWER: Well, I do not think I said that, because I don't think I had ever read the script at that time.

MARGOLIS: The fact is you had not read the script at that time.

BREWER: I do not believe so, so I do not think that I said that. But as to exactly what I said, I don't know.

MARGOLIS: Well, give us your best recollection as to anything at all that you said about the film at that time?

                ... ...

BREWER: Well, I probably said I considered that it was made for propaganda purposes and it would be used for that.

MARGOLIS: That was before you read the script?

BREWER: Yes, that was my opinion.

MARGOLIS: Did you at that time make the statement to the effect that the laboratories probably would not work on the film "because the laboratories here are fully aware of the subversive and un-American purposes of *Salt of the Earth* and its promoters"?

BREWER: I don't believe I made that statement.

MARGOLIS: You saw it in the press, however, did you not?

BREWER: I presume that I did, yes.

MARGOLIS: Did you take any steps to correct the "misquotation"?

BREWER: No.

                ... ...

MARGOLIS: You resigned or left your job with Allied Artists and ran
                as a candidate against Mr. Walsh for the international
                presidency, did you not, sir?

BREWER: Yes, sir.

                ... ...

MARGOLIS: Beginning at least in May of 1954, you began to hold
                press conferences dealing with your criticism of Mr.
                Walsh and your projected candidacy and opposition to
                it, isn't that correct?

                ... ...

MARGOLIS: Did you in that press conference state that Walsh should
                have stopped booth men from projecting the film *Salt of
                the Earth?*

BREWER: Well, at that point I don't know whether I used those
                exact words or not.

MARGOLIS: Well, did you say in substance, whether or not you used
                those exact words?

BREWER: Well, I certainly said that he should be more active,
                more militant.

MARGOLIS: That is not the question.

LANE: He has answered it. I do not think he should badger the
                witness.

THE COURT: Overruled.

                ... ...

MARGOLIS: I am really only concerned with the substance of the
                statement, whether you criticized Mr. Walsh for permit-
                ting members of the I.A. to project the film.

BREWER: I did criticize them, yes.

MARGOLIS: Did you say with respect to this, "I hope it will be pursued vigorously. If they bring in non-union workers to run it we should fight it." Did you say that?

BREWER: Yes, I think I did.

THE COURT: Could we suspend here to take a short recess?

MARGOLIS: Yes.

[jury left the courtroom.]

THE COURT: Mr. Margolis, would you or Mr. Galligan mind if I were to talk briefly and informally with Mr. Lane and Mr. Luddy—Mr. Gould is missing, so we will add only Mr. Mayer. In other words, it has to do with our conversation off the record this morning. It is on that subject.

MARGOLIS: Not at all, your Honor.

THE COURT: And something further occurs to me that I would like them to consider along the lines of how we ended up, you know, what they were going to do and so on. Would you mind that?

MARGOLIS: Perfectly all right with me, your Honor.

THE COURT: Would you come up, gentlemen?

What had been discussed that morning by the judge with a committee of defense counsel and Ben Margolis and Sidney Dickstein—*was settlement of the case.* Following the first part of Roy Brewer's testimony, the judge had called counsel in to state to them that he was going to send the case to the jury. If defense counsel had any notion of coming in at the end of plaintiffs' case and asking to have the complaint dismissed, they could forget it. He suggested that counsel ought to get together and discuss the possibility of a settlement. Each had something to gain from it. He believed the case against the defendants had a chance of being sustained. He believed that the amount of damages the jury would award if they found for the plaintiffs might be small. A settlement now might accomplish everything a longer trial would. The defense counsel talked about a hundred thousand dollars cash settlement—no statements—no press releases. The counteroffer by Ben Margolis was three hundred thousand in cash, and a guarantee of no further interference with the film by any of the defendants. Each side rejected the offer of the other, made tentatively since neither had conferred with principals, but agreed to discuss the matter with their clients.

The readiness of defense counsel to talk settlement at this moment seemed an indication that they shared the apparent opinion of the judge that the equivocal appearance and "testimony" of Roy Brewer was proving disastrous to the defendants' efforts to justify themselves.

The great Brewer of ten years ago, as he sat there now, responding so dully, and so squirmingly, epitomized for me the braggard emptiness of all blind labeling of others whether it is of Negroes in Mississippi, of Jews in Germany, of Communists or alleged Communists in the United States, or of capitalists in the Soviet Union.

The examination which Ben had begun earlier in the day had charted Brewer's rise from a projectionist in a town in Nebraska to "the toughest anti-Communist in the whole of Hollywood." It now approached a climax. Ben began to question Brewer about the MPIC—the Motion Picture Industry Council—another industry organization of which Mr. Brewer had once been president. This had been organized by the producers and included the talent guilds and the unions in addition to the producers and the trade association. It was the realization of Eric Johnston's dream—an industry united "to eliminate subversives." At a moment when we were peacefully engaged in shooting *Salt of the Earth* in the Silver City area of New Mexico, unprecedented statements on the subject of the film by the AF of L Film Council and MPIC rocked the New Mexican community, turned vigilantes loose upon us, caused our leading lady to leave the country, and sent our film underground for the duration of its shooting and processing. Mr. Brewer's close association with MPIC—one of his hats—made it plausible that the action of this organization was what was meant by "the unified opposition of the industry."

MARGOLIS: ... It is a fact, is it not, sir, that a statement was issued just prior to February 13, 1953, by the MPIC, through Mr. Steve Broidy, as follows, and I quote: "None of the motion picture companies represented in the MPIC has any connection whatsoever with this picture or the organization or individuals making it. The studios and groups composing the MPIC membership do not recog-

nize this operation or its product as representing their
own views or interests or policies."

In the whole previous history of the motion picture industry, no
statement of that kind had ever been issued by the industry against any
single film. What is significant in the statement is that it made clear, to
everyone in the industry, that *Salt of the Earth* was out of bounds.

MARGOLIS: That is correct, is it not, sir?

BREWER: To the best of my recollection, it is, yes, sir.

MARGOLIS: You do have a recollection that a statement in substance
              to that effect was issued by the MPIC council at that
              time?

BREWER: Yes, sir.

MARGOLIS: Isn't it a fact that at the same time you issued a state-
              ment in which you said as follows with respect to *Salt of
              the Earth:* "No motion picture made by Communists can
              be good for America. Hollywood has gotten rid of these
              people and we want the government agencies to investi-
              gate carefully."

Ben paused to allow the statement to sink into the jury's minds.

MARGOLIS: Isn't that correct?

BREWER: ... I am sure this was not a written statement. As to
              whether I actually said those words or not, I don't recall.

              ... ...

MARGOLIS: Mr. Brewer, can you explain how it is that you recall the
              substance of the MPIC statement but cannot recall the
              substance of what you yourself said at that time?

KANTOR: Objection, if your Honor please.

THE COURT: Overruled.

BREWER: It was a written statement, the MPIC was.

MARGOLIS: Did you prepare it?

BREWER: No, I did not prepare it, but I am sure that I saw it.

MARGOLIS: You saw it?

BREWER: Yes.

MARGOLIS: And you yourself had conferences with the AF of L Film
                 Council and then made an oral statement, is that right?

BREWER: Well. I say that I don't recall the matter of the oral
                 statement.

                 … … … … … … … …

MARGOLIS: Mr. Brewer, did you ever express opposition to *Salt of the
                 Earth* and ask for a government investigation of the film
                 because you considered it to be Communist propaganda
                 or a propaganda film?

BREWER: Well, the Film Council did that.

MARGOLIS: Did you ever issue a statement on behalf of the Film
                 Council so stating?

BREWER: A statement was issued over my name.

                 … … … … … … … …

MARGOLIS: Isn't it a fact, Mr. Brewer, that in the discussion at the
                 AF of L Council you stated in substance that it was desir-
                 able to have the Film Council state publicly its opposi-
                 tion to the making of *Salt of the Earth?*

BREWER: I don't recall that.

MARGOLIS: You don't recall one way or the other whether you did
                 that?

BREWER: No.

MARGOLIS: Isn't it a fact that at the time that there was this discus-
                 sion in the AF of L Film Council you knew that the
                 MPIC was issuing a statement the same day?

BREWER: I have no recollection of whether I did or I didn't.

MARGOLIS: Isn't it a fact, Mr. Brewer, that these two statements
                 were timed to be issued at the same time so as to get the
                 maximum public impact?

BREWER: I think not.

MARGOLIS: You do not remember for sure, do you?

BREWER: I do not remember, but I don't believe that was the case.

MARGOLIS: Mr. Brewer, following your first receiving information
                with respect to the fact that *Salt of the Earth* was actually
                being filmed in New Mexico, you sent some body to
                New Mexico to investigate *Salt of the Earth*, did you not?

BREWER: A representative of my office went down there to do
                that, yes, sir.

MARGOLIS: And the representative of your office who went down
                there was a Mr. Fairbanks?

BREWER: Yes, sir.

MARGOLIS: Did he go down there to try to sign the union contract?

BREWER: He went down there to investigate the production.

MARGOLIS: Did he go down there to try to get a union contract, Mr.
                Brewer?

BREWER: I would say that he was not instructed to get a union
                contract.

                ... ...

BREWER: His instructions were to report back so that that could be
                determined as to what the next step should be.

MARGOLIS: All right. Mr. Fairbanks went to New Mexico pursuant
                to your instructions, did he not, sir?

BREWER: Yes.

MARGOLIS: He was there for about a day.

BREWER: Yes.

MARGOLIS: At the end of a day he came back and he reported to
                you.

BREWER: Yes.

MARGOLIS: What did he tell you?

BREWER: Well, he told us it was being operated as a non-union project.

MARGOLIS: What else did he tell you?

BREWER: And he told us it was being operated by the persons that it was reported had been—were operating it.

MARGOLIS: You mean that it was being operated by Mr. Biberman, Mr. Jarrico and Mr. Wilson?

BREWER: Yes, sir.

MARGOLIS: Did he tell you how he found out it was a non-union operation?

BREWER: I don't recall that.

MARGOLIS: Did you then give him instructions, say, "Mr. Fairbanks, go back there and sign those people up if you can"?

BREWER: No, I don't think we did.

MARGOLIS: What?

BREWER: I don't remember that was done.

MARGOLIS: As a matter of fact, you did not do that, did you, sir?

BREWER: I would say no.

On being shown the Waldorf Declaration, Mr. Brewer stated his position as follows:

BREWER: I don't think there was any doubt but what—of my view that subversives should not work in the motion picture industry. That was my independent view. It was not in agreement, it was my independent view.

Ben then took this "independent" man through a score of letters to and from heads of studios in which Mr. Brewer exercised his "independence" through a dominating collaboration with the producers.

In a letter submitted as evidence by the plaintiffs, Mr. Kahane, vice-president of Columbia Pictures, wrote to Mr. Brewer: "As requested, I am sending you herewith the testimony of X before the McCarran Committee."

In another letter, Mr. Kahane pleaded with Mr. Brewer to clear an actress who had made amends for past behavior: "Miss H has admitted that she was duped and played for a sucker. I have indicated by red pencil passages in the testimony which it seems to me cover the situation.... Would you please call me after you have read and considered the enclosures."

Mr. Kahane expressed his belief that this actress had passed muster in a letter to Nate Spingold, a vice president of Columbia: "Dear Nate:... as you know, I had Roy come over and meet J.... I felt that J handled herself very satisfactorily and made a good impression on Roy."

More letters followed, referring to M.B., R.S., W.K. In one letter Mr. Kahane referred to "the one citation you have against S" (editorials S had written for the *Bruin*, the student paper while he had been at UCLA).

MARGOLIS: Do you know of any editorials that were published in the UCLA *Bruin* that ever called for the overthrow of the government by force and violence?

BREWER: No, but there were a lot of things going on at UCLA that came in for a great deal of criticism.

MARGOLIS: A lot of things you did not agree with, that's correct, isn't it?

BREWER: That's correct.

Ben's fullest exposure of the character of Brewer of old came later when he quoted from a speech Brewer had delivered to the American Legion:

> When it comes to fighting Hollywood Commies, I will take second place to no one.... Their ignorance of the Communist party and its workings... made them look pretty silly in the eyes of the American people. But let us make clear that this ignorance is not by any means confined to persons in the motion picture industry. It goes to the very top of our government—and I mean the top. It carries into our colleges, our schools, our halls of scientific research and even to the heads of our large industrial institutions.

Ben looked at the jury, his face grim. "Gee, those words have a familiar ring," he said.

It was terrifying to look at the deflated Brewer in the witness chair in that courtroom and to know that only a few years before leaders of a great communications industry had permitted that man to inflate his ambition with the gusting winds of "the times," and with the broken lives of some of the most creative talent that American films had developed.

There followed perhaps the most serious deprivation to the plaintiffs in the trial. They were prevented from bringing before the jury Mr. Howard Hughes' letter to Representative Donald Jackson, in which he called, in language no lawyer could controvert, for an industry-wide boycott of *Salt of the Earth.* (See page 121.) Praising Pathé for its refusal to service the film any longer, Howard Hughes laid out the full gamut of industry power like a blueprint, asking the industry, boldly, to exercise it against Biberman and Jarrico.

But the letter proved to be no letter. With the sagacity in such matters for which Hughes has become famous, the communication apparently was teletyped from the Hughes' Tool Company in Los Angeles to its counterpart in New York, and sent to the congressman from New York. Since the original document could not be found the communication, which had been reprinted by Jackson in the Congressional Record, was declared inadmissible by the judge.

Plaintiffs had tried for four years to serve Mr. Hughes with a subpoena in order to examine him, but had failed. This was no proper cause for self-castigation. Far larger corporations than they all over the country had failed with all the resources at their disposal. Mr. Hughes had the power to hit-and-run, by teletype.

One would have thought that such passion as his would have propelled him proudly into the courtroom to testify concerning his bold advice to the industry. But it did not. To a layman like myself, watching such a powerful piece of evidence disallowed—because of a legal technicality—was shocking. There it was, in the *Congressional Record.* Its effect had been far-reaching to my own knowledge. It had intimidated; it had deprived us of necessary men and machines. But the ruling was *legally* proper. The judge was correct.

VII

While awaiting further settlement discussions we were faced by another plaguing problem. We had failed to find a witness on damages. Without an expert witness it is impossible to make a legal claim for damages. It cannot be established by the attorneys. I had been working on finding a witness for weeks on end. Paul had joined when he arrived from Paris. We needed someone with experience in distribution, someone we could hire to come to court for a day to say, "In my opinion this film should have grossed so and so much money in the theaters if it had had normal access to them." Right or wrong—his opinion. No comment upon the conspiracy, only expert testimony. *There was not one such individual in New York City who was willing to appear on the stand as a witness for us.* Even men who had retired from the business refused, fearful that if they ever wanted to return they would have made it impossible for themselves. In desperation I went into the 16mm distributing field and even there I could find no one willing to express his opinion upon our film in open court.

Damages has to do with value and value has to do with public acceptance and, in the case of this film, value had to do with whether the jury believed the viewing public would find Communist propaganda within it. Not permitted to show the film to the jury, unable to find an expert who would testify as to its commercial value, we sought, at the very least, to find witnesses who could cope, effectively, with the defendants' assertions of Communist propaganda. Two possible witnesses occurred to us at once. Both had been present as invited guests of George Brussel, Jr., in 1954, at the private screening he had requested when we sought to lease the Squire Theater. They were the then Dean of the Cathedral of St. John the Divine in New York, presently Bishop of the Episcopal Diocese of California, the Rt. Rev. James A. Pike, and Rabbi Edward Klein of the Stephen Wise Free Synagogue of New York. Bishop Pike was in New York for a brief period, occupying the pulpit of Trinity Church at Wall Street and Broadway. I telephoned both gentlemen. They remembered the film and asked to view it again in order to refresh their memories. The screening for Bishop Pike was the first arranged. Mrs. G. K. M. Montizambert, in charge of television programming for the Anglican Church of Canada, was in New York and Bishop Pike invited her to see the film with him.

Upon the conclusion of the screening Mrs. Montizambert said she was very moved by the film and would enjoy testifying on the subject of its cinematographic excellence—excellence as film and as profoundly satisfying entertainment. She believed this to be within the area of her professional competence. Bishop Pike said he found the film even more relevant to the American scene than when he had seen it ten years ago and that he wished very much to testify to its positive, moral character. Additionally he wished to inform the court and jury that he had recommended it to members of his staff at St. John's after having viewed it ten years before.

I suggested to the Bishop that, in cross-examination, Myles Lane would confront him with the "sanction order" and undoubtedly would ask him if he would recommend it now, having been apprised of the fact that *for the purposes of the trial* the makers of the film were members of the Communist party.

Bishop Pike said that in his church in San Francisco there was an altar cross—one of the most beautiful he had ever seen. It had been made by a San Franciscan who was a devout, practising Jew. If he were obliged to judge a work of art by the beliefs of its maker rather than by its own inherent values he would be forced to take down the altar piece at St. Paul's—an action he was not about to engage in any more than he was about to refrain from testifying for *Salt of the Earth* because of the alleged beliefs or the real beliefs of its makers. He wished very much to be a witness. Rabbi Klein also wished to testify.

When the court was informed concerning our prospective witnesses Mr. Lane objected strenuously. If these witnesses were permitted to appear he said he would then be obliged to call a Catholic priest who would testify oppositionally. The judge felt that such a wrangle would advance the case not at all. He wished to avoid anything resembling a popularity contest respecting the film's content. Despite their distinguished personal qualities he believed our witnesses were lay people with respect to film and he refused to permit them to testify.

Bishop Pike, on being informed of the judge's ruling, said, "Tell your attorneys that I am a lawyer. I am licensed to practise in the State of New York and to appear before the Supreme Court. If you lose and go up on appeal I wish to associate myself with them as co-counsel. I will join them in argument before the Supreme Court. And I will appear there in full canonicals with mitre."

His robustiousness and moral passion did a great deal to bolster our attorneys. The unexpected deprivation of these distinguished witnesses was a considerable and irreplaceable loss.

The search for an expert witness proceeded in an atmosphere of desperation. When we would find one who would agree to testify, a day or two later it seemed he would be "called upon," reminded that bread is normally buttered only on one side, and, suddenly, he would find it impossible to appear.

Fear of reprisal by the defendants was obviously rife. And this was grimly funny. The general attitude in the courtroom about our case was that it was ancient history. It was about something that had happened in those dismal yesteryears when Joe McCarthy was loose. This sort of thing, surely, had passed into limbo.

Finding witnesses to testify about blacklisting practices was equally impossible. Many of the victims did not want to "go all through that again," and potential witnesses employed in the industry were reluctant to put their jobs in jeopardy.

We had failed to find an expert on damages, or on blacklist. Depress us all as this did, it also added a certain outraged zest to the battle. The terror was *not in limbo*, with the ghost of Joe McCarthy. Limbo was sitting in the courtroom in Foley Square—and it had to be fought with what we had. But we had no expert witness on damages.

It was in these circumstances that the question to settle or not to settle was reviewed. The lawyers consulted with Simon Lazarus on the telephone. They painted the picture in its grimmest colors.

If we settled: after eight years of tenacious litigation, no decision; no judgment upon the defendants; we get a little money to be spread out among creditors and lawyers; we take a little bribe to get off the defendants' backs and go back to anonymity, still blacklisted and blacklistable. The status quo gives up a pittance and goes scot-free. Limbo takes over, uncontested.

But if we did not settle we might lose, and have nothing.

Why had we undertaken this nearly impossible suit? To attempt to expose conspiracy, conspirators. To make them understand that the United States was not their quarry—that its meaning was not hypocrisy and running for cover. It was courage in the face of assault. Despite all the problems, deprivations, witness for witness and point for point, we were at least holding our own. We were in contest. The decision was made. No "calling the whole thing off" for a handout. If they wished to settle, then they must decently reflect the extent of our damage and give assurance securing the re-entrance of the film into the market.

At the next meeting on settlement, the defendants raised their offer to $150,000. Someone mentioned a figure of $182,000. But the settlement was to be cash—period. The offer was rejected. The trial was going to the wire. To a legal decision.

VIII

The plaintiffs continued to present their case. They requested permission for the film to be shown to the jury. The judge refused on the grounds that this was not a case dealing with alleged pornography in which judgment of the film by the jury was significant. It mattered not at all what was in this film, the judge held. The only question was whether it had suffered anti-trust violations as alleged. The artistic or ethical values or lacks were not at issue in the case. Much as I wished the jury to see the film, I could not but feel that the judge's argument was sound. The attorneys were not convinced of it and were waiting for an opportune moment to raise it again on other grounds.

The plaintiffs called fourteen witnesses and presented seven depositions. Paul Jarrico testified for a week, taking the jury through the production and economics of the film. He established his story and it withstood cross-examination unshaken. Mike Wilson flew in from California to testify about his work on the film. Simon Lazarus gave evidence regarding the refusal of the major companies to supply "shorts" to run with the film at the Marcal Theater in Los Angeles. Irving Fajans testified about our ejection from the New York laboratories at the demand of the I.A.T.S.E. John Rossen reported on the two years of frustrated effort to open in Chicago. My testimony was to cover the making of the film, the attempts to distribute it and the abortive negotiations over many months with Mr. Baskind and LLPE of the national AF of L for national commercial distribution.

Mr. Lane had told the plaintiffs' lawyers on various occasions that he doubted I would ever dare testify. He believed that I knew what huge blunderbusses he had to fire.

Making a good witness of me was a major undertaking. Ben Margolis and Art Galligan, who conducted my examination, had to contend with my urge to "expatiate upon themes." How often, in near-desperation, Ben would say, "Herbert, you save your stories for your book. Allow me to give just the bare bones to the jury."

Evidence accumulates slowly. Testimony on any one issue at any one time presents only part of the picture. When the defense lawyers attempted to present their side through the questions they asked me,

I felt I had a right not to give simple answers to complex and artful questions. At one point, when I was having difficulty giving a yes or no answer demanded by Mr. Lane, the judge, understanding my problem, suggested to me that though it seemed difficult at times, it was a good idea to play the game by the rules, to give answers directly, and to allow plaintiff attorneys to fill in the interstices.

My first difficulty as a witness came with Mr. Lane's first shot.

LANE: Mr. Biberman, you testified on your direct examination that the Chicago case was dismissed on plaintiffs' motion, do you recall that?

BIBERMAN: I do.

LANE: You weren't telling the truth when you said that, were you?

GALLIGAN: Objection, your Honor.

Without waiting for a ruling on the objection, I struck back with all vigor.

BIBERMAN: Of course I was telling the truth.

LANE: Do you recall that in the Chicago case you were asked certain questions which you refused to answer?

BIBERMAN: They were interrogatories, Mr. Lane....

             ... ...

LANE: Wasn't it because you didn't answer those questions that the case was dismissed?

BIBERMAN: No, sir.

LANE: It was not?

BIBERMAN: It was because I asked to have the case dismissed.

LANE: You are sure of that?

BIBERMAN: Yes, sir. I am sure of that.

I did not add "to the best of my knowledge" as I had been counseled to do in replying to a hard attack in an area where my memory might be faulty. Lane produced a defendant exhibit and offered it to me.

BIBERMAN: This case was dismissed on the plaintiffs' motion, Mr.
              Lane. I haven't even read this, but I know what hap-
              pened, and I will be glad to relate it to you and then—

LANE: You have answered the question.

BIBERMAN: On the plaintiffs' motion, I said.

Mr. Lane proceeded to read from the record in the Chicago case which stated that it had been dismissed upon motion of the defendants. In re-direct examination Arthur Galligan was able to set the actual facts in clear chronological order. I had asked judge Perry to dismiss the case and he had assented to my request by asking defendants to move dismissal.

I began to learn caution and to believe that my attorneys would be able to put Mr. Lane's legal manoeuvres in their proper perspective. This occurred during examination pertaining to the earnings of the film in Berkeley.

LANE: Showing you Exhibit 3-H for identification, have you
              seen this before [handing]?

BIBERMAN: Yes.

LANE: Was Miss Dahl authorized to write certain letters on
              behalf of the plaintiff corporation I.P.C. Distributors?

BIBERMAN: She was.

LANE: Did she ever write to two persons in Dorchester, Massa-
              chusetts, to the effect that *Salt of the Earth* had enjoyed a
              phenomenal success in Berkeley, California?

BIBERMAN: Yes, apparently she did.

LANE: *Salt*, from the answers to the interrogatories that we
              posed to the plaintiffs, played there for 13 days, from
              June 9th to June 22nd 1954, and the receipts, that is the
              revenue which the plaintiff I.P.C. Distributors obtained
              out of that performance was $800 or $60 a day. Now
              would you agree with Miss Dahl that that was a phe-
              nomenal performance for this picture?

              ... ...

LANE: Mr. Biberman, is that your idea of a phenomenal suc-
               cess, $60 a day?

BIBERMAN: No, sir, I would think that this was an exaggeration....

LANE: I take it, then, that you would agree that this was a
               more or less distorted view of the true facts?

BIBERMAN: I would think that it is an exaggerated statement,
               certainly.

               ... ...

LANE: Do you recall writing to a man in Cambridge, Massachu-
               setts, in November of 1954, at the Brattle Theater about
               Salt of the Earth?

BIBERMAN: I have a memory of having talked with the man or writ-
               ten to him, yes, sir. I don't remember the date, but I
               would be glad to refresh my memory, if you have the
               document.

               ... ...

LANE: Now referring to that letter, you say that the $800 take
               for 13 days was something beyond your greatest expec-
               tations. What had you expected the picture to do at the
               Rivoli Theater in Berkeley, California?

GALLIGAN: I object to the characterization of the letter as an $800
               take. I think the word that was used was receipts, and I
               think we ought to get a definition of what the receipts
               are that is referred to in the letter. There are different
               kinds of receipts.

THE COURT: I will go along with that. You can rephrase it, I think,
               Mr. Lane.

LANE: Keeping in mind the fact that the receipts you obtained
               from the showing of that picture *Salt of the Earth* at the
               Rivoli Theater in Berkeley, California, was $800 for 13
               performances, and you say in your letter that this was
               something beyond your wildest expectations, just
               exactly how much did you anticipate would be made at
               that theater at that time?

… … … … … … … …

GALLIGAN: Your Honor, this is the same objection. We still haven't
              defined receipts, as I understand his question. Are we
              talking about receipts to the distributor or total receipts
              taken at the box office?

THE COURT: Instead of wrangling, let's ask Mr. Biberman.

BIBERMAN: I don't know, sir, what the receipts were. I don't have
              the books with me. I don't have a memory as to what
              the receipts were. I don't know whether they were $800
              or more or less.

LANE: For your information the theater gross was about
              $4200, $4250, but your take, the I.P.C. take—and you
              know what I mean by take—was $800.

BIBERMAN: My dear Mr. Lane, this is a very different thing than you
              said first. You talked about receipts of $800 without
              identifying it. Now I will say that I am impressed that
              $4200 in two weeks in a theater in Berkeley, near the
              University, may have been exactly what Miss Dahl char-
              acterized it as being and what I apparently did in my let-
              ter, and also what the owner estimated it to be. I don't
              think that was fairly represented.

Mr. Dickstein made use of Mr. Lane's sally in his summation. He pointed out to the jury that if the money paid to the corporation from the Berkeley engagement had been repeated on a per capita basis all over the United States, the film would have brought a gross revenue to the corporations of $1,200,000.

For his blockbuster to end his cross-examination of me, Mr. Lane referred to a sworn affidavit presented to judge Sugarman, stating that I had rendered no services to the corporations after the fall of 1956. Having asked me to identify the affidavit, Mr. Lane then brought into evidence two letters written by Mr. Lazarus in the spring of 1957 upon which, in my hand, was written a list of the countries where prints of the film existed. Mr. Lane asked me how it was possible that I had done this six months after the date at which my affidavit swore to my having ceased all service to the corporations. I replied that the assistance I had given with the letters had been an inconsequential act, one that I had obviously forgotten about when I gave my affidavit. With a quiet and ominous "No further questions," Mr. Lane ended. In his summation, at the end of the case, Mr. Lane came back for a last shot, and said that any man who would lie to a federal judge was not worthy of belief. I took this failure of memory on my part very seriously. I believe I blushed, visibly.

Ben took this up in his summation. He said that this failure on my part and two others which Mr. Lane exposed during more than a week on the stand, against depositions and a parade of cross-examining lawyers, attested to the kind of memory in a client for which any lawyer would get down on his knees and give thanks. "And out of that to stand up and say liar? When you have to resort to that kind of exaggeration, you are in bad shape, bad shape."

IX

The defendants summoned twenty-two witnesses and presented five depositions.

Mr. Steve D'Inzillo, business agent of the New York Projectionists' local, took the stand to deny that he had ever informed Paul and myself of the industry–union conspiracy. He also denied on the stand that he had followed the orders of Mr. Richard F. Walsh and directed projectionists to leave the booth of the Preview Theater and the New Dyckman.

Mr. Daniel Ruffini, projectionist at the Preview Theater, "corroborated" Mr. D'Inzillo's version of the story. Mr. Ruffini ran the film seven or eight times under the deceptive title *Vaya con Dios* which painstakingly we had had etched on the film itself and printed on the can. His memory of the event was different as was brought out by Ben Margolis's cross-examination:

MARGOLIS:	When you first began to show, project, *Salt of the Earth*, the fact is that it didn't have a title on it, isn't that correct?
RUFFINI:	It did have a title.
MARGOLIS:	It had the title *Salt of the Earth* on it?
RUFFINI:	It had a title on the can, *Salt of the Earth* also.
MARGOLIS:	It had a title on the can?
RUFFINI:	Yes, outside the can.
MARGOLIS:	Did it have a title on the picture that you were projecting?
RUFFINI:	I don't remember. I don't recall, sir.
MARGOLIS:	Do you recall, as a matter of fact, that you ran the film seven or eight times when it did not have the title on it, and that the first time that the title was put on the film you refused to run it?
	… … … … … … … …

RUFFINI: I don't know if it happened. You are telling me it hap-
              pened. I didn't say it happened. You said it happened. If
              it did happen, it would be a coincidence. I don't know
              and I don't recall it.

MARGOLIS: You don't recall one way or the other?

RUFFINI: That is right.

MARGOLIS: Tell us, when you saw this film you decided that it was
              Communist propaganda, is that right?

RUFFINI: Well, yes.

MARGOLIS: Now tell us about all the Communist propaganda in the
              film, will you please?

RUFFINI: Well, in the first place, it was made by the union of
              Mine, Mill and Smelter Workers Union which was
              thrown out of the CIO as being a communistic union.

MARGOLIS: Just one question. Was that on the can?

RUFFINI: It was in the picture, in banners.

What Mr. Ruffini remembered were scenes in the union ball
where a sign above the platform identified the union hall as that of
the International Union of Mine, Mill and Smelter Workers.

MARGOLIS: All right. And that made the Communist propaganda?

RUFFINI: I didn't say that made it. I said that it was sponsored and
              it was made by that union, which was a communistic
              union. I am sure they are not going to make a picture
              conducive to capitalism.

MARGOLIS: When did you first find out that the Mine, Mill and
              Smelter Workers Union was one of the sponsors of the
              picture?

RUFFINI: By officials that were at our theater at one time.

              ... ...

MARGOLIS: Anything else that you found that was Communist pro-
              paganda in the film?

RUFFINI: The whole general tone of the picture I didn't like.

... ...

MARGOLIS: ... Can you give me any more specific than the whole
              general tone?

... ...

RUFFINI: In specific, everything about it. The sheriffs in there
              were bullies. They hit women, they clubbed women in
              the picture there on the picket line, shoved them, threw
              a pregnant woman down. This is picture making? This is
              entertainment and that is supposed to be what is here,
              as happening here in this country?

MARGOLIS: You have never seen anything like that?

RUFFINI: No.

MARGOLIS: All right. Anything else?

RUFFINI: The general tone of the whole picture was down with
              the bosses and—

MARGOLIS: Have you ever seen violence in pictures before, where
              police shoved people around and beat them over the
              heads with clubs?

RUFFINI: News reels?

Obviously things such as depicted in *Salt of the Earth* did not happen in America, according to Mr. Ruffini. Not in the "real America of
movies," only in the unreal America of news reels.

MARGOLIS: I am not talking about news reels. I am talking about
              motion picture features.

RUFFINI: Features? Make believe, yes.

MARGOLIS: Well, I am talking about motion pictures. You have seen
              motion pictures in which police have beaten people
              over the head with clubs, haven't you?

RUFFINI: Yes.

MARGOLIS: And you refused to run them?

RUFFINI: No.

MARGOLIS: I have no further questions.

    So much for Mr. Ruffini.

Mr. Gullette, his boss, the owner of the Preview Theater, was a pleasant
    looking, well-spoken gentleman, who, it seemed to me,
    would rather have been anywhere but on that stand.
    Ben showed him a newspaper clipping.

MARGOLIS: Did you tell anyone of the press that it was your under-
    standing "that unofficial instructions had been issued to
    the men regarding *Salt* which was made in New Mexico
    last year by a group which included several unfriendly
    Red probe witnesses"? Did you ever tell that to anybody
    in the press?

GULLETTE: No.

MARGOLIS: You saw that in the press, didn't you?

GULLETTE: Yes.

MARGOLIS: Did you take any steps to have that statement corrected?

GULLETTE: No.

    … … … … … … … …

MARGOLIS: Did you tell any press representative that you could not
    fight a phantom battle against the I.A. which would ruin
    your business?

GULLETTE: No.

MARGOLIS: You saw that in the press?

GULLETTE: Yes.

MARGOLIS: Did you take any steps to have it corrected?

GULLETTE: No.

MARGOLIS: Did you ever tell anybody from the press that you had
    been given to understand that if you fired your projec-
    tionists, replacements would be hard to come by?

GULLETTE: No.

MARGOLIS: You saw that in the press, didn't you? You are quoted to
              that effect?

GULLETTE: Yes.

MARGOLIS: Did you take any steps to correct it?

GULLETTE: No.

MARGOLIS: No further questions.

So much for Mr. Gullette.

Mr. Walsh, international president of the I.A.T.S.E. union, on
cross-examination by Ben, was asked whether it was true that in the
issue of the I.A.T.S.E. bulletin in January of 1954 there had appeared
a special box carrying this legend:

NOTICE TO ALL LOCAL UNION AND PROJECTIONIST MEM-
BERS OF THE I.A.T.S.E. BEFORE HANDLING OR PROJECTING
THE FILM ENTITLED *Salt of the Earth* YOU ARE HEREBY
INSTRUCTED TO CONTACT THE GENERAL OFFICE FOR
INFORMATION PERTAINING TO THIS PRODUCTION.

When he was asked why he had caused the notice to be published he replied that there was "no special reason." When he was
asked if there had appeared any other such notice respecting any
other motion picture, he replied that there had not. He claimed he
had never instructed anyone in the office how to handle any calls
that came in response to the notice. And he stated that, to the best of
his knowledge, no call ever came to the office in response to the
bulletin.

Mr. Walsh readily admitted that when Mr. Baskind met with him
to discuss the desire of LLPE of the AF of L to support national theater
distribution of *Salt of the Earth* he told him he would oppose it. He also
said that he had *never seen the film, had never read the script.* His opposition was based upon what Mr. Brewer had told him, what he had
read in the newspapers and what he had been told by a couple of
actors whose names he could not recall. All he could remember was
his uninvestigated opposition.

In his cross-examination of Mr. Walsh, Ben Margolis wished to
set the record straight on the history of the I.A.T.S.E. and its "anti-

Communist" crusade. He questioned Mr. Walsh about the Conference of Studio Unions which Brewer and Walsh had attacked as "Communist-dominated."

MARGOLIS: You went into the history of your union associations and of the CSU. Do you remember about when the CSU was organized?

WALSH: No, sir. It's quite a number of years ago.

MARGOLIS: As a matter of fact, wasn't it organized about or shortly before you became international president?

WALSH: That's very possible.

MARGOLIS: Wasn't it—

WALSH: It's very possible it was. It definitely was before I became international president.

MARGOLIS: And you succeeded Brown and Bioff, did you not, sir?

WALSH: No, I succeeded Brown.

MARGOLIS: You succeeded Brown but Bioff had also been in office before; is that correct?

LUDDY: I object as immaterial, and if he pursues it, I shall have another motion to make.

THE COURT: I agree. Sustained. We got an answer, in any event. He succeeded Mr. Brown.

It was at this point that Ben asked to approach the bench and he addressed the judge out of hearing of the jury.

MARGOLIS: ... I wanted to ask some questions to establish not the truth of the matters, but the nature of the contentions between the parties: that the cry of Communism was first raised by his predecessors, Brown and Bioff, and that the CSU raised the cry of corruption; that one was crying corruption and the other was crying Communism, and that the CSU was formed around this issue... of the fight against corruption.

> It seems to me, your Honor, that if they're allowed to
> show that the issue around which the I.A. was fighting
> was Communism, we should be able to show—

THE COURT: No, I am sorry. That is denied.

Had Ben been permitted to describe the origins of the I.A.T.S.E.–CSU battle, the jury would have learned that the CSU was born in an effort to rally the workers of Hollywood against the collusion of studios and I.A.T.S.E. executives Brown and Bioff to extort money. When the CSU raised the cry of corruption, the classic reply of both industry and the union's thieving leaders was "Communism." Although both the union leaders were tried and went to jail, along with one of the top studio executives, the role of the CSU in exposing the extortion was never forgotten. It was repaid for its insurgency in the 1945–46 strike when it was broken apart and ended up in the arms of Mr. Brewer.

Since this testimony was barred, the I.A.T.S.E. remained, for the jury, what Mr. Lane had described it to be, a fine, old-line, AF of L union, with an unblemished record in its leadership.

X

In our extremity in the area of a witness on damages, David Shapiro discovered that, by law, an owner may testify concerning damage to his property. And as I was a registered owner of undistributed shares of I.P.C. Distributors Inc., I was privileged to testify as our "expert" on damages. The judge was probably at a loss to understand why, out of the whole of New York City, we could not come up with one reasonably expert expert. However, counsel thought it preferable to risk his bafflement than to tax his credulity in attempting to explain the simple fact that we had not been able to find one. I was put on the stand.

Admitted as a witness on damages only through a legal technicality, my veracity and ability as a distributor attacked by Mr. Lane, labeled a subversive, and, at the very least a most interested party in the litigation, I was obliged to attempt to convince the judge and jury of the reasonableness of plaintiffs' estimate of the damages they had suffered.

GALLIGAN: Mr. Biberman, predicated upon your experience in the motion picture industry as an associate producer, as a participant in the exploitation and projection of revenue you derived from motion pictures, and so on, can you give us your opinion as to what the value of this film was in 1956 at the time this suit was instituted?

LANE: Objection, your Honor. The man is not qualified—

THE COURT: Whether the man is qualified or not, Mr. Lane, at the moment doesn't bother me as much as a couple of other things bother me. I don't know what he means by value. As a piece of film? Or what is he talking about?

              ... ...

GALLIGAN: Did you arrive at a valuation at that time, Mr. Biberman?

BIBERMAN: I did.

GALLIGAN: What did you take into account in arriving at that valuation?

              ... ...

BIBERMAN: ... I would like to begin with 1954. We were then about
                 to begin exhibition of the film.... We asked ourselves
                 what is the potential audience for this particular film. It
                 doesn't appeal to everyone. If one made a football pic-
                 ture it would not appeal to non-football lovers. If one
                 made a stark tragedy it would not appeal to people who
                 didn't like stark tragedies. We said to ourselves: "There is
                 no doubt, based upon our experience, that this film does
                 appeal to the general area of people who work for a liv-
                 ing, in organized trade union relations to industry."

                 And we said, "There are fifteen million such people and
                 their families. Let's say this is an area."—

KANTOR: I object to conversations among this group.

THE COURT: Well, this is not necessarily being offered for that, Mr.
                 Kantor. This is the opinions of three men who are prin-
                 cipals of the suing company. On that basis I will allow it
                 as long as it is confined to the considerations.

                 You go ahead. You considered the audience, and in your
                 opinion that was fifteen million more or less.

BIBERMAN: Well, we arrived at a figure of sixty million of potential
                 audience. That doesn't mean we would get them all.
                 This was the potential field with special interests,
                 women, minority groups, labor. Now we said to our-
                 selves: What portion of that audience can we hope to
                 get? There are certain limitations upon this film. It is a
                 very sober film. People who want light entertainment
                 are not going to come to this film. We said there are no
                 stars in the film and the American audience likes stars; it
                 likes the identification. This might limit the audience.
                 We said the sound is not good in a number of places,
                 and those people who can't find other virtues in a film
                 won't come for that reason.

                 ... ...

BIBERMAN: We said that balancing the limitations and the advan-
                 tages of the film, thinking that we had out of the whole
                 country sixty million people only who might be a poten-

tial audience, that we believe that we had a right to expect that 5 per cent of that potential audience would come to see this film.... That would give us an audience of three million people, the full potential that we were anticipating.

Let's say that that audience paid only fifty cents apiece entrance to the motion picture, which is a pretty low average... that would give us $1,500,000.

And we said: —Suppose only half of that ever comes into the company. That is $750,000.

Now, allowing for all the error that it is reasonable to expect, we said we ought to be able to get $400,000, reducing the $750,000 on the limited basis down to a $400,000 figure.

Now, in March, as we estimated our potential we said this film has a value at this moment of $400,000. That is one calculation, your Honor.

... ...

[Jury left the courtroom.]

LANE: Before the jury comes in I want to make a motion to strike all this testimony as being completely incompetent because the man has not been qualified as an expert, and I think it is quite obvious from the record.

THE COURT: I have heard you now for the fourth time on this subject and you may be right, but I am the one who is calling the shots, and that application is denied.

CAMHY: For the record, your Honor, the same type of motion based on the form of the questions.

THE COURT: That motion is denied.

At a later point the matter was opened again. My testimony, at least in the view of the defense counsel, must have had some effect upon the jury.

HOWELL: I think the difficulty, if I may, your Honor, with Mr. Biberman's speculation—and I call it that advisedly, because clearly the 1954 calculation is simply a speculation, this adding up a potential market of 60,000,000, et cetera.

THE COURT: It was kind of modest, though, don't you think?

HOWELL: It depends upon whether or not you consider this a family picture. I think he included the families of all organized labor in there.

THE COURT: If he did he only got 3,000,000 of them in.

YOUNG: He got all the women, though, your Honor.

THE COURT: No, he did not.

... ...

THE COURT: ... He is a man who is an officer of these companies. If his testimony is to be believed, he invested a lot of time in sales, distribution. He was doing everything but running the machines. Maybe you will get a certain amount of expertise, or at least I am willing to let the jury decide that.

What a difference in authority came from the expert witness called by the defense, Mr. Milton E. Cohen, national director of road show sales for United Artists. Well-spoken, at ease, brilliantly versed in the multiple facets of distribution of motion pictures, he was an impressive witness in his direct testimony. Mr. Frohlich, an associate of Mr. Lane, of the office of Schwartz and Frohlich, examined him. It was immediately evident that they had worked long and hard together and that they had his testimony well in hand. He described the distribution business interestingly and ably. He told of its hazards. So many pictures failed. He told the story of *Twelve Angry Men* starring Henry Fonda, a film which had a fine script, a fine star, a fine distribution organization, and which cost only the modest sum of $600,000. Despite excellent reviews, awards and much appreciation among the cognoscenti, it was a failure. It lost the producers $375,000. He went on to Charles Chaplin's *Limelight,* a beautiful film, which, sadly, because of the controversial nature of its maker, lost money.

Having established the perilous nature of the business, Mr. Cohen went on into further mysteries. The small picture, the second feature, often received as little as 3 per cent of the theater take. *Salt of the Earth,* he went on, was not derived from a well known novel or play. It did not have a top flight producer, or star or any salable element through which an audience might relate its desires toward it. It had no distributor, only a few prints. It was therefore in no sense qualified to be a percentage picture, it would play on a flat rental as a second feature—and regrettably, these earned as little as 3 per cent of the gross.

And if *Twelve Angry Men*, upon which $190,000 had been spent on advertising alone, and *Limelight*, starring the most celebrated actor in the world, could fail, how could a picture like *Salt of the Earth*, with nothing merchandisable, hope to succeed? Mr. Frohlich was ready for the question of questions!

FROHLICH: Now, sir, based upon those facts which I have asked you to assume, do you have an opinion as to whether the motion picture had any commercial value?

COHEN: Yes, I have an opinion.

FROHLICH: What is your opinion?

COHEN: That it has no commercial value—had no commercial value.

Mr. Frohlich then outlined each of the thirteen engagements the film had had and quoted the receipts for each of them and then asked whether this changed his judgment.

COHEN: No. It would confirm my judgment.

FROHLICH: I have no further questions.

There was no question but that he had been a telling witness for the defense. He left the stand and trailed the atmosphere of a funeral behind him. Not only for our film, but for the entire motion picture industry. One felt ready to make a small contribution toward the erection of a monument to those brave souls who risked so much and lost so heavily in the abortive effort to make a buck.

Ben, in his cross-examination of Mr. Cohen, cut through the lugubriousness with a bright voice which seemed to say, "Cheer up, Mr. Cohen, maybe we can rescue that poor business, yet."

MARGOLIS: The motion picture business is a very tricky business, isn't it?

COHEN: A very difficult business.

MARGOLIS: Well, a lot of surprises in the business, aren't there?

COHEN: Yes, sir.

MARGOLIS: In other words, all the experts in the world will think
                that a particular picture is going to be great and that it
                turns out not to be quite as great as they think, that is
                right, isn't it?

COHEN: It has happened.

MARGOLIS: Then it happens that experts will think that a picture is
                going to be a total flop and it turns out to be pretty good
                sometimes; that happens, too, doesn't it?

COHEN: Yes.

MARGOLIS: And it has happened to you in your judgments, hasn't
                it?

COHEN: Yes.

MARGOLIS: In the ultimate sense, the people who determine
                whether the picture is going to make any money or not
                are the audience and they decide sometimes contrary to
                the way the experts think they are going to decide, that
                is right, isn't it?

COHEN: Yes.

MARGOLIS: So the only way that you can really know whether a
                picture is going to make any money is to give an audi-
                ence of the United States an opportunity to see it, that is
                true, isn't it? The only way you can really know?

COHEN: Yes, the audience decides.

It was clear in that courtroom that Mr. Cohen's hour had come
and fully gone. It was just a matter of how long Ben planned to have
at him, and whether he would come out of the courtroom head or
feet first. But Ben was striving to make a point beyond the obvious
one. And he bore on:

MARGOLIS: Now, you based your opinion, sir, upon seeing this pic-
                ture just a few days ago.

COHEN: Yes.

MARGOLIS: And without that you could have had no opinion?

COHEN: I had none.

MARGOLIS: Your Honor, at this time I renew my motion to exhibit
                the motion picture to the jury on the grounds that with-
                out it, it is impossible for them to evaluate the testimony
                of this witness to judge the credibility of the witnesses
                who said that they refused to run the picture because it
                was Communist propaganda or to arrive at any measure
                of damages in the event that they should find for the
                plaintiff.

THE COURT: Denied.

MARGOLIS: I didn't hear it.

THE COURT: Denied.

MARGOLIS: Does your Honor have in mind the fact that it was left
                open?

THE COURT: His Honor has that in mind, among many other things.

MARGOLIS: All right, sir.

                The picture *Twelve Angry Men* has been discussed at con-
                siderable length here, has it not, sir?

COHEN: Yes.

MARGOLIS: Did that picture have all the ingredients for a success?

COHEN: Well, it had many of them.

MARGOLIS: What did it lack?

COHEN: Public acceptance.

MARGOLIS: Why?

COHEN: I wish I could tell you.

MARGOLIS: You don't know, do you?

COHEN: No.

MARGOLIS: You don't know what makes the public accept or reject a picture, do you?

COHEN: Nobody knows.

MARGOLIS: Nobody does. And therefore it is impossible for anybody to tell what a picture is going to do, isn't it?

    … … … … … … … …

MARGOLIS: It is true, is it not, that there have been pictures without any stars in them that have been great successes?

COHEN: Yes.

    … … … … … … … …

MARGOLIS: It is true is it not, that there have been controversial pictures that have been a dud at the box office?

COHEN: Yes.

MARGOLIS: It is also true, is it not, sir, that there have been controversial pictures which have made a lot of money?

COHEN: Well, I don't know without looking over a long list of pictures—I couldn't cite any.

MARGOLIS: All right. We will come back to that a little later, sir.

    It is true, is it not, that there have been films which have dealt with labor and labor strikes which have been flops, that is true, isn't it?

COHEN: Well, I don't know whether that is true or not. If you would tell me what the titles of the pictures are, I would be in a better position to answer that.

MARGOLIS: I thought you were the expert, sir, and I am trying to find out what you know, sir, not what I know. It is true, is it not, sir, that there have been pictures concerning labor strikes which have made a lot of money?

COHEN: Well, I would have to give you the same answer. You show me the list of answers and I will be glad to answer the question.

    … … … … … … … …

MARGOLIS: Well, you have been in the industry all these years and are familiar with pictures, aren't you, sir?

              … … … … … … … …

MARGOLIS: And it is also true, is it not, that there have been pictures which have been labeled as propaganda pictures which have made a lot of money?

COHEN: I must ask you to show me those pictures, the titles of those pictures. I don't know.

MARGOLIS: Did you ever hear of a picture called *The Best Years of Our Lives*?

COHEN: Yes, sir.

MARGOLIS: Did you know that the hearings of the House Committee on Un-American Activities attacked that picture as being Communist propaganda?

COHEN: I didn't know.

MARGOLIS: You didn't know that?

COHEN: No.

MARGOLIS: Didn't you see that in the newspaper at the time?

COHEN: I handled the picture.

MARGOLIS: You handled the picture and you didn't see that in the newspaper at the time?

COHEN: I have no recollection of it.

MARGOLIS: None at all?

COHEN: No, sir.

MARGOLIS: You didn't read that it was labeled as Communist propaganda because it showed a banker as being hard-hearted and not willing to make a loan to a veteran who had just returned from the war?

              … … … … … … … …

MARGOLIS: Do you remember a picture called *Crossfire*?

COHEN: Yes, sir.

MARGOLIS: Did that do quite well?

COHEN: Yes, sir.

MARGOLIS: Was that a propaganda picture?

COHEN: It was a controversial picture.

MARGOLIS: That's one controversial picture that was a low budget
              picture that did very well, didn't it?

COHEN: I don't know the cost. I handled the picture, also. It had
              a story of anti-Semitism. It did very well. It was very
              well received. It had a fine star in it. It had a fine direc-
              tor, a fine producer.

              … … … … … … … …

MARGOLIS: Do you recall anything about its director or its producer,
              who they were?

COHEN: It was produced, I believe, by Dore Schary.

MARGOLIS: Well, he was the over-all man. Who was the actual pro-
              ducer of the picture, do you know?

COHEN: I don't know.

MARGOLIS: You do not know?

COHEN: No.

MARGOLIS: Who was the director?

COHEN: I don't know.

              … … … … … … … …

MARGOLIS: Were you aware of the fact that Edward Dmytryk was
              the director of that picture?

COHEN: Now that you mention it, yes, I do recall.

MARGOLIS: Were you aware that Edward Dmytryk was one of the
              so-called Hollywood Ten?

COHEN: I was aware that there was some controversy over Mr.
              Dmytryk. I don't recall what the extent of it was.

MARGOLIS: You don't recall the nature of the controversy at all?

COHEN: No, sir.

MARGOLIS: Wasn't the matter of importance to you?

COHEN: No.

MARGOLIS: It did not affect the question of your handling any picture?

COHEN: No.

MARGOLIS: Did you know that Adrian Scott was the producer of the picture?

COHEN: No, I didn't know....

            ... ...

MARGOLIS: Did you know that Adrian Scott was also one of the Hollywood Ten?

COHEN: No, sir.

            ... ...

MARGOLIS: Suppose that you have a quality picture, one that the public would buy, but for some reason the picture is unable to get a release, what is the effect upon the value of the motion picture?

COHEN: It has no value.

MARGOLIS: Destroyed, isn't it?

COHEN: It has no value. Its only value is what it can bring in in the market. If it has no market, it has no value.

To conclude Ben took Mr. Cohen on a Cook's tour of controversial films in the history of American motion pictures. The expert's lack of knowledge of them, or his unwillingness to discuss them, was beyond even plaintiffs' credulity. He was asked whether he knew the film *The Grapes of Wrath*. Yes, the expert testified, he did. But he didn't know that it had been regarded as an insane venture by the motion picture industry and turned into a most spectacular success. He did not remember that it showed agricultural employers acting in inhuman manner to their workers, or that it showed police brutality. But most astonishing of all, he didn't know that it had been a big money-maker. He had only a vague recollection that *Born Yesterday* had any controversy attached to it and no knowledge about its great success at the box office. When he was shown weekly *Variety* grosses, he said he did not trust them. He knew nothing of the film *Fury*, with Paul Muni; he did not remember *The Corn Is Green*; and he did not recall anything about How *Green Was My Valley* except its title.

When he was asked whether he knew that *Limelight* had been withdrawn from circulation and that that probably accounted for its small gross, he admitted that he did know that. Ben asked one final question. Did he remember an Arthur Miller film *Death of a Salesman*? Mr. Cohen said, "No." It seemed an appropriate question with which to end the cross-examination of the salesman for United Artists. In three hours Ben had turned their expert witness into ours.

XI

Following the last defense witness judge Tyler referred to Ben's "rather emotional appeals" during the cross-examination of two of the witnesses about showing the film to the jury. His Honor stated that he had always been troubled at the prospect of taking the jury uptown to some large commercial building and into a commercial screening room. If Mr. Margolis would modify his application to the extent of having the film shown to the jury in the courtroom, he would consider it. Further, he thought at this point he should see the film himself and thereafter allow counsel to state their positions respecting a screening for the jury.

The debate exploded at once. And it went into high gear after the judge had viewed the film. Defense counsel did not want that film run for the jury! Was this trial to be turned into a debate over whether the film should or should not have been denied public exhibition? That was not the issue! The issue was whether there had been a conspiracy! The film need not be seen. Showing it would be most prejudicial to the defense! But the defendants' lawyers had overcooked the brew by allowing Mr. Cohen to state that the film had no value whatsoever. Judge Tyler agreed that to consider the question of its value, the jury now must be able to see the film. But he insisted that it could not be shown anywhere but in the courtroom. Since this necessitated showing it in 16mm film, with two breaks in the screening to change reels, which would create a "home movie" character for the film, plaintiffs' counsel first refused the judge's offer.

That night we debated the question the judge had left open. But our great desire to have the jury experience the film won. The following morning, after a preview of a reel of the 16mm print for the judge, he ruled that the film could be seen by the jury to help them "determine its value and marketability at the time back when it was produced and distributed."

In perhaps a hundred screenings of this film, in all sorts of places and before all kinds of audiences I had not before encountered an audience so totally unreacting. If not a sound could be heard, it was also true that one could have heard a feather drop. If they did not laugh in many places where no audience had ever before been unresponsive, they proffered a greater attentiveness than any previous audience.

The film over, the judge called upon counsel to begin summation, beginning with the defense. The summations and the judge's charge to the jury lasted three days and took over six hundred pages of transcript. Hence only the briefest indication can be given here, which, again, will represent what seems to me significant.

Mr. Young, representing Fox West Coast Theaters, opened the defense. He had called no witnesses and he contended that if every word uttered by plaintiffs was taken at face value there would still be no possible case for any conspiratorial connivance by his client. He closed on a philosophical note:

YOUNG: But I think the final irony or the supreme irony of this
            case is that the principals here—whether they are Com-
            munists or not, I don't know. If they are, they obviously
            don't believe in God. It seems to me that the two terms
            are incompatible. But I hope it won't astonish you to
            know that the title of this picture comes from the words
            of Jesus himself, from the Sermon on the Mount. It is
            the fifth chapter of Matthew and the 13th Verse. They
            misquoted it. There is nothing in there which says, "Ye
            shall inherit the earth." It says: "Ye are the salt of the
            earth, but if the salt have lost his savor wherewith shall
            it be salted; it is henceforth good for nothing but to be
            cast out and to be trodden under the foot of men."

            Now a few words about the picture itself. Except for the
            Christening scene, did you see a church or a synagogue
            anywhere in that picture...? God is certainly conspicu-
            ous in this case by the almost complete absence of any of
            his representatives.

            ... I ask your verdict, ladies and gentlemen, in favor of
            the Fox West Coast defendants because it is the only
            verdict that the law and the facts can support.

            There is a favorite line of mine from Isaiah: "How beau-
            tiful upon the mountains are the words of Him who
            bringeth good tidings." I am sure that you will exercise
            your function as the trier of the facts and bring us tid-

ings that the verdict will be in favor of the Fox West
Coast defendants.

Mr. Sand spoke next, representing Steve D'Inzillo, business
agent of the New York Projectionists' local union. Mr. D'Inzillo, he
said, should have been the last man on earth sued in this action; he
had tried to help Biberman and Jarrico. There was no evidence tying
him to Walsh or Brewer or anyone else. Mr. Sand concluded:

SAND: I will avoid the Bible for a minute. I will try Shakes-
                peare. In Julius Caesar, Brutus was complaining, as I
                recall, or Cassius was complaining to Caesar, and Caesar
                said, "The fault, dear Brutus, lies not in the stars, but in
                ourselves."

                … This very publicity, these very reputations, their own
                beliefs, their own film, this was the fault. It lay not in
                the stars, and I request that you find, quite respectfully,
                that the fault was not in Mr. D'Inzillo, who at the very
                least helped these people rather than hindered them.

Mr. Camhy, addressing the jury for Pathé Laboratories, explained
to the jury that Pathé's decision to cease processing the film was uni-
lateral and was based upon a superintendent's report to the manager
that the film was Communist propaganda. They had been able to tell
from the bits and pieces of film seen in the laboratory that

CAMHY: … there were Mexicans, that they were living in pov-
                erty, that they had organized a strike and they were on
                picket lines, that the Sheriffs and the police were also
                involved and appeared to be lined up against them, and
                that there were women and children in jail banging
                their cups against the bars.…

This Mr. Camhy thought was more than an adequate basis for
Pathé to refuse, individually, to have any more to do with it. His
opinion of the whole venture was that:

                Finding themselves out of work, Biberman and Jarrico
                got together with other unhappy people like themselves
                and decided to make movies about what a rotten coun-
                try this is.

Mr. Howell addressed the jury for RKO. His documentation was
minute and he reviewed many aspects of the case. He still believed

that it was almost beyond belief that an industry could not protect itself. But on the specifics, he contended that RKO had set up a screening policy before Waldorf and although his client was present there it did little more than to reassert its own independent and previously established position. He closed:

HOWELL: This isn't a conspiracy case. This is a broken dreams case.... Sometimes people will stand on a foolish principle and adhere to it as their proudest accomplishment, and they will look for a scapegoat. They always have an alibi, they always have a reason why they are not nationally recognized or internationally recognized.

               And that is about where I put Jarrico and Biberman. They have hung on to that foolish consistency which Emerson wrote "is the hobgoblin of small minds."

   Mr. Luddy followed for defendants Walsh and Brewer.

LUDDY: This is a unique case. It is the most unique case I have ever been in. Isn't it a bit ironical to think that people who believe in the overthrow of the laws of our country, and who believe in the overthrow of our government, could come here into this court—and legalistically, I admit, they have a right to do so—and ask for the enforcement of a particular law of the United States, which laws, if they had their way, would be overthrown.

               But, anyway, we are here.

               ... as I said before, Jarrico, Biberman, Michael Wilson, if you want to just take the word "right" and put quotation marks around it, sure they have a right to make a living. They have a right if they could to make a living in a shoe factory, plow factory or a hardware factory, but they didn't have a right to make a living in a sensitive industry which depended upon public acceptance of a product such as a motion picture. Their very connection with motion pictures would detract from the public acceptance of the product which the companies had to sell. Now, that being true, let's not talk about rights, rights to work and so on. [*]

... You know I nearly fell out of my chair when Mr. Biberman said that he went into this picture to make money. I said: my word, that is capitalism.

... Now here were these men, their country had given them an opportunity of a brilliant education, an opportunity to get into creative work and make a lot of money, and yet when it came to selling their product not one of them had the slightest idea how to do it. Not a one of them. No practicality about them at all.

... You saw the picture the other day. So far as you are concerned, the picture might represent conditions that existed last week. You are not told that this is some time back in 1950 or 1948, back in the days when labor and management were on a dog-eat-dog basis.

... I tell you now, speaking as a labor lawyer—and I am in favor of strikes if they are necessary, although my union has a record of not doing it—that those conditions are not realistic today.

Mr. Lane was the closing attorney for the defendants, and was given the major portion of the defense task. He sought to create a framework for the jury to follow. The picture had failed for five reasons: it was Communist created, it was exhibited when the industry was at its lowest ebb, it was distributed by two men who didn't know how to do the job, insufficient money was spent on advertising and it was co-sponsored by the Mine-Mill Union.

His summation was, comparatively, so mild as to be almost unrecognizable as the final statement of the same man who had taken off with such a flamboyant opening. It seemed to me his most effective work in the trial.

LANE: Then, when Mr. Margolis attempts to tell you, ladies and gentlemen, that the subject matter of the Waldorf was

*As Mr. Luddy spoke, and as he well knew, five of the original Hollywood Ten were working for the studios under their own names—one, Edward Dmytryk, an informer "rehabilitated" by Mr. Luddy's client, Brewer; and four, Dalton Trumbo, Albert Maltz, Ring Lardner, Jr. and Adrian Scott, rehabilitated by their own talents, unblemished by the helping hand of Mr. Brewer.

the matter of eliminating all Communists from the
industry, ask yourselves what you have seen in the
record to show that this meeting touched on any other
matter but employees at the respective studios.

I say this: That the absence of any evidence showing any
connection between this meeting and the two corporations formed many years later is so remote and so without basis that the plaintiffs have necessarily changed
their theory and have now attempted to change what
happened at the Waldorf meeting.

... ...

They are trying to convince you, ladies and gentlemen,
that the meeting at the Waldorf was so broad in purpose
as to have affected the plaintiffs which weren't even in
existence at that time.

Mr. Lane then went on to the MPIC statement. He read it to the
jury again, including the last line in which MPIC's industry members
stated that they did not recognize this operation or its product as
reflecting their own views, or interests or policies. Then he
continued:

LANE: Ladies and gentlemen, if that constitutes one of the two
             bits of information against my clients, then I think it is a
             travesty, a travesty that we were brought into this court-
             house to undergo the trouble and expense of trying this
             case, let alone the fact that it has taken you people out
             of your busy lives to spend almost ten weeks in this
             courtroom.

And so it had rung out from six defense lawyers: the defendants
did nothing conspiratorial. Whatever they did, they did individually.
They had a legal and moral right to act individually, *if they did*, against
a group of inept Communists and their flimsy film, so anti-American
in content as to have had no right to be aided in entering the American marketplace—where it failed on its own because it was Communist propaganda.

Six lawyers asked the jury to believe that all that this book
records of instances of interference with, vilification and ostracism of

the makers of the film and of the film itself, was without a trace of conspiracy.

Sidney Dickstein was the first of two lawyers to sum up for the plaintiffs, stating the case for damages. He began by discussing the estimate of the film's potential commercial success.

DICKSTEIN: Plaintiffs do not contend that this motion picture as Mr.
               Howell put it, was a sure—fire commercial success. All
               we say is that we never had the opportunity to find out.
               On the other hand, it was not, as Mr. Howell also put it,
               a jerry-built little picture, a pathetic little project, a com-
               mercial dog.

He then read excerpts from reviews, the *New York Times*, the *Herald-Tribune*, which criticized the film but also stated: "The movie craftsmanship is excellent. There is a severe beauty in the location photography of a desperately poor community, and enormous affection and sympathy for these olive-skinned Americans." He quoted from leading AF of L journals. Then he picked up Mr. Lane on the film's controversial character, which, according to defense counsel, was fated to keep people away from the theater. And he spoke directly to the jury.

DICKSTEIN: Mr. Camhy, he said, "Well, back in Pathé we saw that
               this film dealt with Mexicans that were living in pov-
               erty." This is supposed to be communistic? If it is com-
               munistic to depict poverty in the United States, then *Life*
               magazine, the *New York Times* and President Johnson
               himself, in trying to open our eyes on this subject, are
               purveyors of Communism. We are told, oh, gee, this
               must be communistic; there are policemen who beat up
               people. Where have defense counsel been?

               Well, you saw the motion picture. I would not hazard a
               guess how many of you liked it and how many of you
               did not like it. I have no idea whatsoever, but there is
               one thing I am absolutely certain about; you, after hear-
               ing two months of controversy about this particular
               motion picture, certainly wanted to see it, and it might
               have been enough to get you into a motion picture
               house in 1954 and away from the television which

defendants would have you believe glued everybody to
their homes. This is not a film for everyone, but it
doesn't have to be. It did not have to recoup a negative
cost of $35,000,000.

Mr. Dickstein carefully analyzed all costs, relating them to the
budget and measuring the increase caused by interference and refusal
to service. Then he came to his conclusion:

I think perhaps the best single evidence of the value of
this motion picture is the fact that the defendants could,
if they had wanted to, have allowed the picture to have
a normal commercial run... just let this film die on the
normal commercial vine, as they now tell you it would
have done anyway. No, they had to push, they had to
shove, because they were afraid—they were afraid—
that this film might have had a reasonably successful
commercial run.

It seemed to us that the jury was affected by Mr. Dickstein's presentation. He left with the jury the "spectre" this film's possible success had raised as a threat to the industry's "program."

XII

As Ben had left for the court that morning he said that he wished he could have three days for his summation to make all the necessary delicate connections for the jury. He was granted only three and a half hours. He built his summation around a few major points:

MARGOLIS: It serves no useful purpose in a case like this, as defense counsel has done, to pick up each little piece of this picture puzzle and say "Look at this little piece. It doesn't say anything. It is innocuous. It doesn't prove anything." But that's the nature of this kind of puzzle. It is its character. It wouldn't be a puzzle if you could pick up each little piece and get a complete picture.

And this is the nature of a conspiracy.

… … … … … … … …

We have to prove that it is more probable that there was a conspiracy than that there wasn't such a conspiracy; that is what the preponderance of the evidence is.

… … … … … … … …

There is one very unusual feature in this case for a conspiracy case, and that is that there is one aspect of the conspiracy, a basic aspect that was carried out in broad daylight, out in the open, frankly and unashamedly… because the very object of the combination was to give publicity to what they were doing, and if they did it secretly they wouldn't have accomplished their object.

He went into the Waldorf meeting and he examined it from a score of points of view.

They had fine lawyers there, I agree. Some of the best in the country. Some who said, "Look you are taking a legal risk when you do this," and they went ahead despite this.

Those fine lawyers, they would know how to draft a document that was an individual statement. Even one document, not fourteen or fifteen.

....

What in the English language is more of a collective
term, of a joint term, than "we"...? "We will forthwith
discharge." Not individually. "We will and we will not
reemploy...." Without ever a statement that this is
intended to be individual action.

....

If you had a price-fixing agreement... would it be any
less a violation of the anti-trust laws because the implementation was left to the individual act?

As a matter of fact in most conspiracies that is the way it
is done.

....

On February 16, 1952, there was a statement issued by
Mr. Eric Johnston, Exhibit 7, nobody has paid any attention to this so far.... "This policy has been adhered to
unswervingly.... "This policy has resulted in our members being sued in court for large sums and suits are still
in progress. This has not deterred us and will not."

Law? What difference does a law make. Don't talk to us
about law.

Ben strung Brewer to the industry, with the multiple threads
provided by the evidence. Then he turned to the arguments of the
defense lawyers.

Mr. Luddy argued, in effect, that persons who refuse to
answer questions, or who are named as Communists,
could be excluded from the motion picture industry by a
private combination.

Ben turned to the jury and said with quiet force:

We wouldn't be here if that were the law. We couldn't
be here. We would be thrown out of court.

....

Mr. Howell argued that a private industry has a right to
take a public position. I couldn't agree with him more, if
it is a legal thing that they are doing.

> ... ...
> ... It isn't the question of... right to take a public posi-
> tion, but the question of... right to commit an illegal act.

Ben picked up the Waldorf Agreement and read from it. "There is the danger of hurting innocent people. There is the risk of creating a climate of fear."

> ... did they conduct themselves in such a way as to really prevent this climate of fear if they spread this thing?

> It became something that permeated the life and soul of this industry.

> Mr. Broidy (president of Allied Artists) testified and had a little joke. In talking about the situation in Hollywood, he testified that he had had a conversation in which he was told to be careful of what he joined, *and he said he was scared to join the temple.* I thought it was humorous but it was not funny.

The jury had laughed when Mr. Broidy had delivered the remark rather jocularly. Ben turned its reverse and true side to the jury to expose its grimness:

> If the head of a major industry can use this kind of joke, how about the little people whose livelihoods, whose businesses depend upon this very big mogul who himself made this little *joke?*

He recapped the acts of each defendant and then brought his argument to a close.

> ... It was the inevitable result of the powers and the forces which the defendants in this case set in the meeting at Waldorf. They created it, they are responsible for it, they should bear the burden of it.

He asked that the perpetrators not be permitted to go scot free. And Ben had concluded.

A ten-week trial is like a ten-week-long horse race. One evaluates one's posture every hour, often every few minutes. When Ben had finished we believed our case had been solidly summed up. There was only one unknown factor left—the judge's instructions to the jury.

The following morning the judge gave his charge; counsel on both sides had submitted scores of requests for the judge to include. Those from the plaintiffs were the days-and-nights-long work of David Shapiro, aided by Sidney Dickstein. The charge covered seventy-five pages, and plaintiffs' counsel estimated that the judge had included 95 per cent of their requests. His instructions on the law were full, clear and, in the opinion of plaintiffs' counsel, they were the law. The more delicate instructions were direct and without equivocation.

Five essential elements were to be found present by the jury before any defendant could be found liable for the conspiratorial conduct alleged by the plaintiffs. The jury was required to find that by the preponderance of the evidence the plaintiffs had established:

> (1) That between the latter weeks of November 1947 and the first weeks of 1960 there existed a conspiracy substantially as pleaded in the complaint.

> (2) That a purpose and object of the conspiracy was to restrain trade by boycotting or refusing to deal with plaintiff corporations in their production and distribution of the film *Salt of the Earth*.

> (3) That the defendants or some of them were knowing members of the conspiracy as charged.

> (4) That the trade or commerce involved or affected by such conspiracy was interstate or, to put it a little more specifically and accurately, that the activities of the combination or conspiracy had some discernible impact upon commerce between the several states.

> (5) That the conspiracy had an impact upon plaintiff corporations to the extent of proximately causing injury to their business or property.

The judge continued: "As you can see, and as I believe the plaintiffs frankly recognize, the gist of the complaint which they must prove is conspiracy."

His Honor then carefully spelled out the nature of conspiracy, the fact that formal agreements are unusual, that once it is formed it continues until affirmatively terminated, that the evidence taken by the judge as "subject to connection" was reserved for the jury as triers of the facts to determine whether and to whom it applied.

Then the judge moved into the more delicate areas of this case.

> Under our law, motive of the conspirators... that they were pressured by public clamor or otherwise, to join the conspiracy, makes no difference to the crucial issues of the conspiracy or the claimed membership of the defendants therein.
>
> I emphasize here as clearly as I know how a number of propositions which you should keep in mind in connection with the evidence, such as it is, bearing on Communism or pro-Communism or Communist party affiliations of certain principals or agents of plaintiffs.
>
> In the first place... our law contains no rule or proposition to the effect that Communists or alleged Communists in this country cannot sue under the anti-trust laws or that they are barred from recovery if they can prove the claims of violations of such laws with resultant damages to them.
>
> In the second place, assuming you were to find that the defendants... acted with the highest and most understandable and praiseworthy motives of, for example, routing communism out of the movie industry this finding in and of itself would have no bearing so long as you were to determine that a conspiracy of the kind alleged in the complaint existed....

The judge enunciated the principle that if any defendant acted independently, stimulated by accounts that persons involved in the film were pro-Communists or party members or subversives, such a defendant is not liable. The test was not motive, but whether the action was independent or conspiratorial.

Then judge Tyler came to the "sanction order."

> I ask you to derive no connotation unfavorable toward plaintiffs or any defendant from the word "sanction" or

"sanction order." This order has been entered but the fact of its entry, as such, should not be construed against any of the parties. By reason of this order thus imposed against the plaintiff corporations, I instruct you that, *for the purpose of this case*, plaintiffs' principal officers and employees and certain members of *Salt*'s cast and production crew were members of the Communist party.

I further charge you, however, that you may not consider these facts as bearing on the credibility of any witness of this kind who appeared here and testified at this trial.

His Honor then asked the jury to keep in mind another matter with respect to Messrs. Jarrico, Wilson, Lazarus and Biberman, who had appeared before the House Committee on Un-American Activities and invoked their constitutional privileges not to testify before that body, at least on certain subjects.

Particularly, I wish to emphasize that you should not consider the fact that these witnesses invoked their First and Fifth Amendment privileges when you assess their credibility. Obviously, if our laws and Constitution confer a privilege upon an individual, its exercise can not be used to assail the credibility of that person.

He stated that under our system a unanimous verdict was required.

At 1:20 P.M. on the 11th of November, 1964, the jury retired to begin their deliberations.

XIII

The courtroom was empty, the jury was still out. Waiting for the verdict, I found myself repeating Esperanza's lines in her quarrel scene with her husband, late in the film.

ESPERANZA: But why must you say to me "stay in your place." Do
              you feel better having someone lower than you?

RAMÓN: : Shut up, you're talking crazy.

ESPERANZA: Whose neck shall I stand on to make me feel superior?
              And what will I get out of it? I don't want anything
              lower than I am. I am low enough already. I want to
              rise. And push everything up with me as I go.

Mr. Howell had referred to a line in the film in which the union president advocated the necessary "unity of working men" in carrying out a strike. He also quoted Esperanza's line, "I want to rise. And push everything up with me as I go."

HOWELL: In your judgment, would it seem a fair conclusion that
              those two items of dialogue really amount to "Workers
              of the world, arise. You have nothing to lose but your
              chains"?

GALLIGAN: Objection.

BIBERMAN: It does not

GALLIGAN: Objection.

BIBERMAN: —imply anything of the kind—

GALLIGAN: Objection, Mr. Biberman.

BIBERMAN: —in my opinion.

THE COURT: We have gotten an answer. Let it stand.

In that moment, I believe I knew more clearly than ever before why I hoped we might win this case. Not for the sake of triumph, or for money with which to pay off debts or beyond that to stuff our own pockets. It was that Esperanza might prevail. Esperanza, the embodiment of the passionate cry of all decent human beings for the right to elevate themselves to the side of all their kind in loving respect. Esperanza's plea had been the birth cry of this country. The promise of human rights and of human liberty is and always has been the promise of America. And to hear it scorned, branded as subversive! A victory in this case, would, in its small way, reassert the right of all Americans to communicate their feeling of unself-centered human fraternity.

At 2:42 P.M. a note was received from the jury and given to the judge. They requested all exhibits exclusive of the film. Attorneys from both sides were assigned to make them available.

At 4 P.M. the jury asked for a copy of the five points the judge had described as necessary to find that a conspiracy had existed. The judge called the jury into the court room and recited the five points for them verbally.

At 6 P.M. the jury was excused for dinner, their foreman stating to the judge that they probably required another hour before reaching a verdict.

At 9:45 P.M. the jury was reconvened. It had not yet reached a verdict. The judge ordered the jury taken to a hotel for the night. The odds stood at even money. From a rating of not a chance of reaching trial eight years ago, we were running even money with worried defendants. As we rode back to the hotel Ben said that if we wished we had the right, that night, in his opinion, to have some hope, some modest hope.

Next morning, at 11:45, the jury announced that it was ready to report a verdict. When they had been brought into the courtroom and were seated in the jury box, the Clerk of the court addressed them.

THE CLERK: Mr. Foreman, have you agreed upon a verdict?

THE FOREMAN:Yes, we have.

THE CLERK: How say you?

THE FOREMAN:We the members of the jury, find the defendants *not guilty*.

XIV

Leaving the courtroom, one of the defense counsel stopped me. "You didn't win—but you are a hell of a long way from having lost. We sweated too much for comfort. I doubt if you are going to have to take what you took any longer. It was a hell of a fight. If you are not greedy, you have cause to celebrate your accomplishment."

A moment later I learned that on the first ballot we had three votes. One juror said to me, "We all felt that there had been a conspiracy against the film and that the film had been done in by it. But, finally, there was just not enough concrete evidence of it for us to find that it was so."

I addressed the juror who made the observation.

"But if you were convinced that there had been a conspiracy why could you not find for the plaintiffs through inference? How much, if you could be frank and quite direct with me, please, did the labeling hold you back from that harder choice?"

He thought briefly and then replied, "We hope we acted free of prejudice. Of course we all know we have some." Then he took hold of my arm.

"Mr. Biberman, I want you to know how much I admire you. I wish I possessed some of your courage, energy and confidence. And, admiring you as I do, I would like to have you think the way I do. *And you don't think the way I think at all.*"

I was interested especially in the intensity of his remark.

"How do you know what I think?"

"Well, you're a ———"

As we stood looking at each other the meaning of seventeen years of my life raised itself for instantaneous review. Suppose I had never moved away from the more or less comfortable conformity which he so wished we might cohabit! I had once lived there. Everyone must make his choice.

Was he suggesting that if we had surrendered our consciences to the committee, we might have been able to make our film without opposition, or, might have won the trial? Perhaps. But there is also the possibility that under those circumstances we would never have

made the film. And, today, we might be envying in others the qualities of "courage, energy and confidence"?

Perhaps the truth is that both he and I are necessary to any viable society, since I believe it to be moot, at the very least, whether the
accommodators or the "subversives" are the progenitors of a free
society. All in all, apparently, he was content with his views, opinions
and intellectual posture. So was I. At the cost of denying myself, victory in this case would have been too dear, and perhaps saddest of all,
not even necessary.

No, I had no apologies to make to myself, or to offer him.

The American, the human struggle for dignity and the "right to push
everything up with us," must not be labeled and thereby discarded.
Labeling deprives a man of his greatest gift to his country—himself. It
also destroys his country's greatest gift to him —himself. Of all things,
patriotism may not be weighed, cannot be weighed in a scales of public polls. The poll of polls remains the individual conscience. It is the
seed of America as a great society.

By all reasonable standards we had had a fair trial. Our jury was
conscientious, our judge scrupulously judicious. No reasonable basis
for appeal existed. No reasonable basis! It was my belief that because
of the "sanction order" we had lost this case—and it was my belief
that the "sanction order" was unjust—that though judge Tyler had
minimized it, perhaps to the limit of his ability to do so, it had clung
to us. Should we now appeal the case and carry it, perhaps to the
Supreme Court, on this issue, meet Bishop Pike there as co-counsel,
and there ask whether we were not entitled to appear in Court, unla-
beled, as do all other anti-trust litigants? But it would cost—what?
Fifty thousand dollars? And take—how many years? No—we would
take opposing counsel's advice because nothing else was possible for
us. We would not be greedy. We had not won. But we *had been felt.*
We had lost. But we had had success. The case was over.

In 1947 I offered a statement to the Un-American Activities Committee which they would not permit me to read and would not read
themselves. Its last lines seem as appropriate to end my part of this
book as they seemed to me to be then:

"In this hearing I will not merely rely upon the Constitution. I will fight for it and defend it against all possible intimidation. Here, as well, I am a free man—accustomed to slow, hard, patient, and passionate defense of what I believe to be American."

PHOTOGRAPHS FROM
SALT OF THE EARTH

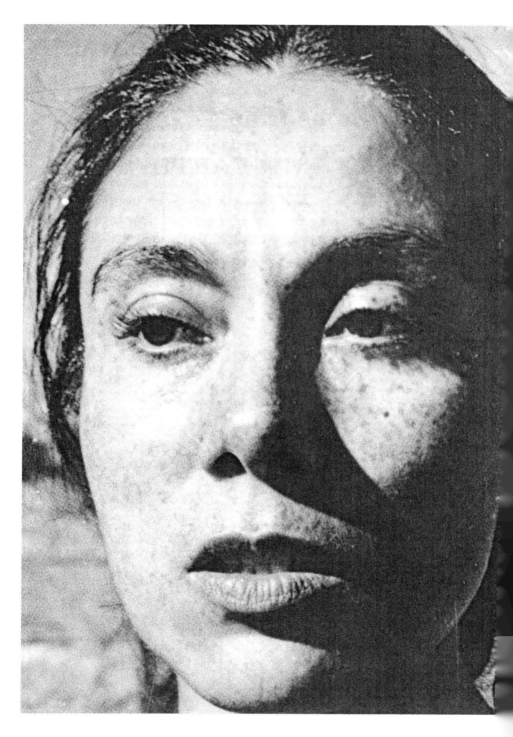

Left: ESPERANZA: "It was my Saint's Day. I was thirty-five years old. And on that day I had a wish... so sinful... I prayed to God to forgive me for it."

Above: Juan Chacon as RAMÓN QUINTERO: "First we got to get equality on the job. Then we'll work on these other things. Leave it to the men."

Ernest Velasquez as CHARLEY VIDAL, Clinton Jencks as FRANK
BARNES, and miners listening to an off-scene debate: FOREMAN: "You
work alone, savvy? You can't handle the job, I'll find someone who
can." RAMÓN: "Who? A scab?" FOREMAN: "An American."

RAMÓN and his daughter ESTELLA (Mary Lou Castillo). LUÍS, off-scene: "Papa, is there going to be a strike?"

Left: Henrietta Williams as TERESA VIDAL, Virginia Jencks as RUTH BARNES, Angie Sanchez as CONSUELO RUIZ: "The ladies have been talking about sanitation. And if the issue is equality, like you say it is, then maybe we ought to have equality in plumbing too...."

Above: David Wolff as FOREMAN: "You're a liar, Pancho...." RAMÓN lunges at him....

Left: The men vote to strike. They look up to see their womenfolk atop a hill holding a sign: "We Want Sanitation Not Discrimination." The men stare at their women, perplexed....

Above: At a birthday party for ESPERANZA: "We all forgot our troubles at the mañanita. I had never had so nice a party. It was like a song running through my mind."

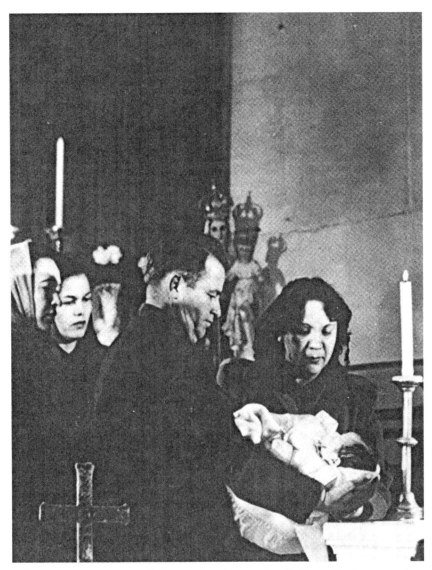

Left: In the relaxation of the mañanita tender feelings find expression:
ESPERANZA: "Forgive me for saying you never thought of me." RAMÓN:
"I did forget. Luís told me."

Above: TERESA and ANTONIO (Charley Coleman). ESPERANZA'S VOICE: "I
decided to postpone the christening until Ramón got out of jail. Antonio was
his godfather, and Teresa Vidal his godmother. We christened him Juan."

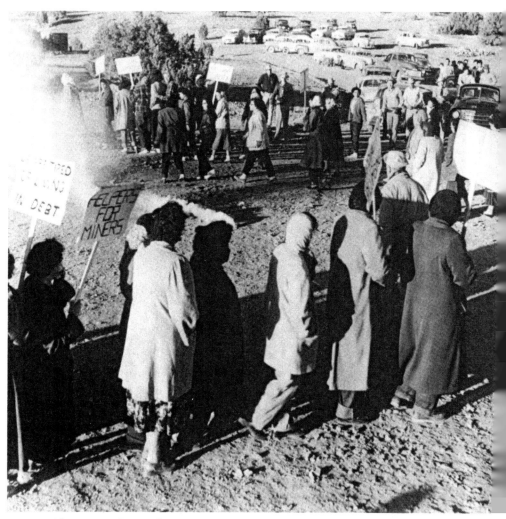

Above: A Taft-Hartley injunction ordered the miners to stop picketing. After fierce debate, the women are permitted to take over the picket lines. ESPERANZA: "They came... the women. They came from Zinc Town and from the hills beyond... women we had never see before...."

Right: Frank Talavera as LUÍS QUINTERO: "Boy, did you see the way Mama whopped that deputy!"

Left: Women and children are hauled off to jail. THE CHILDREN: "Let us out. Let us out!"

Above: Will Geer as the harassed SHERIFF: "You girls got nobody but yourselves to blame and you can be home with your families in an hour. All you have to do is sign a pledge that you won't go back to the picket line."

The men—in the beer parlor—beef at bosses and women. One suggests they take off to hunt some venison. RAMÓN: "Why ask me? If you want permission to go over the hill, go ask the Ladies Auxiliary."

The last company attempt to break the strike—an eviction. It brings the long strike and the older "woman question" to simultaneous resolution.

Director Herbert Biberman (under the camera) and crew on location during the filming of *Salt of the Earth*.

CPSIA information can be obtained at www.ICGtesting.com
Printed in the USA
LVOW011026060112

262709LV00005B/47/P